A Guide to America's Sex Laws

A GUIDE TO AMERICA'S SEX LAWS

Richard A. Posner
and Katharine B. Silbaugh

THE UNIVERSITY OF CHICAGO PRESS
CHICAGO AND LONDON

The University of Chicago Press, Chicago 60637
The University of Chicago Press, Ltd., London

Paperback edition 1998
Printed in the United States of America
05 04 03 02 01 00 99 98   2 3 4 5

ISBN: 0-226-67564-5 (cloth)
ISBN: 0-226-67565-3 (paperback)

Library of Congress Cataloging-in-Publication Data

A guide to America's sex laws / Richard A. Posner and Katharine B. Silbaugh.
p. cm.
Includes bibliographical references.
1. Sex and law—United States. I. Posner, Richard A.
II. Silbaugh, Katharine B.
KF9325.G85 1996
345.73′0253—dc20
[347.0305253]

96-3306
CIP

∞ The paper used in this publication meets the minimum requirements of the American National Standard for Information Sciences—Permanence of Paper for Printed Library Materials, ANSI Z39.48-1992.

Contents

Introduction

Sex, although considered by many the quintessential private activity in our culture, is blanketed by laws. These laws have received an increasing amount of popular, scholarly, and media attention in recent years as the sexual mores of the society have become ever more heterogeneous and contested. It seemed to us that the time had come when a published compendium of the nation's sex laws might serve a useful purpose, or rather several purposes: revealing gaps, anachronisms, anomalies, inequalities, irrationalities; providing an empirical basis for studies of sexual regulation; and satisfying the legitimate interests of individuals in ascertaining the legality of contemplated behavior.

This book is that compendium. It distributes the statutes (or pertinent provisions of statutes) in broad subject areas, such as "Adultery" and "Sodomy," with brief introductions to provide background and context. Within each subject area, the statutes (both state and federal) are arrayed alphabetically by state or federal jurisdiction. Each statute is summarized briefly, and the citation to where it can be found in the statute books is also given so that anyone who wants to read the full text of the statute can find it in a law library or computerized legal database. Although we do not quote the statutes in full, our summaries generally employ the statutes' terminology in order to convey the flavor as well as content of the statutes. As a result, there are some verbal differences between summaries of statutes that actually have the same meaning, much stilted language, and some legal jargon. The Glossary at the end of the book defines the handful of terms (such as "dower" and "curtesy") whose meaning would not be apparent to a nonlawyer. The date the statute was enacted is given in parentheses at the end of the citation. This should be useful to readers who want to estimate the social context from which the laws arose, or ascertain how recently the laws of a given state have been revised. References throughout to the "Model Penal Code" are to an influential "ideal" criminal code drafted by the American Law Institute; provisions of the Code have been adopted in a number of states.

Is such a compilation really necessary or useful? Or are we engaged in filling the proverbial long-needed gap?

When law tracks the moral beliefs held by all or at least the vast majority of the members of a society, as is true of the laws prohibiting murder and theft, people do not have to "know" the law in order to comply with it; they have only to follow their conscience. Given the diversity of moral opinion regarding sex in the United States, conscience is not a sure guide to legality any more. No longer is it "obvious" (if it ever was) that sexual relations between consenting adults of the same sex is a crime, or that the age of consent to marriage should be lower for females than for males, or that marital rape is not a crime, or that adultery and fornication are crimes. By the same token, moral diversity in a federal system in which the regulation of some field of activity is dominated by state law (as is the case with the regulation of sex) is likely to lead to a crazy quilt of laws, and, as readers of this book will discover, has indeed done so. So far as the regulation of sexual behavior is concerned, by crossing a state boundary one may be stepping into a different moral universe.

We said that sex in this country today is blanketed by laws, but before beginning this project we did not know how many blankets there were. The number and variety of laws regulating sex are staggering. This book, we hope, will convey that complexity while giving the reader some help in sorting things out. But it will not answer all questions, and we want to emphasize the constraints we imposed on ourselves for the sake of clarity and a manageable size.

- The book is limited to state, federal, and District of Columbia statutes. Excluded are regulations governing Indian and noncontinental territories as well as local ordinances (regulating such things as public nudity and prostitution—practices also regulated by statute, however). An even more significant exclusion is of common law—judge-made law not embodied in statutes, which has to be extracted from a sequence of judicial decisions. An example is the tort of seduction, for which damages are obtainable in many states.
- The book is limited to the texts of the statutes, as distinct from judicial interpretations of the texts. Judicial interpretation is important in clarifying the meaning of statutory language. Often it gives that language a nonobvious gloss, so that the statute as interpreted and applied may mean something different from what a reading of the text would

suggest. Some laws may be held unconstitutional by the courts, and so be unenforceable, yet remain on the statute books—and so appear in this book. We have tried in the introduction to each of the chapters to indicate the major respects in which judicial interpretation has altered the apparent meaning or significance of the statutes that we summarize.

• The book is limited in the main to statutes that impose criminal penalties, even though there are many statutory and administrative regulations that impose civil rather than criminal sanctions (injunctions and damages rather than imprisonment and fines).

• We indicate whether the statute creates a felony or a misdemeanor, but not the precise sentence or range of sentences that the statute authorizes; and of course not all felony statutes, or misdemeanor statutes, carry the same penalties. In general, misdemeanor statutes do not authorize imprisonment for more than a year, while felony statutes authorize both longer imprisonment and larger fines than misdemeanor statutes authorize.

• We have ignored the exercise of enforcement discretion by police and prosecutors. Many criminal laws are not enforced, or are enforced only rarely, as a matter either of deliberate law enforcement policy or because of the practical difficulties of enforcement. Both conditions are frequently encountered in the area of sex crimes. For example, although many states retain on their statute books criminal prohibitions against adultery and fornication, these laws are almost never enforced. Sodomy laws are with very rare exceptions enforced only when the offender has committed other crimes in which the authorities are also interested. Some sex laws are enforced sporadically (laws against prostitution are a good example), others consistently, such as those involving children. Sexual regulation is a particularly clear example of the frequent divergence between the law on the books and the law in action. A compilation of current police and prosecutorial policies with regard to the range of sexual activities nominally criminalized by state statutes would be a formidable undertaking, which we have not attempted.

• Finally, we have limited our consideration to statutes that regulate personal sexual activity as distinct from entrepreneurial activity related to sex, such as producing or distributing pornographic materials as distinct from buying pornography for personal consumption. The line between the personal and the entrepreneurial is sometimes faint, as in the case of prostitution. We include statutes that prohibit people from working as or patronizing prostitutes, but not statutes that regulate or prohibit the maintenance of a house of prostitution. We include the Mann Act because it can be applied to personal conduct such as transporting an underage female across state lines with intent to have sexual relations with her, although it is also enforced against the interstate traffic in prostitutes.

Because of the limitations and exclusions that we have mentioned and because statutes are frequently amended, this book should not be regarded as a definitive statement of current law. (Our summaries reflect amendments through September 1, 1994.) Nevertheless we believe that many people both within and outside the legal profession—specialists in the regulation of sexual behavior, students of the legislative process, lawyers involved in family and sex law, persons interested in social and political issues involving sexual orientation and sexual morality generally, and even persons who have or are contemplating a change in residence from one state to another—will find this compendium of statutory regulations, limited though it is as a guide to that mysterious entity, "the law," informative and even fascinating.

We acknowledge with gratitude the research assistance of Andrew Trask and of the following students at the University of Chicago and Boston University law schools: Stephen Armbruster, Douglas Y'Barbo, Scott Gaille, Heather Hostetter, Richard Hynes, Marie-Flore V. Johnson, Lorraine Jones, Maria Lopotukhin, Betsy Mukamal, Steven Neidhardt, Kimberly Ockene, Kevin Perez, and Clinton Uhlir. We also thank Elizabeth B. Clark and Daniel H. Jurayj for helpful suggestions.

1

Rape and Sexual Assault

Most states treat rape and sexual assault together in one section or series of sections in the state's code. In this chapter, we have summarized the laws on sexual assault between adults who are not spouses and do not stand in some relationship of trust, and where the victim does not consent to the sexual act.

Assaults by spouses are often treated differently under sexual assault laws. Because the question of whether such assaults should be legal has generated much debate, we have treated it in a separate chapter (chap. 2), where we sketch the spousal exemption where one exists. We have also treated separately acts that become offenses because of a special relationship of trust between the offender and victim (chap. 9). Many states prohibit conduct between psychotherapists and clients, for example, that would not be prohibited between strangers.

Many states use identical terms in defining the offense; others use a different term or set of terms for the same idea. For example, some states say "sexual penetration" where others say "sexual penetration and sexual intrusion" to mean the same thing. For the sake of simplicity, we have not repeated the definitions of some very frequently used and uniformly defined terms, such as "physically helpless."

Rape, which had been defined as sexual intercourse by a man with a woman, not his wife, by force and against her will, was a serious felony at common law. "Common law" means, roughly, judge-made as distinct from statutory law. Most crimes, such as rape, were originally common law crimes. Sexual assaults that did not involve intercourse were treated under the assault and battery provisions of the criminal law rather than as a separate offense of sexual battery.

Rape law has received an extraordinary amount of attention and commentary over the past thirty years. The particular aspects of the old law of rape that have received the most criticism are the exemption from rape for married people (covered in chapter 2), the common requirement that a conviction for rape cannot be obtained on the testimony of the victim unless it is corroborated by a third party or by physical evidence, a requirement that there be evidence of the victim's utmost physical resistance, evidentiary rules that made evidence of the victim's past sexual conduct admissible in a rape trial, and instructions to a jury to consider the victim's past conduct closely.

Rape reform laws have swept the states since the early 1970s. In addition to addressing some of the concerns just listed, states have struggled with the difference between objective manifestations of force, created by the defendant's conduct, and the subjective concept of the victim's nonconsent.

Degrees of sexual assault are another novelty in the laws of rape. Gradations have been added to apply different punishments to rapes, depending on the degree of force used. The gradations themselves have been controversial, evoking debate over what is the most injurious rape or what behavior can be most deterred by law. Sexual assaults that do not involve intercourse are now usually treated in the same code section as rape, but in most cases with less severe punishment.

Some rape statutes have not been significantly changed in the modern era; these statutes often do not define rape, or do so in relatively brief terms. Though the reforms in other states are so varied as to make classification tentative, the reforms tend to take their lead from one of three sources: the Michigan statute, the New York statute, or the Model Penal Code. No state uses the Model Penal Code language in its entirety, but it is reflected in the laws of Massachusetts, North Dakota, and South Dakota. The most significant difference among the statutory formulations of rape is whether the critical element is nonconsent, no matter how much evidence of force and coercion is available. The Model Penal Code emphasizes consent but avoids questions of the victim's subjective nonconsent as much as possible, focusing on outward manifestations of nonconsent such as physical resistance, corroborating testimony, or fresh complaint. In this the Code resembles the common law requirement of utmost resistance, although the Code takes resistance as important evidence of nonconsent rather than as essential evidence.

Reformers in Michigan removed the inquiry into resistance from the statute, instead focusing almost exclusively on the conduct of the defendant, termed "force or coercion," that constitutes sexual assault or imposition. The concept of "nonconsent" is not a part of the Michigan definition of rape, in keeping with Michigan's focus on the defendant's conduct alone.

The Model Penal Code downgrades the offense of sexual assault where the parties were voluntary social companions. The Michigan statute removes the language of rape entirely from its code, relying instead on degrees of sexual assault. The Michigan reformers believed that alignment with the traditional law of assault rather than rape would bring an easier set of evidentiary expectations to victims of rape. The Michigan statute was also the first to use gender-neutral language and to grade offenses equally regardless of the sex of the parties, a practice that is now very common in sexual assault statutes.

The New York statute, on which several other statutes are based, is closer to the Model Penal Code than to the Michigan statute, but departs from the Code in several respects. The New York statute does not focus on the resistance of the victim to the extent that the Model Penal Code does, and it is possible to be guilty of the highest level of offense without severe physical injury to the victim or where the victim and the defendant are social companions, unlike the approach of the Model Penal Code. Most states combine elements from the three models.

ALABAMA: It is a felony to engage in sexual intercourse or deviate sexual intercourse under the following circumstances: by forcible compulsion; or where the victim is incapable of consent because physically helpless, mentally incapacitated, or mentally defective. ALA. CODE §§ 13A-6-60 (enacted 1977), 13A-6-61 (enacted 1977), 13A-6-62 (enacted 1977), 13A-6-63 (enacted 1977), 13A-6-64 (enacted 1977). It is a felony to engage in sexual contact by the use of forcible compulsion or where the victim is incapable of consent because physically helpless or mentally incapacitated. ALA. CODE §§ 13A-6-60 (enacted 1977), 13A-6-66 (enacted 1977). It is a misdemeanor to engage in sexual intercourse or deviate sexual intercourse without the victim's consent or where consent is obtained by the use of any fraud or artifice. ALA. CODE §§ 13A-6-60 (enacted 1977), 13A-6-65 (enacted 1977). It is a misdemeanor to engage in sexual contact where the victim is incapable of consent because mentally defective. ALA. CODE §§ 13A-6-70 (enacted 1977), 13A-6-67 (enacted 1977). Forcible compulsion means physical force that overcomes earnest resistance or a threat, express or implied, that places a person in fear of immediate death or serious physical injury to any person. ALA. CODE § 13A-6-60 (enacted 1977).

ALASKA: It is a felony to engage in sexual penetration or sexual contact with another person: without that person's consent; where the victim is incapacitated or unaware that a sexual act is being committed; or when the offender knows the victim is mentally incapacitated. ALASKA STAT. §§ 11.41.410 (enacted 1978), 11.41.420 (enacted 1978), 11.41.425 (enacted 1988).

ARIZONA: It is a felony to intentionally or knowingly engage in sexual penetration, sexual contact (not defined as including contact over clothing), or oral sexual contact with any person without that person's consent. ARIZ. REV. STAT. ANN. §§ 13-1406 (enacted 1977), 13-1404 (enacted 1977). Without consent means either the victim is coerced by the immediate use or threatened use of force against a person or property, or the victim is incapable of consent by reason of mental disorder, drugs, alcohol, sleep, or any other similar impairment of cognition and such condition is known or should have reasonably been known to the defendant. ARIZ. REV. STAT. ANN. § 13-1401 (enacted 1977).

ARKANSAS: It is a felony to engage in sexual intercourse, deviate sexual intercourse, or sexual contact with another person by forcible compulsion or where the victim is incapable of consent because physically helpless. ARK. CODE ANN. §§ 5-14-103 (enacted 1975), 5-14-108 (enacted 1975). It is a felony to engage in sexual intercourse or deviate sexual intercourse, and a misdemeanor to engage in sexual contact, with another person where the victim is incapable of consent because mentally defective or mentally incapacitated. ARK. CODE ANN. §§ 5-14-105 (enacted 1975), 5-14-109 (enacted 1975).

CALIFORNIA: It is a felony to engage in sexual penetration where the offender knows or reasonably should know that the victim is incapable, because of a mental disorder or developmental or physical disability, of giving legal consent; where the act is accomplished against the victim's will by means of force, violence, duress, menace, or fear of immediate and unlawful bodily injury to any person; where the victim is mentally incapacitated; where the offender knows that the victim is unconscious of the nature of the act; where the victim submits under the belief that the offender is the victim's spouse, and this belief is induced by any artifice, pretense, or concealment practiced by the offender with the intent to induce the belief; where the act is accomplished against the victim's will by threatening to retaliate in the future against the victim or any other person, and there is a reasonable possibility that the perpetrator will execute the threat; or where the victim's consent is procured by false or fraudulent representation or pretense that is made with the intent to create fear, that does induce fear, and that would cause a reasonable person in like circumstances to act contrary to that person's free will. CAL. PENAL CODE §§ 261 (enacted 1872), 266c (enacted 1985), 286 (enacted 1872), 288a (enacted 1921), 289 (enacted 1978). It is a felony to take a woman unlawfully against her will, and by force, menace, or duress, compel her to marry any person, or to be defiled. CAL. PENAL CODE § 265 (enacted 1872). It is a felony for a person to take any victim unlawfully, and against the victim's will, and by force, menace, or duress, compel the victim to live with the offender or any other person in an illicit relation, against the victim's will. CAL. PENAL CODE § 266b (enacted 1905). Threatening to retaliate means a threat to kidnap or falsely imprison, or to inflict extreme pain, serious bodily injury, or death. Duress means a direct or implied threat of force, violence, danger, hardship, or retribution sufficient to coerce a reasonable person of ordinary susceptibilities to perform or acquiesce in an act which otherwise would not have occurred. Menace means any threat, declaration, or act which shows an intention to inflict an injury upon another. CAL. PENAL CODE § 261 (enacted 1872). Consent means positive cooperation, in act or attitude, pursuant to an exercise of free will where the person acts freely and voluntarily with knowledge of the nature of the act or transaction; a current or previous dating relationship does not constitute consent. CAL. PENAL CODE § 261.6 (enacted 1982). A person also receives a three-year sentence enhancement for the commission of certain specified crimes, such as rape and sodomy, when the offender commits such offenses with the knowledge that he or she has AIDS or the HIV virus at the time of commission. CAL. PENAL CODE § 12022.85 (enacted 1988).

COLORADO: It is a felony to engage in sexual penetration or sexual contact where the offender causes the victim's submission through the actual application of physical force or physical violence; by threat of imminent death, serious bodily injury, extreme pain, or kidnapping to be inflicted on anyone if the victim believes that the offender has the present ability to execute these threats; or by threatening to retaliate against any person, including threats of kidnapping, death, serious bodily injury, or extreme pain, if the victim reasonably believes that the offender will execute the threat. COLO. REV. STAT. §§ 18-3-401 (enacted 1975), 18-3-402 (enacted 1975), 18-3-404 (enacted 1975). It is a felony to engage in sexual penetration by any means reasonably calculated to cause submission against the victim's will; where the victim is mentally incapacitated; where the victim is physically helpless and the offender knows the victim is helpless and has not consented; where the offender knows that the victim is incapable of appraising the nature of the victim's conduct; or where the offender knows that the victim submits in the erroneous belief that the offender is the victim's spouse. COLO. REV. STAT. §§ 18-3-401 (enacted 1975), 18-3-402 (enacted 1975), 18-3-403 (enacted 1975). It is a misdemeanor to engage in sexual contact when the offender knows that the victim does not consent; where the victim is mentally incapacitated; where the victim is physically helpless and the offender knows it; or where the offender knows that the victim is incapable of appraising the nature of the conduct. COLO. REV. STAT. § 18-3-404 (enacted 1975). Consent means cooperation, in act or attitude, pursuant to an exercise of free will and with knowledge of the nature of the act; submission under the influence of fear does not constitute consent, nor does a previous or current relationship. COLO. REV. STAT. § 18-3-401 (enacted 1975).

CONNECTICUT: It is a felony to engage in sexual penetration where the victim is compelled by the use of force against the victim or a third person; is compelled by the threat of the use of force against any person which reasonably causes the victim to fear physical injury to any person; is mentally defective or mentally incapacitated to the extent of being unable to consent to the act; or is physically helpless. CONN. GEN. STAT. ANN. §§ 53a-65 (enacted 1969), 53a-70 (enacted 1969), 53a-70a (enacted 1975), 53a-71 (enacted 1969). It is a felony to engage in sexual contact with another person where the offender compels the victim to submit by the use of force against the victim or a third person or where the victim is compelled by the threat of the use of force against any person which reasonably causes the victim to fear physical injury to any person. CONN. GEN. STAT. ANN. §§ 53a-65 (enacted 1969), 53a-72a (enacted 1975). It is a misdemeanor to engage in sexual contact with another person where the victim is mentally defective or mentally incapacitated to the extent of being unable to consent to the act; the victim is physically helpless; or the offender acts without the victim's consent. CONN. GEN. STAT. ANN. §§ 53a-65 (enacted 1969), 53a-73a (enacted 1975). Use of force means use of a dangerous instrument, or use of actual physical force or violence or superior physical strength, against the victim. CONN. GEN. STAT. ANN. § 53a-65 (enacted 1969).

DELAWARE: It is a felony to engage in sexual penetration without the victim's consent or to intentionally place one or more fingers or thumbs or an object inside the vagina or anus of a person without the victim's consent. DEL. CODE ANN. tit. 11, §§ 770 (enacted 1953), 771 (enacted 1953), 772 (enacted 1953), 773 (enacted 1953), 774 (enacted 1953), 775 (enacted 1953). For these purposes, without consent means: the defendant compelled the victim to submit by force, gesture, or threat of death, physical injury, pain, or kidnapping to be inflicted upon the victim or a third party, or by any other means which would compel a reasonable person under the circumstances to submit. It is not required that the victim resist such force or threat to the utmost, or resist if the resistance would be futile or foolhardy, but the victim need resist only to the extent that is reasonably necessary to make the victim's refusal to consent known to the defendant. Without consent also means the offender knew that the victim was unconscious, asleep, or otherwise unaware that a sexual act was being performed; or the offender knew that the victim suffered from a mental illness or mental defect which rendered the victim incapable of appraising the nature of the sexual conduct; or the offender had substantially impaired the victim's power to appraise or control his or her conduct by administering or employing without the other person's knowledge or against his or her will drugs, intoxicants, or other means for the purpose of preventing resistance. DEL. CODE ANN. tit. 11, § 761 (enacted 1953). It is a felony for a person intentionally to compel or induce another to engage in any sexual act involving contact, penetration, or intercourse with the offender or a third person by means of instilling in the victim fear that, if the sexual act is not performed, the offender will cause physical injury to anyone; cause damage to property; engage in other conduct constituting a crime; accuse anyone of a crime or cause criminal charges to be instituted against the victim; expose a secret or publicize an asserted fact, whether true or false, intending to subject anyone to hatred, contempt, or ridicule; falsely testify or provide information or withhold testimony or information with respect to another's legal claim or defense; or perform any other act which is calculated to harm another person materially with respect to his or her health, safety, business, calling, career, financial condition, reputation, or personal relationships. DEL. CODE ANN. tit. 11, § 776 (enacted 1992). It is a misdemeanor to engage in sexual contact with another person with knowledge that the contact is offensive to the victim or occurs without the victim's consent. DEL. CODE ANN. tit. 11, § 767 (enacted 1953). If the victim is physically injured as a result of the offense or the offender displays what appears to be a deadly weapon or dangerous instrument, the offender is guilty of a felony. DEL. CODE ANN. tit. 11, § 769 (enacted 1953).

DISTRICT OF COLUMBIA: Whoever has carnal knowledge of a female forcibly and against her will, or whoever carnally knows and abuses a female under sixteen, is guilty of a felony. D.C. CODE § 22-2801 (enacted 1901).

FLORIDA: It is a felony to engage in sexual penetration with another person without that person's consent where the offender uses or threatens to use a deadly weapon; where the offender uses actual physical force likely to cause serious personal injury; where the victim is physically helpless to resist; where the offender coerces the victim to submit by threatening to use force or violence likely to cause serious personal injury to the victim, and the victim reasonably believes the offender has the present ability to execute the threat; where the offender coerces the victim to submit by threatening to retaliate against the victim or any other person, and the victim reasonably believes that the offender has the ability to execute the threat in the future; where the victim is mentally incapacitated; where the offender knows or has reason to believe that the victim is mentally defective; where the victim is physically incapacitated, meaning bodily impaired or handicapped and substantially limited in his or her ability to resist or flee an act. Consent must be intelligent, knowing, and voluntary, and may not be construed to include coerced submission. Retaliation includes, but is not limited to, threats of future physical punishment, kidnapping, false imprisonment or forcible confinement, or extortion. FLA. STAT. ANN. § 794.011 (enacted 1992). It is a misdemeanor to observe the commission of any of the above offenses, to have the ability to seek assistance by immediately reporting the incident to law enforcement, and to fail to seek assistance, if it would not expose one to any threat of physical violence and if the victim or offender is not one's husband, wife, parent, grandparent, child, grandchild, brother, or sister, by consanguinity or affinity. FLA. STAT. ANN. § 794.027 (enacted 1984).

GEORGIA: It is a capital felony to have carnal knowledge of a female forcibly and against her will. Carnal knowledge occurs when there is any penetration of the female sex organ by the male sex organ. GA. CODE ANN. § 16-6-1 (enacted 1833). It is a felony to perform or submit to any sexual act involving the sex organs of one person and the mouth or anus of another where the offender acts with force and against the will of the other person. GA. CODE ANN. § 16-6-2 (enacted 1833). It is a felony to intentionally penetrate with a foreign object the sexual organ or anus of another person without that person's consent. GA. CODE

ANN. § 16-6-22.2 (enacted 1981). It is a misdemeanor to intentionally engage in sexual contact with another person without that person's consent. GA. CODE ANN. § 16-6-22.1 (enacted 1981).

HAWAII: It is a felony to subject another person to sexual penetration under any of the following circumstances: the offender acts in the absence of consent; the offender uses a threat, express or implied, that places the victim in fear of bodily injury to or kidnapping of the victim or a third person; the offender uses a dangerous instrument; the offender uses physical force; the victim is mentally defective, mentally incapacitated or physically helpless; or the offender uses a threat, express or implied, that places the victim in fear of public humiliation, property damage, or financial loss. HAW. REV. STAT. §§ 707-700 (enacted 1972), 707-730 (enacted 1986), 707-731 (enacted 1986), 707-732 (enacted 1986). It is a felony for a person to engage in sexual contact with another person under any of the following circumstances: the victim is mentally defective, mentally incapacitated or physically helpless; the offender uses a threat, express or implied, that places a person in fear of bodily injury to or kidnapping of the victim or a third person; or the offender uses a dangerous instrument, or physical force to overcome the victim. HAW. REV. STAT. §§ 707-700 (enacted 1972), 707-732 (enacted 1986). It is a misdemeanor to subject a person to sexual contact in the absence of consent or where the offender uses a threat, express or implied, that places the victim in fear of public humiliation, property damage, or financial loss. HAW. REV. STAT. §§ 707-700 (enacted 1972), 707-733 (enacted 1986).

IDAHO: Rape, a felony, is an act of sexual intercourse accomplished with a female, or penetration of the oral or anal opening of a male with the offender's penis, under any of the following circumstances: the victim is incapable, through unsoundness of mind, whether temporary or permanent, of giving legal consent; the victim resists but his or her resistance is overcome by force or violence; the victim is prevented from resistance by threats of immediate and great bodily harm, accompanied by apparent power of execution; the victim is prevented from resistance by any intoxicating narcotic or anesthetic substance administered by or with the consent of the offender; the victim is at the time unconscious of the nature of the act and this is known to the offender; or the victim submits under the belief that the person committing the act is her husband, and the belief is induced by artifice, pretense, or concealment practiced by the offender with intent to induce the belief. IDAHO CODE

§§ 18-6101 (enacted 1972), 18-6108 (enacted 1990). It is a felony to cause the penetration of the genital or anal opening of another person by any object, instrument, or device against the victim's will by use of force or violence or by duress, or by threats of immediate and great bodily harm, accompanied by apparent power of execution, for the purpose of sexual arousal, gratification, or abuse. IDAHO CODE. § 18-6608 (enacted 1983).

ILLINOIS: It is a felony to commit an act of sexual penetration by use of force or threat of force, or where the offender knows that the victim is unable to understand the nature of the act or is unable to give knowing consent. ILL. ANN. STAT. ch. 720, para. 5/12-13 (enacted 1961). It is a felony to engage in sexual contact with a person by the use of force or threat of force or where the offender knows that the victim is unable to understand the nature of the act or is unable to give knowing consent under any of the following circumstances: where the offender displayed, threatened to use, or used a dangerous weapon or any object fashioned or utilized in such a manner as to lead the victim to reasonably believe it to be a dangerous weapon, or where the victim was sixty years old or older at the time of the offense. ILL. ANN. STAT. ch. 720, para. 5/12-16 (enacted 1961). It is a misdemeanor to engage in sexual contact with a person by the use of force or threat of force or where the offender knows that the victim is unable to understand the nature of the act or is unable to give knowing consent. ILL. ANN. STAT. ch. 720, para. 5/12-15 (enacted 1961). Force or threat of force means the use of force or violence, including but not limited to the following situations: when the offender threatens to use force or violence against the victim or a third person and the victim under the circumstances reasonably believes that the offender has the ability to execute the threat; or where the offender has overcome the victim by use of superior strength or size, physical restraint, or physical confinement. ILL. ANN. STAT. ch. 720, para. 5/12-12 (enacted 1961). The crime of sexual relations within families becomes criminal sexual assault if the child was under eighteen years of age. ILL. ANN. STAT. ch. 720, para. 5/12-13 (enacted 1961).

INDIANA: It is a felony to engage in sexual penetration where the victim is compelled by force or imminent threat of force, is unaware that the act is occurring, or is so mentally disabled or deficient that consent to the act cannot be given. IND. CODE ANN. §§ 35-41-1-9 (enacted 1983), 35-42-4-1 (enacted 1976), 35-42-4-2 (enacted 1976). It is a felony for a person, with the intent to arouse or satisfy the sexual desires of any person, to touch another person where the victim is compelled to submit to the touching by force or imminent threat of force, or is so mentally disabled or deficient that consent to the touching cannot be given. IND. CODE ANN. §§ 35-42-4-8 (enacted 1987).

IOWA: It is a felony to engage in a sex act by force or against the will of the victim, meaning in any case where the consent or acquiescence of the victim is procured by threats of violence toward any person, or where the victim suffers from a mental defect or incapacity which precludes giving consent, or lacks the mental capacity to know the right and wrong of conduct in sexual matters. IOWA CODE ANN. §§ 702.17 (enacted 1976), 709.1 (enacted 1976), 709.3 (enacted 1976), 709.4 (enacted 1976). Mental defect and mental incapacity are not defined. Sex act means any sexual contact between two or more persons, by penetration of the penis into the vagina or anus, by contact between the mouth and genitalia, by contact between the genitalia of one person and the genitalia or anus of another person, or by use of artificial sex organs or substitutes therefor in contact with the genitalia or anus. IOWA CODE ANN. § 702.17 (enacted 1976).

KANSAS: It is a felony to engage in sexual penetration with a person who does not consent to the act when the victim is overcome by force or fear; when the victim is unconscious or physically powerless; when the victim is incapable of giving consent because of a mental deficiency or disease, and that condition is known by or reasonably apparent to the offender; or when the victim is mentally incapacitated. KAN. STAT. ANN. §§ 21-3501 (enacted 1969), 21-3502 (enacted 1969), 21-3506 (enacted 1969).

KENTUCKY: It is a felony to engage in sexual intercourse, deviate sexual intercourse, or sexual contact with another person by forcible compulsion, or where the victim is physically helpless. KY. REV. STAT. ANN. §§ 510.040 (enacted 1974), 510.070 (enacted 1974), 510.110 (enacted 1974). It is a felony to engage in sexual intercourse or deviate sexual intercourse with a person who is incapable of consent because mentally defective or mentally incapacitated. KY. REV. STAT. ANN. §§ 510.060 (enacted 1974), 510.090 (enacted 1974). It is a misdemeanor to engage in sexual contact with a person who is incapable of consent because mentally defective or mentally incapacitated or where the victim does not expressly or impliedly acquiesce in the actor's conduct . KY. REV. STAT. ANN. §§ 510.120 (enacted 1974), 510.130 (enacted 1974), 510.020 (enacted 1974). It is a misdemeanor to engage in sexual intercourse or deviate sexual intercourse with another person without the latter's consent, meaning through forcible compulsion or where the victim lacks capacity to consent. KY. REV. STAT. ANN. §§ 510.140 (enacted 1974), 510.020 (enacted 1974). Forcible compulsion means physical force that overcomes earnest resistance or a threat, express or implied, that overcomes earnest resistance; by placing the victim in fear of immediate death or physical injury to the victim or another person or in fear that the victim or another person will be immediately kidnapped. KY. REV. STAT. ANN. § 510.010 (enacted 1974).

LOUISIANA: It is a felony to engage in anal or vaginal intercourse with another person where the victim resists the act to the utmost, but where resistance is overcome by force; where the victim is prevented from resisting by threats of great and immediate bodily harm, accompanied by apparent power of execution; where the victim is prevented from resisting the act because the offender is armed with a dangerous weapon; where two or more offenders participate in the act; where the victim is prevented from resisting the act by force or threats of physical violence under circumstances where the victim reasonably believes that such resistance would not prevent the rape; where the victim is mentally incapacitated or suffers from a mental defect; or where the female victim submits under the belief that the person committing the act is her husband and such belief is intentionally induced by any artifice, pretense, or concealment practiced by the offender. It is a felony to engage in sexual contact with a person where the offender acts without the consent of the victim. LA. REV. STAT. ANN. §§ 14:41 (enacted 1978), 14:42 (enacted 1978), 14:42.1 (enacted 1978), 14:43 (enacted 1978), 14:43.1 (enacted 1978). It is a felony to engage in any of the following acts where the offender compels the victim to submit by placing the victim in fear of receiving bodily harm: the touching of the anus or genitals of the victim by the offender or the offender by the victim using the mouth or tongue. LA. REV. STAT. ANN. § 14:43.3 (enacted 1978).

MAINE: It is a felony to engage in contact between the genitals of a person, an animal, or an object being manipulated by that person and the anus, genitals, or mouth of another under any of the following circumstances: the victim submits because of the use of physical force, a threat to use physical force, or a combination thereof that makes the victim unable to physically repel the actor or produces in the victim a reasonable fear that death, serious bodily injury, or kidnapping might be imminently inflicted upon any person; the actor has substantially impaired the victim's power to appraise or control his or her sexual acts by administering or employing drugs, intoxicants, or other similar means where the victim did not voluntarily consume the substance with knowledge of its nature or did so pursuant to medical treatment; the offender compels or induces the victim to engage in the conduct by any threat; the victim suffers from mental disability that is reasonably apparent or known to the actor and renders the victim substantially incapable of appraising the nature of the conduct or his or her right to deny or withdraw consent; or the victim is unconscious or otherwise physically incapable of resisting and has not consented to the sexual act. ME. REV. STAT. ANN. tit. 17-A, §§ 251 (enacted 1975), 253 (enacted 1975). It is a felony to engage in sexual contact with a person who has not expressly or impliedly acquiesced in the sexual contact; where the victim is unconscious or otherwise physically incapable of resisting and has not consented to the sexual contact; or the victim suffers from mental disability that is reasonably apparent or known to the actor and renders the victim substantially incapable of appraising the nature of the conduct or his or her right to deny or withdraw consent; or the victim submits as a result of compulsion. ME. REV. STAT. ANN. tit. 17-A, § 255 (enacted 1975). Compulsion is defined so that the victim is not required to resist in order for compulsion to be present. ME. REV. STAT. ANN. tit. 17-A, § 251 (enacted 1975).

MARYLAND: It is a felony to engage in sexual penetration by force or threat of force against the will and without the consent of the victim, or where the victim is mentally defective, mentally incapacitated, or physically helpless. MD. ANN. CODE, art. 27, §§ 461 (enacted 1976), 462 (enacted 1976), 463 (enacted 1976), 464 (enacted 1976), 464A (enacted 1976). It is a felony to engage in sexual contact with another person against the will and without the consent of the other person where the offender employs or displays a dangerous or deadly weapon or an article which the victim reasonably concludes is a dangerous or deadly weapon; the offender inflicts suffocation, strangulation, disfigurement, or serious physical injury upon the victim or upon anyone else in the course of committing the offense; the offender threatens or places the victim in fear that the victim or any person known to the victim will be imminently subjected to death, suffocation, strangulation, disfigurement, serious physical injury, or kidnapping; or the offender is aided and abetted by one or more other persons. It is also a felony to engage in sexual contact where the offender knows or should reasonably know that the victim is mentally defective, mentally incapacitated, or physically helpless. MD. ANN. CODE, art. 27, §§ 461 (enacted 1976), 464B (enacted 1976). In Maryland, the definition of sexual contact includes the penetration by any part of the offender's body, other than the penis, mouth, or tongue, into the genital or anal opening of the victim's body. MD. ANN. CODE, art. 27, § 461 (enacted 1976). It is a misdemeanor to engage in sexual contact with another person against the will and without the consent of that person. MD. ANN. CODE, art. 27, §§ 461 (enacted 1976), 464C (enacted 1976).

MASSACHUSETTS: It is a felony to engage in sexual intercourse or deviate sexual intercourse with another person where the victim is compelled to submit by force and against his or her will or is compelled to submit by threat of bodily injury. MASS. GEN. LAWS ch. 265, § 22 (enacted 1974). A person who applies, administers, or causes to be taken by the victim any drug, matter, or thing with intent to stupefy or overpower the victim in order to enable any person to engage in unlawful sexual intercourse with the victim commits a felony. MASS. GEN. LAWS ch. 272, § 3 (enacted 1978). Persons who with offensive or disorderly acts accost or annoy persons of the opposite sex; lewd, wanton, and lascivious persons in speech or behavior; commit a misdemeanor. MASS. GEN. LAWS ch. 272, § 53 (enacted 1943).

MICHIGAN: It is a felony to engage in sexual penetration or sexual contact with another person under any of the following circumstances: the offense occurs involving the commission of any other felony; the offender is armed with a weapon or any article used or fashioned in a manner to lead the victim to reasonably believe it to be a weapon; the actor causes personal injury to the victim and either knows that the person is mentally incapable, mentally incapacitated by a narcotic or other substance administered by the offender, or physically helpless; or force or coercion is used to accomplish the offense. Force or coercion means that the offender overcomes the victim through the actual application of physical force or physical violence; the actor coerces the victim to submit by threatening to use force or violence on the victim, and the victim believes that the offender has the present ability to execute these threats; the offender coerces the victim to submit by threatening to retaliate, including threats of physical punishment, kidnapping, or extortion, in the future against the victim or any other person and the victim believes that the offender has the ability to execute this threat; or the actor engages in medical treatment or examination of the victim in a manner or for purposes that are medically recognized as unethical or unacceptable. It is also a felony to engage in sexual penetration or sexual contact with another person where the offender is aided or abetted by one or more other persons and knows or has reason to know that the victim is mentally incapable, mentally incapacitated by a narcotic or other substance administered by the offender, or physically helpless, or the offender uses force or coercion. MICH. COMP. LAWS ANN. §§ 750.520a (enacted 1974), 750.520b (enacted 1974), 750.520c (enacted 1974). It is a felony to engage in sexual penetration if the offender uses force or coercion to accomplish the offense or if the actor knows that the victim is mentally incapable, mentally incapacitated, or physically helpless; however, sexual contact under these circumstances is only a misdemeanor. MICH. COMP. LAWS ANN. §§ 750.520d (enacted 1974), 750.520e (enacted 1974).

MINNESOTA: It is a felony to engage in sexual penetration or sexual contact if circumstances existing at the time of the act cause the victim to have a reasonable fear of imminent great bodily harm to the victim or a third person; the offender is armed with a dangerous weapon or any article fashioned in a manner to lead the victim to reasonably believe it to be a dangerous weapon, and uses or threatens to use the weapon or article to cause the victim to submit; the offender uses force or coercion to accomplish the act; or the offender knows or has reason to know that the victim is mentally impaired, mentally incapacitated, or physically helpless. MINN. STAT. ANN. §§ 609.341 (enacted 1975), 609.342 (enacted 1975), 609.343 (enacted 1975), 609.344 (enacted 1975), 609.345 (enacted 1975). Mentally impaired means that the victim, as a result of inadequately developed or impaired intelligence or a substantial psychiatric disorder of thought or mood, lacks the judgment to give a reasoned consent to sexual contact or penetration. MINN. STAT. ANN. § 609.341 (enacted 1975). Force means the infliction, attempted infliction, or threatened infliction by the offender of bodily harm, or the commission or threat of any other crime by the offender against any person which causes the victim to believe that the actor has the present ability to execute the threat and causes the victim to submit. MINN. STAT. ANN. § 609.341 (enacted 1975). Coercion means words or circumstances that cause the victim reasonably to fear that the offender will inflict bodily harm upon, or hold in confinement, the victim or another, or force the victim to submit to sexual penetration or contact, but proof of coercion does not require proof of a specific act or threat. MINN. STAT. ANN. § 609.341 (enacted 1975). Nonconsensual sexual contact is a misdemeanor. MINN. STAT. ANN. § 609.3451 (enacted 1988). The meaning of sexual contact for the purposes of a single misdemeanor offense only does not include the intentional touching of the clothing covering the immediate area of the buttocks, but does include the intentional removal or attempted removal of clothing covering the victim's intimate parts or undergarments, if the action is performed with sexual or aggressive intent. MINN. STAT. ANN. § 609.3451 (enacted 1988). Consent means a voluntary uncoerced manifestation of a present agreement to perform a particular sexual act with the offender. MINN. STAT. ANN. § 609.341 (enacted 1975).

MISSISSIPPI: It is a felony to forcibly ravish any person, or to have carnal knowledge of a victim without the victim's consent by administering to the victim any substance or liquid which shall produce such stupor or imbecility of mind or weakness of body as to prevent effectual resistance. MISS. CODE ANN. § 97-3-65 (enacted 1848). It is a felony to assault with intent to forcibly ravish any female of previous chaste character. MISS. CODE ANN. § 97-3-71 (enacted 1906). It is a felony to take a person unlawfully, against his or her will, and by force, menace, fraud, deceit, stratagem, or duress, compel or induce him or her to marry the offender or to marry any other person or to be defiled. MISS. CODE ANN. § 97-3-1 (enacted 1848).

MISSOURI: It is a felony to engage in sexual intercourse, deviate sexual intercourse, or sexual contact with another person without that person's consent by the use of forcible compulsion. MO. ANN. STAT. §§ 566.030 (enacted 1977), 566.060 (enacted 1977), 566.100 (enacted 1977). It is a felony to engage in sexual intercourse or deviate sexual intercourse with a person who is incapacitated. MO. ANN. STAT. §§ 566.040 (enacted 1977), 566.070 (enacted 1977).

MONTANA: It is a felony to engage in sexual penetration and a misdemeanor to engage in sexual contact without the victim's consent. Sexual contact without consent becomes a felony where the offender inflicts bodily injury on anyone in the course of committing the offense. Without consent means the victim is compelled to submit by force against any person, or the victim is incapable of consent because the victim is mentally defective, mentally incapacitated, or physically helpless. The definition of mentally incapacitated does not include a requirement that the victim consumed an intoxicating substance involuntarily. MONT. CODE ANN. §§ 45-5-501 (enacted 1973), 45-2-101 (enacted 1973), 45-5-502 (enacted 1973), 45-5-503 (enacted 1973).

NEBRASKA: It is a felony to subject another person to sexual penetration and overcome the victim by force, express or implied, coercion, or deception, or know or have reason to know that the victim is mentally or physically incapable of resisting or appraising the nature of his or her conduct. NEB. REV STAT. § 28-319 (enacted 1977). It is a misdemeanor to subject any person to sexual contact under any of these circumstances or a felony if serious personal injury is caused to the victim. NEB. REV STAT. § 28-320 (enacted 1977).

NEVADA: It is a felony to subject another person to sexual penetration, or to force another person to make a sexual penetration on himself or herself or on another, against the victim's will or under conditions in which the offender knows or should know that the victim is mentally or physically incapable of resisting, or understanding the nature of, the conduct. NEV. REV. STAT. ANN. §§ 200.364 (enacted 1977), 200.366 (enacted 1977).

NEW HAMPSHIRE: It is a felony to engage in sexual penetration with another person where the offender overcomes the victim through the actual application of physical force, physical violence, or superior strength; where the victim is physically helpless to resist; where the offender coerces the victim to submit by threatening to use physical violence or superior physical strength on the victim and the victim believes the offender has the present ability to execute the threat; where the offender coerces the victim to submit by threatening to retaliate against the victim or any other person by actions including but not limited to physical or mental torment or abuse, kidnapping, false imprisonment, extortion, public humiliation, or disgrace, and the victim believes the offender has the present ability to execute the threat; where the victim submits under circumstances involving false imprisonment, kidnapping, or extortion; where the offender, without the prior knowledge or consent of the victim, administers or has knowledge of another person administering to the victim any intoxicating substance which mentally incapacitates the victim; where the actor engages in the medical treatment or examination of the victim in a manner or for purposes that are not medically recognized as ethical or acceptable; where, except as between legally married spouses, the victim is mentally defective and the actor knows or has reason to know that the victim is mentally defective; where the actor through concealment or by the element of surprise is able to cause sexual penetration with the victim before the victim has an adequate chance to flee or resist. N.H. REV. STAT. ANN. § 632-A:1 (enacted 1975), 632-A:2 (enacted 1975). It is a misdemeanor to subject any person thirteen or over to sexual contact under any of the circumstances named above. N.H. REV. STAT. ANN. § 632-A:4 (enacted 1975). It is also a felony to subject a person to sexual contact under any of the circumstances named above if serious personal injury is caused to the victim. N.H. REV. STAT. ANN. § 632-A:4 (enacted 1975).

NEW JERSEY: It is a felony to engage in sexual penetration or sexual contact under the following circumstances: the act is committed during the commission, or attempted commission, of robbery, kidnapping, homicide, aggravated assault on another, burglary, arson, or criminal escape; the offender is armed with a weapon or object fashioned in such a manner as to lead the victim to reasonably believe it to be a weapon and threatens by word or gesture to use the weapon or object; or the offender is aided or abetted by one or more persons and either the offender uses physical force or coercion or the victim is physically helpless, mentally defective, or mentally incapacitated. N.J. STAT. ANN. §§ 2C:14-1 (enacted 1978), 2C:14-2 (enacted 1978), 2C:14-3 (enacted 1978). It is a felony to engage in sexual penetration and a misdemeanor to engage in sexual contact if the offender uses physical force or coercion, but the victim does not sustain severe personal injury, or the victim is physically helpless, mentally defective, or mentally incapacitated. N.J. STAT. ANN. §§ 2C:14-1 (enacted 1978), 2C:14-2 (enacted 1978), 2C:14-3 (enacted 1978). The sexual contact must be for the purpose either of sexually arousing or gratifying the offender, or of degrading or humiliating the victim. N.J. STAT. ANN. §§ 2C:14-1 (enacted 1978). Coercion means to threaten, with the purpose of restricting another's freedom of action to engage or refrain from engaging in conduct, to do any of the following: inflict bodily injury on anyone or commit any other offense; accuse anyone of an offense; expose any secret which would tend to subject any person to hatred, contempt, or ridicule, or to impair a person's credit or business repute; take or withhold action as an official, or cause an official to take or withhold action; bring about or continue a strike, boycott, or other collective action; testify or provide information or withhold testimony or information with respect to another's legal claim or defense; or perform any other act which would substantially benefit the actor but which is calculated to substantially harm another person with respect to his or her health, safety, business, calling, career, financial condition, reputation, or personal relationship. N.J. STAT. ANN. §§ 2C:14-1 (enacted 1978).

NEW MEXICO: It is a felony to engage in sexual penetration with a person by the use of force or coercion or in the commission of any other felony. Force or coercion means the use of physical force or physical violence; the use of threats to use physical violence or physical force against the victim or a third person when the victim believes that there is a present ability to execute such threats; the use of threats, including threats of physical punishment, kidnapping, extortion, or retaliation directed against the victim or another person when the victim believes there is ability to execute such threats; or perpetrating criminal sexual penetration or sexual contact when the offender knows or has reason to know that the victim is unconscious, asleep, or otherwise physically helpless, or suffers from a mental defect. Physical or verbal resistance by the victim is not an element of force or coercion. N.M. STAT. ANN. §§ 30-9-10 (enacted 1975), 30-9-11 (enacted 1975). It is a felony to engage in sexual contact under the following circumstances: by the use of force or coercion which results in personal injury to the victim; by the use of force or coercion where the offender is aided or abetted by one or more persons; or where the offender is armed with a deadly weapon. Sexual contact includes a requirement that the intimate parts be unclothed. N.M. STAT. ANN. §§ 30-9-10 (enacted 1975), 30-9-12 (enacted 1975). Sexual contact is a misdemeanor when perpetrated through the use of force or coercion. N.M. STAT. ANN. § 30-9-12 (enacted 1975).

NEW YORK: A male is guilty of rape, a felony, when he engages in sexual intercourse with a female by forcible compulsion or where the female is incapable of consent because physically helpless. N.Y. PENAL LAW § 130.35 (enacted 1965). It is a felony to engage in deviate sexual intercourse with another person by forcible compulsion or where the victim is physically helpless, mentally defective, or mentally incapacitated. N.Y. PENAL LAW §§ 130.05 (enacted 1965), 130.40 (enacted 1965), 130.50 (enacted 1965). It is a felony to insert a foreign object into the vagina, urethra, penis, or rectum of another person causing physical injury to that person or to subject another person to sexual contact by forcible compulsion or where the victim is physically helpless. N.Y. PENAL LAW §§ 130.65 (enacted 1965), 130.70 (enacted 1978).

It is a misdemeanor to subject another person to sexual contact who is mentally defective or mentally incapacitated or where the victim does not expressly or impliedly acquiesce in the offender's conduct. N.Y. PENAL LAW §§ 130.05 (enacted 1965), 130.55 (enacted 1965), 130.60 (enacted 1965). It is a misdemeanor for a male to engage in sexual intercourse with a female who is mentally defective or mentally incapacitated. N.Y. PENAL LAW §§ 130.05 (enacted 1965), 130.20 (enacted 1965). Forcible compulsion means to compel by either the use of physical force or a threat, express or implied, that places a person in fear of immediate death or physical injury to himself, herself, or another person, or in fear that any person will be kidnapped. N.Y. PENAL LAW § 130.00 (enacted 1965).

NORTH CAROLINA: It is a felony to engage in or to attempt to engage in a sexual act by force and against the will of the victim, or where the offender knows or should reasonably know that the victim is mentally defective, mentally incapacitated, or physically helpless. N.C. GEN. STAT. §§ 14-27.1 (enacted 1979), 14-27.2 (enacted 1979), 14-27.3 (enacted 1979), 14-27.4 (enacted 1979), 14-27.5 (enacted 1979).

NORTH DAKOTA: It is a felony to engage in sexual penetration or sexual contact where the offender compels the victim to submit by force or by threat of imminent death, serious bodily injury, or kidnapping, to be inflicted on any human being, or the offender compels the victim to submit by any threat that would render a person of reasonable firmness incapable of resisting. N.D. CENT. CODE §§ 12.1-20-02 (enacted 1973), 12.1-20-03 (enacted 1973), 12.1-20-04 (enacted 1973). It is a felony to engage in sexual penetration if the victim is mentally incapacitated, the offender knows that the victim is unaware that the act is being committed, or the offender knows or has reasonable cause to believe that the victim has a mental defect. N.D. CENT. CODE § 12.1-20-03 (enacted 1973). It is a misdemeanor to engage in sexual contact if the offender knows or has reason to believe that the contact is offensive to the victim; the offender knows or has reason to believe that the victim has a mental defect; or the victim is mentally incapacitated. N.D. CENT. CODE § 12.1-20-07 (enacted 1973).

OHIO: It is a felony to engage in sexual penetration or sexual contact if the victim is mentally incapacitated and the offender has facilitated the incapacity for the purpose of preventing resistance, or if the offender purposely compels the victim to submit by force or threat of force. Physicial resistance by the victim to the offender need not be proved. OHIO REV. CODE ANN. §§ 2907.01 (enacted 1972), 2907.02

(enacted 1972), 2907.05 (enacted 1972). It is a felony to engage in sexual penetration where the offender knowingly coerces the victim to submit by any means that would prevent resistance by a person of ordinary resolution; the offender knows that the victim's ability to appraise the nature of or control his or her conduct is substantially impaired; or the offender knows that the victim submits either because the victim is unaware that the act is being committed or because the victim mistakenly identifies the offender as his or her spouse. OHIO REV. CODE ANN. § 2907.03 (enacted 1994). It is a felony to engage in sexual contact where the offender knows that the victim's judgment or control is substantially impaired as a result of the influence of any drug or intoxicant administered to the victim with the victim's consent for the purpose of any kind of medical or dental examination, treatment, or surgery. OHIO REV. CODE ANN. § 2907.05 (enacted 1993). It is a misdemeanor to engage in sexual contact if the offender knows that the sexual contact is offensive to the victim or is reckless in that regard, or the offender knows that the victim's ability to appraise the nature of or control the offender's or the victim's conduct is substantially impaired. A person cannot be convicted of this misdemeanor solely on the victim's testimony unsupported by other evidence. OHIO REV. CODE ANN. § 2907.06 (enacted 1990).

OKLAHOMA: It is a felony to engage in sexual penetration with another person under any of the following circumstances: where the victim is incapable through mental illness or any other unsoundness of mind, temporary or permanent, of giving legal consent; where force or violence is used or threatened, accompanied by apparent power of execution against the victim or a third person; where the victim is mentally incapacitated; where the victim is unconscious of the nature of the act and the offender knows this; or where the victim submits under the belief that the person committing the act is a spouse and this belief is induced by artifice, pretense, or concealment by the accused (if the artifice is achieved in collaboration with the spouse, both are guilty). OKLA. STAT. ANN. tit. 21, §§ 1111 (enacted 1981), 1111.1 (enacted 1981), 1113 (enacted 1981), 1114 (enacted 1981), 1115 (enacted 1965), 1116 (enacted 1887). It is a felony to seduce and have illicit connection with any unmarried female of previous chaste character under promise of marriage; later marriage is a defense. OKLA. STAT. ANN. tit. 21, §§ 1120 (enacted 1887), 1121 (enacted 1887). It is a felony to force another person to engage in the detestable and abominable crime against nature under any of the following circumstances: where the victim is incapable through mental illness or any other unsoundness of mind, temporary or permanent, of giving legal consent; or where force or violence is used or threatened, accompanied by apparent power of execution. OKLA. STAT. ANN. tit. 21, § 888 (enacted 1981).

OREGON: It is a felony for a person to engage in sexual penetration under any of the following circumstances: where the victim is subjected to forcible compulsion, meaning physical force that overcomes earnest resistance, or a threat, express or implied, that places the victim in fear of immediate or future death or physical injury to, or kidnapping of, the victim or another; where the victim is incapable of consent by reason of mental defect, mental incapacitation, or physical helplessness; or where the victim does not consent. OR. REV. STAT. §§ 163.305 (enacted 1971), 163.375 (enacted 1971), 163.405 (enacted 1971), 163.411 (enacted 1981), 163.425 (enacted 1971). It is a felony to engage in sexual contact with a person where the victim is subjected to forcible compulsion by the offender. OR. REV. STAT. § 163.427 (enacted 1991). It is a felony to intentionally cause a person under eighteen to touch or contact the mouth, anus, or sex organs of an animal for the purpose of arousing or gratifying the sexual desire of a person. OR. REV. STAT. § 163.427 (enacted 1991). It is a misdemeanor to engage in sexual contact with a person where the victim does not consent or is incapable of consenting because mentally defective, mentally incapacitated, or physically helpless. OR. REV. STAT. § 163.415 (enacted 1971).

PENNSYLVANIA: It is a felony to engage in sexual penetration or deviate sexual intercourse under any of the following circumstances: by forcible compulsion; by threat of forcible compulsion that would prevent resistance by a person of reasonable resolution; where the complainant is unconscious or where the person knows that the complainant is unaware that sexual intercourse is occurring; where the person has substantially impaired the complainant's power to appraise or control his or her conduct by administering or employing, without the knowledge of the complainant, drugs, intoxicants, or other means for the purpose of preventing resistance; where the complainant suffers from a mental disability which renders the complainant incapable of consent; or generally without the complainant's consent. As used in this section, the term "forcible compulsion" includes, but is not limited to, compulsion resulting in another person's death, whether the death occured before, during, or after the sexual intercourse. 18 PA. CONS. STAT. ANN. §§ 3121 (enacted 1972), 3123 (enacted 1972), 3124.1 (enacted 1995), 3125 (enacted 1990). It is a misdemeanor for a person to engage in sexual contact with a person under the circumstances defined above. 18 PA. CONS. STAT. ANN. § 3126 (enacted 1992).

RHODE ISLAND: It is a felony to engage in sexual penetration with a person where the offender knows or has reason to know that the victim is mentally incapacitated, mentally disabled, or physically helpless; the offender uses force or coercion; the offender, through concealment or by the element of surprise, is able to overcome the victim; or the accused engages in medical treatment or examination of the victim for the purpose of sexual arousal, gratification, or stimulation. R.I. GEN. LAWS §§ 11-37-2 (enacted 1979), 11-37-3 (enacted 1979). Assault with attempt to do any of the above is also a felony. R.I. GEN. LAWS § 11-37-8 (enacted 1979). Force or coercion means any of the following: the offender uses or threatens to use a weapon or any article used or fashioned in a manner to lead the victim to reasonably believe it to be a weapon; the offender overcomes the victim through the application of physical force or physical violence; the offender coerces the victim to submit by threatening to use force or violence on the victim and the victim reasonably believes the offender has the present ability to execute the threats; or the offender coerces the victim to submit by threatening to, at some time in the future, murder, inflict serious bodily injury upon, or kidnap the victim or a third person, and the victim believes that the offender has the ability to execute the threat. R.I. GEN. LAWS § 11-37-1 (enacted 1979). It is a misdemeanor for any person other than the victim, who knows or has reason to know that a sexual assault involving sexual penetration is taking place in his or her presence, to fail to immediately notify the state police or local police department; provided that no one can be charged with failure to report without a signed complaint by the victim. R.I. GEN. LAWS §§ 11-37-3.1 (enacted 1983), 11-37-3.2 (enacted 1983), 11-37-3.3 (enacted 1983). It is a felony to engage in sexual contact with another person under any of the following circumstances: the offender knows or has reason to know that the victim is mentally incapacitated, mentally disabled, or physically helpless; the offender uses force or coercion; or the offender engages in the medical treatment or examination of the victim for the purpose of sexual arousal, gratification, or stimulation. R.I. GEN. LAWS §§ 11-37-4 (enacted 1979), 11-37-5 (enacted 1979).

SOUTH CAROLINA: It is a felony for a person to engage in sexual penetration or commit assault with intent to do the same under any of the following circumstances: the offender uses aggravated force, meaning physical force or physical violence of a high and aggravated nature to overcome the victim or includes the threat of the use of a deadly weapon; the victim is also the victim of forcible confinement, kidnapping, robbery, extortion, burglary, housebreaking, or any other similar offense or act; the offender uses aggravated coercion, meaning that the actor threatens to use force or violence of a high and aggravated nature to overcome the victim or a third person and the victim reasonably believes that the offender has the present ability to carry out the threat, or the offender threatens to retaliate in the future by the infliction of physical harm, kidnapping, or extortion under circumstances of aggravation; the offender uses force or coercion; or the offender knows or has reason to know that the victim is mentally defective, mentally incapacitated, or physically helpless. S.C. CODE ANN. §§ 16-3-651 (enacted 1977), 16-3-652 (enacted 1977), 16-3-653 (enacted 1977), 16-3-654 (enacted 1977), 16-3-656 (enacted 1977). It is a felony for a person who knows that he or she is infected with HIV to forcibly engage in vaginal, anal, or oral intercourse without the consent of the other person including the legal spouse of the offender. S.C. CODE ANN. § 44-29-145 (enacted 1988).

SOUTH DAKOTA: It is a felony to engage in sexual penetration with a person under any of the following circumstances: using force, coercion, or threats of immediate and great bodily harm against the victim or a third party in the victim's presence accompanied by apparent power of execution; where the victim is incapable, because of physical or mental incapacity, of giving consent to the act; or where the victim is incapable of giving consent because of some intoxicating, narcotic, or anesthetic agent, or hypnosis. S.D. CODIFIED LAWS ANN. § 22-22-1 (enacted 1877). It is a felony for a person to knowingly engage in sexual contact with another person who is incapable, because of physical or mental incapacity, of consenting. S.D. CODIFIED LAWS ANN. § 22-22-7.2 (enacted 1985). It is a misdemeanor for a person to knowingly engage in sexual contact with a person who is capable of consenting but has not consented. S.D. CODIFIED LAWS ANN. § 22-22-7.4 (enacted 1991).

TENNESSEE: It is a felony to engage in sexual penetration or sexual contact with a person under any of the following circumstances: force or coercion is used; the offender causes bodily injury to the victim; the offender knows or has reason to know that the victim is mentally defective, mentally incapacitated, or physically helpless; or the act is accomplished by fraud. Coercion includes threat of kidnapping, extortion, force, or violence to be performed immediately or in the future, or the use of parental, custodial, or official authority over a child under fifteen. TENN. CODE ANN. §§ 39-13-501 (enacted 1989), 39-13-502 (enacted 1989), 39-13-503 (enacted 1989), 39-13-504 (enacted 1989), 39-13-505 (enacted 1989).

TEXAS: It is a felony to intentionally or knowingly engage in sexual penetration with a person without that person's consent. Without consent means any of the following: the offender compels the victim to submit or participate by the use of physical force or violence; the offender compels the victim to submit or participate by threatening to use force or violence against the victim and the victim believes that the offender has the present ability to execute the threat; the victim has not consented and the offender knows that the victim is unconscious or physically unable to resist; the offender knows that the victim is mentally defective or incapable of resisting the act; the victim has not consented and the offender knows that the other person is unaware that the act is occurring; the victim is mentally incapacitated; or the offender compels the victim to submit or participate by threatening to use force or violence against any person and the victim believes that the offender has the ability to execute the threat. TEX. PENAL CODE ANN. § 22.011 (enacted 1983).

UTAH: It is a felony for a person to engage in sexual penetration or sexual contact with another person without that person's consent. UTAH CODE ANN. §§ 76-5-402 (enacted 1973), 76-5-402.2 (enacted 1983), 76-5-403 (enacted 1973), 76-5-404 (enacted 1973). These acts are without consent under the following circumstances: the victim expresses lack of consent through words or conduct; the offender overcomes the victim through the actual application of physical force or violence; the offender is able to overcome the victim through concealment or by the element of surprise; the offender coerces the victim to submit by threatening to retaliate, including threats of the use of physical force, kidnapping, or extortion in the future and the victim believes that the offender has the ability to execute the threat; the victim has not consented and the offender knows the victim is unconscious, unaware that the act is occurring, or physically unable to resist; the victim has a mental defect or is mentally incapacitated; or the offender knows that the victim is participating in the belief that the offender is the victim's spouse. UTAH CODE ANN. § 76-5-406 (enacted 1973). An HIV positive individual wih actual knowledge of his or her infection suffers enhanced penalties. UTAH CODE ANN. § 76-10-1309 (enacted 1993).

VERMONT: It is a felony to engage in sexual penetration with another person under any of the following circumstances: without the consent of the victim; by threatening or coercing the victim; by placing the victim in fear that any person will suffer imminent bodily injury; or where the victim is mentally incapacitated. VT. STAT. ANN. tit. 13, § 3252 (enacted 1977). Consent means words or actions by a person indicating a voluntary agreement to engage in the sexual act. VT. STAT. ANN. tit. 13, § 3251 (enacted 1977). Lack of consent may be shown without proof of resistance. An offender shall be deemed to have acted without consent where the actor knew that the victim was mentally defective, physically helpless, or unaware that a sexual act was being committed. VT. STAT. ANN. tit. 13, § 3254 (enacted 1977).

VIRGINIA: It is a felony to engage in or attempt to engage in sexual penetration where the act is accomplished against the victim's will, by force, threat, or intimidation of or against the victim or another person; or through the use of the victim's mental incapacity or physical helplessness. VA. CODE ANN. §§ 18.2-61 (enacted 1950), 18.2-67.1 (enacted 1981), 18.2-67.2 (enacted 1981), 18.2-67.5 (enacted 1981). It is a misdemeanor called sexual battery for a person to engage in or attempt to engage in sexual conduct with a victim against the victim's will, by force, threat, or intimidation; or through the use of the victim's mental incapacity or physical helplessness. VA. CODE ANN. §§ 18.2-67.4 (enacted 1981), 18.2-67.5 (enacted 1981). Sexual battery is a felony when the offender causes serious bodily or mental injury to the victim or uses or threatens to use a dangerous weapon. VA. CODE ANN. §§ 18.2-67.3 (enacted 1981), 18.2-67.5 (enacted 1981). Proof that the victim cried out or physically resisted the offender is not necessary for a conviction, but absence of such proof may be used in the offender's defense. VA. CODE ANN. § 18.2-67.6 (enacted 1981).

WASHINGTON: It is a felony for a person to engage in sexual penetration with another person by forcible compulsion; where the victim is incapable of consent by reason of being physically helpless or mentally incapacitated; where the victim did not consent to sexual penetration with the offender and such lack of consent was clearly expressed by the victim's words or conduct; or where there is threat of substantial unlawful harm to property rights of the victim. WASH. REV. CODE ANN. §§ 9A.44.010 (enacted 1975), 9A.44.040 (enacted 1975), 9A.44.050 (enacted 1975), 9A.44.060 (enacted 1975). Consent means that at the time of the sexual penetration there are actual words or conduct indicating freely given agreement to engage in sexual penetration. Forcible compulsion means physical force which overcomes resistance, or a threat, express or implied, that places the victim in fear of death or physical injury to or kidnapping of the victim or a third person. WASH. REV. CODE ANN. § 9A.44.010 (enacted 1975). The definition of mentally incapacitated does not include a requirement that the offender is in some way responsible for the victim's incapacitated state, as long as the offender knew or reasonably should have known of the victim's condition. WASH. REV. CODE ANN. §§ 9A.44.010 (enacted 1975), 9A.44.030 (enacted 1975). It is a felony for a person to knowingly cause a victim to have sexual contact with that person by forcible compulsion or where the victim is incapable of consent by reason of being mentally defective, mentally incapacitated, or physically helpless. WASH. REV. CODE ANN. § 9A.44.100 (enacted 1975).

WEST VIRGINIA: It is a felony for a person to engage in sexual penetration with another person without that person's consent where the lack of consent results from forcible compulsion; the offender inflicts serious bodily injury on anyone; or the victim is physically helpless, mentally defective, or mentally incapacitated. W. VA. CODE ANN. §§ 61-8B-1 (enacted 1976), 61-8B-3 (enacted 1976), 61-8B-4 (enacted 1976), 61-8B-5 (enacted 1976). Forcible compulsion means physical force that overcomes such earnest resistance as might reasonably be expected under the circumstances, or threat or intimidation, express or implied, that place the victim in fear of immediate death or bodily injury to or kidnapping of any person. W. VA. CODE ANN. § 61-8B-1 (enacted 1976). It is a felony for a person to engage in sexual contact with another person where lack of consent results from forcible compulsion or where the victim is physically helpless. W. VA. CODE ANN. § 61-8B-7 (enacted 1976). It is a misdemeanor to engage in sexual contact with another person where that person is mentally defective or mentally incapacitated. W. VA. CODE ANN. § 61-8B-8 (enacted 1976).

WISCONSIN: It is a felony to engage in sexual penetration or sexual contact under any of the following circumstances: where the offender acts without the victim's consent and causes pregnancy or great bodily harm to the victim; where the offender acts without the victim's consent by use or threat of use of a dangerous weapon or any article used or fashioned in a manner to lead the victim to reasonably believe it to be a dangerous weapon; where the offender acts without the victim's consent by use or threat of force or violence; where the offender acts without the victim's consent and causes injury, illness, disease, or impairment of a sexual or reproductive organ, or mental anguish requiring psychiatric care for the victim; where the victim suffers from a mental illness or deficiency which renders that person temporarily or permanently incapable of appraising his or her conduct, and the offender knows of the condition; where the victim is unconscious; or where the offender is aided or abetted by one or more persons and acts without the consent of the victim. Sexual penetration without the victim's consent is a felony. Sexual contact without the victim's consent is a misdemeanor. Consent means words or overt actions by a person who is competent to give informed consent indicating a freely given agreement to engage in sexual penetration or sexual contact. The following people are presumed to be incapable of consent but the presumption may be rebutted: a person suffering from a mental illness or defect which impairs capacity to appraise personal conduct; or a person who is unconscious or for any other reason unable to communicate unwillingness to act. WIS. STAT. ANN. § 940.225 (enacted 1987).

WYOMING: It is a felony for any person to engage in sexual penetration or sexual contact with another person under any of the following circumstances: the offender causes submission of the victim through the actual application, reasonably calculated to cause that submission of the victim, of physical force or forcible confinement; the offender causes submission by threat of death, serious bodily injury, extreme physical pain, or kidnapping to be inflicted on anyone and the victim reasonably believes that the offender has the present ability to execute these threats; the victim is physically helpless; the victim is incapable of appraising the nature of his or her conduct due to mental illness, mental deficiency, or developmental disability, and the offender knows or reasonably should know of the incapacity; the offender causes submission by threatening to retaliate in the future, including threats of kidnapping, death, serious bodily injury, or extreme physical pain, against the victim or the victim's spouse, parents, brothers, sisters, or children, and the victim reasonably believes the offender will execute this threat; the offender causes submission of the victim by any means that would prevent resistance by a victim of ordinary resolution; the victim is mentally incapacitated; or the offender knows or should reasonably know that the victim submits erroneously believing the offender to be the victim's spouse. WYO. STAT. §§ 6-2-301 (enacted 1982), 6-2-302 (enacted 1982), 6-2-303 (enacted 1982), 6-2-305 (enacted 1982).

UNITED STATES: A person commits the felony of aggravated sexual abuse who, in the special maritime and territorial jurisdiction of the United States or in a Federal prison, knowingly causes or attempts to cause another person to engage in a sexual act by using force against that other person; or by threatening or placing that other person in fear that any person will be subjected to death, serious bodily injury, or kidnapping; or who knowingly renders another person unconscious and thereby engages in a sexual act with that other person; or who administers to another person by force or threat of force, or without the knowledge or permission of that person, a drug, intoxicant, or other similar substance and thereby substantially impairs the ability of that other person to appraise or control conduct, and engages in a sexual act with that other person. 18 U.S.C.A. § 2241 (enacted 1986). A person commits the felony of sexual abuse who, in the special maritime and territorial jurisdiction of the United States or in a Federal prison, knowingly causes or attempts to cause another person to engage in a sexual act by threatening or placing that other person in fear (other than by threatening or placing that other person in fear that any person will be subjected to death, serious bodily injury, or kidnapping); or engages in a sexual act with another person if that other person is incapable of appraising the nature of the conduct, or physically incapable of declining participation in, or communicating unwillingness to engage in, that sexual act. 18 U.S.C.A. § 2242 (enacted 1986). It is a felony to knowingly engage in or cause sexual contact with another person if to do so would have constituted aggravated sexual abuse or sexual abuse had the contact been a sexual act. It is a misdemeanor to knowingly engage in sexual contact with another person without that other person's permission. 18 U.S.C.A. § 2244 (enacted 1986). Any of the above offenses are capital offenses if the conduct results in the death of a person. 18 U.S.C.A. § 2245 (enacted 1994).

It is a capital offense for two or more persons to conspire to injure, oppress, threaten, or intimidate any person in any state, territory, or district in the free exercise or enjoyment of any right or privilege secured to him by the Constitution or laws of the United States, or because of his having exercised the same, if such acts include aggravated sexual abuse or an attempt to commit aggravated sexual abuse. 18 U.S.C.A. § 241 (enacted 1948). It is a capital offense to travel in interstate or foreign commerce to intentionally obstruct or attempt to obstruct, by force or threat of force, any person in the enjoyment of that person's free exercise of religious beliefs, if such acts include aggravated sexual abuse or an attempt to commit aggravated sexual abuse. 18 U.S.C.A. § 247 (enacted 1988).

2

Marital Exemptions from Rape and Sexual Assault

This chapter incorporates some definitions that are found in the chapter on sexual assault (chap. 1); reference to that chapter will provide additional understanding of the nature of the exemption.

Some states provide that marriage is "not a defense" in particular circumstances, leaving it ambiguous whether it is a defense in other circumstances. Other states are more explicit about when spouses are exempt from the criminal law.

At common law, it was not possible to try a man for raping his wife. In the nineteenth century, when the states of the United States began codifying the English common law, legislatures usually wrote in an explicit marital exemption. States that did not adopted it by judicial interpretation instead. The exemption was originally rationalized as resting on the principle that consent to marriage was permanent consent to sexual availability, and its persistance is often explained by reference to difficulties in evaluating testimonial evidence and concerns about false accusations. Many states have repealed their marital exemptions on the basis of arguments that the evidentiary issues are similar to those in nonmarital cases.

Some states have taken the intermediate step of repealing the exemption only for spouses who are under a court-ordered separation or are living apart with or without a court order. Other states have repealed the exemption only for violent forms of rape. The Model Penal Code recommended keeping the marital exemption. It also suggested expanding the exemption to include couples who voluntarily cohabit without marrying, and several states have adopted that provision.

This chapter does not discuss spousal exemptions where the offense is not against the victim's will, but is illegal only because there is a relationship of trust between victim and offender. For example, many states do not permit sexual contact between prisoners and state prison employees; spouses are exempted from these prohibitions.

ALABAMA: No exemptions.

ALASKA: Spouses are not subject to laws making it an offense to engage in sexual penetration or contact where the victim is mentally incapable, incapacitated, or unaware that a sexual act is being committed, unless the spouses have filed for a legal separation or divorce. ALASKA STAT. §§ 11.41.420 (enacted 1978), 11.41.425 (enacted 1988), 11.41.432 (enacted 1988).

ARIZONA: Sexual assault on a spouse means intentionally or knowingly engaging in sexual intercourse or oral sexual contact with a spouse without consent, and by the immediate or threatened use of force against the spouse or another. It is in the judge's discretion whether to treat the offense as a felony or misdemeanor. ARIZ. REV. STAT. ANN. § 13-1406.01 (enacted 1988). It is a defense to all other sexual assault charges that the offender was the victim's spouse at the time of the assault. ARIZ. REV. STAT. ANN. § 13-1407 (enacted 1977).

ARKANSAS: A spouse is exempted from prosecution for engaging in sexual intercourse, deviate sexual intercourse, or sexual contact with a spouse who is mentally defective or mentally incapable. ARK. CODE ANN. §§ 5-14-105 (enacted 1975), 5-14-109 (enacted 1975). No other exemptions.

CALIFORNIA: Spouses are exempted from the general provision for offenses involving sexual intercourse, but not from offenses involving other forms of sexual penetration. It is a felony to engage in sexual intercourse against the will of a spouse by means of force, violence, duress, or creation of a fear of immediate and unlawful bodily injury on the spouse or another; where the victim is mentally incapacitated; where the offender knows that the victim is unconscious of the nature of the act; or where the act is accomplished against the victim's will by threatening to retaliate in the future against the victim or a third person and there is a reasonable possibility that the offender will execute the threat. CAL. PENAL CODE §§ 261 (enacted 1872), 262 (enacted 1979), 286 (enacted 1872), 288a (enacted 1921), 289 (enacted 1978).

COLORADO: No exemptions.

CONNECTICUT: Spouses and cohabitors are exempted from the general sexual offense statutes and are subject only to the following provision: it is a felony for any spouse or cohabitor to compel the other spouse or cohabitor to engage in sexual penetration by the use of force or by the threat of the use of force against the victim which reasonably causes the victim to fear physical injury. CONN. GEN. STAT. ANN. §§ 53a-65 (enacted 1969), 53a-70b (enacted 1981). Use of force means use of a dangerous instrument or use of actual physical force or violence or superior physical strength against the victim. CONN. GEN. STAT. ANN. § 53a-65 (enacted 1969).

DELAWARE: No exemptions.

DISTRICT OF COLUMBIA: No exemptions.

FLORIDA: No exemptions.

GEORGIA: No exemptions.

HAWAII: No exemptions.

IDAHO: Rape of a spouse, a felony, is sexual penetration of a female where she resists but her resistance is overcome by force or violence or the victim is prevented from resistance by threats of immediate and great bodily harm, accompanied by apparent power of implementation. IDAHO CODE ANN. §§ 18-6101 (enacted 1972), 18-6107 (enacted 1977).

ILLINOIS: Any prosecution for offenses involving sexual penetration against the spouse of the offender is barred unless the victim reported the offense to a law enforcement agency or the State's Attorney's office within thirty days after the offense was committed, unless the court finds good cause for the delay. ILL. ANN. STAT. ch. 720, para. 5/12-18 (enacted 1961). No other exemptions.

INDIANA: No exemptions.

IOWA: The only exemption from the sexual assault laws is that it is not a crime to engage in a sex act with a spouse where the lack of consent results from a mental defect or mental incapacity that precludes giving consent. The exemption also applies to people who are cohabiting as husband and wife at the time of the offense. IOWA CODE ANN. § 709.4 (enacted 1976).

KANSAS: No exemptions.

KENTUCKY: There is a marital exemption from all sexual assault laws, whether they involve sexual intercourse, deviate sexual intercourse, or sexual contact. The marital exemption extends to all people living together as husband and wife regardless of the legal status of their relationship, but does not include spouses living apart under a decree of judicial separation. KY. REV. STAT. ANN. § 510.010 (enacted 1974).

LOUISIANA: Spouses are exempt from the sexual battery and rape provisions of the criminal law. A separate code section governs assault on a spouse. It is a felony to engage in anal or vaginal intercourse with a spouse, or to engage in the intentional touching of the genitals or anus of a spouse by the mouth or tongue under the following circumstances: when the victim resists the act to the utmost, but resistance is overcome by force; when the victim is prevented from resisting by threats of great and immediate bodily harm, accompanied by apparent power of execution; when the victim is prevented from resisting the act because the offender is armed with a dangerous weapon; or where two or more offenders participated in the act. It is a felony to engage in anal or vaginal intercourse with a spouse where the victim is prevented from resisting the act by force or threats of physical violence in circumstances where the victim reasonably believes that such resistance would not prevent the rape. LA. REV. STAT. ANN. §§ 14:41 (enacted 1978), 14:42 (enacted 1978), 14:42.1 (enacted 1978), 14:43.4 (enacted 1985). It is a felony to engage in sexual contact with a spouse where the offender inflicts serious bodily injury on the spouse, meaning unconsciousness, extreme physical pain, protracted and obvious disfigurement, protracted loss or impairment of the function of a bodily member, organ, or mental faculty, or a substantial risk of death. LA. REV. STAT. ANN. § 14:43.2 (enacted 1983). A person is not a spouse if a judgment of separation has been rendered, or if the offender and the victim are living separate and apart and the offender knows that a temporary restraining order, preliminary or permanent injunction, or other order or decree has been issued prohibiting or restraining the offender from sexually or physically abusing, intimidating, threatening violence against, or in any way physically interfering with the victim. LA. REV. STAT. ANN. § 14:43 (enacted 1978).

MAINE: No exemptions.

MARYLAND: Spouses may be prosecuted for engaging in vaginal intercourse with a spouse if the offender uses force against the victim's will and without the victim's consent. Spouses may also be prosecuted for sexual contact against the will and without the consent of the victim where: the offender employs or displays a dangerous or deadly weapon or an article that the victim reasonably concludes is a dangerous or deadly weapon; or the offender inflicts suffocation, strangulation, disfigurement, or serious physical injury upon the other person or upon anyone else in the course of committing that offense. These offenses are felonies. MD. ANN. CODE, art. 27, §§ 461 (enacted 1976), 462 (enacted 1976), 463 (enacted 1976), 464B (enacted 1976), 464D (enacted 1976). Spouses are exempted from prosecution for all other sexual offenses, unless the parties live separate and apart without cohabitation and without interruption either pursuant to a written separation agreement, a decree of limited divorce, or for six months prior to the offense. MD. ANN. CODE, art. 27, § 464D (enacted 1976).

MASSACHUSETTS: No exemptions.

MICHIGAN: An express provision makes all sexual assault laws applicable between legal spouses, with the exception of lack of consent due to age or mental incapacity. MICH. COMP. LAWS ANN. § 750.520l (enacted 1974).

MINNESOTA: No exemptions.

MISSISSIPPI: No exemptions.

MISSOURI: No exemptions.

MONTANA: No exemptions.

NEBRASKA: No exemptions.

NEVADA: It is no defense to the general laws prohibiting sexual penetration under certain circumstances that the offender was, at the time of the assault, married to the victim, if the assault was committed by force or by threat of force. NEV. REV. STAT. § 200.373 (enacted 1967).

NEW HAMPSHIRE: An express provision makes all sexual assault laws applicable between legal spouses. N.H. REV. STAT. ANN. § 632-A:5 (enacted 1975).

NEW JERSEY: No exemptions.

NEW MEXICO: No exemptions.

NEW YORK: There is a marital exemption from all sexual assault laws whether they involve deviate sexual intercourse, sexual intercourse, or sexual contact. The exemption does not extend to spouses living apart pursuant to a court order, judgment of separation, or a separation agreement that contains provisions specifically opening the parties to prosecution for sexual assault. N.Y. PENAL LAW § 130.00 (enacted 1965).

NORTH CAROLINA: A person may not be prosecuted for engaging in sexual penetration under any circumstances if the victim is the offender's legal spouse at the time of the commission of the crime, unless the parties are living separate and apart. N.C. GEN. STAT. §§ 14-27.1 (enacted 1979), 14-27.8 (enacted 1979).

NORTH DAKOTA: No exemptions.

OHIO: The only sexual offenses possible against a spouse are the following: sexual penetration where the offender purposely compels the victim to submit by force or threat of force; or sexual penetration where the victim is mentally incapacitated, and the offender has facilitated the incapacity for the purpose of preventing resistance, and the parties are living separate and apart. OHIO REV. CODE ANN. § 2907.02 (enacted 1993). These limitations on the ordinary sexual assault provisions apply where the parties are married at the time of the offense, except that they do not apply if the parties have entered into a written separation agreement, after the effective date of a judgment for legal separation; or during the pendency of an action for annulment, divorce, dissolution of marriage, or legal separation. OHIO REV. CODE ANN. § 2907.01 (enacted 1990).

OKLAHOMA: Spouses are exempt from rape and sexual assault charges unless: force or violence is used or threatened accompanied by apparent power of execution against the victim or a third person; and a petition for divorce or legal separation is pending or has been granted, or a petition for a protective order is pending, or the victim and offender are living separate and apart from each other. OKLA. STAT. ANN. tit. 21, § 1111 (enacted 1981).

OREGON: No exemptions.

PENNSYLVANIA: Spouses are exempt from the ordinary sexual assault and rape statutes, and are subject instead to a spousal sexual assault provision. Under that provision, it is a felony to engage in sexual penetration with one's spouse under any of the following circumstances: by forcible compulsion; by threat of forcible compulsion that would prevent resistance by a person of reasonable resolution; or where the victim is unconscious; provided that in all cases the crime must be reported by the victim or the victim's agent within ninety days. 18 PA. CONS. STAT. ANN. § 3128 (enacted 1984). This limitation applies to all people living as husband and wife, whether legally married or not, but excludes spouses living in separate residences, or in the same residence but under the terms of a written separation agreement or a court order. 18 PA. CONS. STAT. ANN. § 3103 (enacted 1972).

RHODE ISLAND: The felony prohibitions applicable to sexual penetration apply to spouses except that a spouse will not be convicted where the circumstances making the sexual penetration a felony are that the offender knows or has reason to know that the victim is mentally incapacitated, mentally disabled, or physically helpless. R.I. GEN. LAWS § 11-37-2 (enacted 1979).

SOUTH CAROLINA: Spouses are exempt from sexual assault prosecutions unless the couple is living apart and the offender accomplishes sexual penetration by aggravated force or aggravated coercion, or unless the victim is also the victim of forcible confinement, kidnapping, robbery, extortion, burglary, housebreaking, or any other similar offense or act. S.C. CODE ANN. §§ 16-3-658 (enacted 1977), 16-3-652 (enacted 1977), 16-3-653 (enacted 1977).

SOUTH DAKOTA: Spouses may not be convicted of sexual offenses involving sexual contact but no penetration. For offenses involving sexual penetration, there are no exemptions for spouses. S.D. CODIFIED LAWS ANN. §§ 22-22-7.2 (enacted 1985), 22-22-7.4 (enacted 1991).

TENNESSEE: Spouses are not subject to the ordinary rape and sexual battery statutes unless the spouses are living apart and one of them has filed for separate maintenance or divorce. There is a separate provision for spousal rape and spousal sexual battery. It is a felony for a person to engage in sexual penetration or sexual contact with a spouse where the offender is armed with a weapon or any article used or fashioned in a manner to lead the victim to reasonably believe it to be a weapon, or where the offender causes serious bodily injury to the victim. TENN. CODE ANN. § 39-13-507 (enacted 1989).

TEXAS: Any prosecution for sexual penetration without consent of a spouse under the general sexual assault provision requires a showing of bodily injury or a threat of bodily injury. People are not considered spouses who do not reside together or where there is an action pending for dissolution of the marriage or separate maintenance. TEX. PENAL CODE ANN. § 22.011 (enacted 1983).

UTAH: No exemptions.

VERMONT: No exemptions.

VIRGINIA: A person cannot be convicted for sexual penetration against the will of his or her spouse where the absence of consent is due to mental incapacity or physical helplessness. Neither may a person be convicted for sexual penetration against the will of his or her spouse under the statutory provisions that are applicable to nonmarital offenses unless at the time of the offense the spouses were living separate and apart or the offender caused serious physical injury to the spouse by the use of force or violence. VA. CODE ANN. §§ 18.2-61 (enacted 1950), 18.2-67.1 (enacted 1981), 18.2-67.2 (enacted 1981). It is a felony called marital sexual assault to engage in sexual penetration with a spouse where the act is accomplished against the spouse's will by force or a present threat of force. The violation must be reported to a law enforcement agency within ten days of the crime, unless the victim is restrained or otherwise prevented from reporting the violation. VA. CODE ANN. § 18.2-67.2:1 (enacted 1986).

WASHINGTON: It is not a felony to engage in sexual penetration with a spouse under the following circumstances: where the victim is developmentally disabled and the offender has supervisory authority over the victim; where the victim has not consented but no other factor making the act an offense is present; or where the act is achieved through the threat of substantial unlawful harm to property rights of the victim. It is also not a felony to engage in sexual contact with a spouse under any circumstances. All other behavior criminalized for people who are not married to one another is criminalized for married people. WASH. REV. CODE ANN. §§ 9A.44.050 (enacted 1975), 9A.44.060 (enacted 1975), 9A.44.100 (enacted 1975). These exemptions apply to people who are legally married but exclude a person who is living separate and apart from his or her spouse and who has filed for legal separation or for dissolution of the marriage. WASH. REV. CODE ANN. § 9A.44.010 (enacted 1975).

WEST VIRGINIA: Sexual assault on a spouse is governed by a separate statutory provision. It is a felony for a person to engage in sexual penetration with a spouse without the spouse's consent under any of the following circumstances: the lack of consent results from forcible compulsion; the offender inflicts serious bodily injury upon anyone; or the offender employs a deadly weapon in the commission of the offense. W. VA. CODE ANN. § 61-8B-6 (enacted 1984). In addition to legally married couples, this provision applies to persons living together as husband and wife regardless of the legal status of their relationship. W. VA. CODE ANN. § 61-8B-1 (enacted 1976).

WISCONSIN: A defendant shall not be presumed to be incapable of violating any sexual assault provisions because of marriage to the victim. WIS. STAT. ANN. § 940.225 (enacted 1987).

WYOMING: The fact that the offender and the victim are married to each other is not by itself a defense to a violation of any of the offenses involving sexual penetration under the following circumstances: the offender causes submission of the victim through the actual application, reasonably calculated to cause submission of the victim, of physical force or forcible confinement; the offender causes submission of the victim by threat of death, serious bodily injury, extreme physical pain, or kidnapping to be inflicted on anyone and the victim reasonably believes that the offender has the present ability to execute these threats; the victim is physically helpless; the offender causes submission by threatening to retaliate, including threats of kidnapping, death, serious bodily injury, or extreme physical pain, in the future against the victim or the victim's parents, brothers, sisters, or children, and the victim reasonably believes the offender will execute this threat; the offender causes submission of the victim by any means that would prevent resistance by a victim of ordinary resolution; the victim is mentally incapacitated; or the offender is in a position of authority over the victim and uses this position of authority to cause the victim to submit. WYO. STAT. §§ 6-2-307 (enacted 1982), 6-2-301 (enacted 1982), 6-2-302 (enacted 1982), 6-2-303 (enacted 1982).

UNITED STATES: No exemptions.

3
Age of Consent

This chapter covers two related subjects: conduct that is criminal solely because of the age of the parties, and the legal marriage age, since marriage authorizes sex. Crimes that turn solely on the age of one of the parties are commonly called age of consent crimes, or statutory rape. Most states grade the level of offense depending on the circumstances of the crime. Some conduct is criminal under any circumstances, but the offense is graded more severely for children. Those offenses can be found in chapters 1, 6, 9, 10, 12, and 13. Prostitution offenses, for example, are routinely upgraded where one party is a child.

The law governing the age of consent has changed dramatically in the United States during this century. Most states codified a statutory age of consent during the nineteenth century, and the usual age was ten years. In the twentieth century the age of consent has crept higher. In most states it is not possible to identify a single age of consent, the statutory age varying with the age of the defendant and with the particular sexual activity involved. Nonetheless, in every state there is some age at which a person may engage in any sexual conduct permitted to adults within that state; this age may best fit the name "age of consent." No state goes as low as ten years old now; the ages range from fourteen to eighteen. In the vast majority of states the age of consent is either fifteen or sixteen.

Many states used to require that the victim be "of previous chaste character." Reforms enacted in the 1950s through 1980s eliminated that requirement in almost all states, but a few still retain it. Some states will not convict on a charge of statutory rape if the defendant made a reasonable mistake as to the victim's age.

Before the reform era, most statutory rape statutes explicitly protected females from males. In most states, gender neutral reforms have made it possible to convict both men and women of statutory rape.

Nonetheless, the Supreme Court has held that stricter rules for males do not violate the equal protection clause of the Constitution, on the theory that men lack the disincentives associated with pregnancy that women have to engage in sexual activity, and the law may thus provide men with those disincentives in the form of criminal sanctions. *Michael M. v. Superior Court*, 450 U.S. 464 (1981).

Many state codes now criminalize sexual conduct between adults and adolescents that would not be criminal between two adolescents of similar ages. These states may also punish conduct between adults and young children. Many states have a lower age of consent for sexual contact than for sexual penetration, and a few states are more permissive of underaged heterosexual activity than of underaged same-sex activity.

We have reported the minimum age for marriage without parental approval (usually eighteen), as well as the kinds of approval needed for underage marriages. Many states have elaborate provisions governing which parent must give consent and who qualifies as a custodial parent or guardian; we have omitted those details. Some states provide that where parental approval is unreasonably withheld, judicial approval will suffice; we describe these as states that require parental or judicial approval. Many states do not permit someone under sixteen to marry under any circumstances. When the age of consent to sexual relations and the age of consent to marriage statutes are looked at in combination, it is evident that some states will allow a minor to marry with parental permission at an age when the minor cannot engage in legal sexual activity, while others allow a minor to engage in sexual activity years before he or she can marry without parental approval.

ALABAMA: It is a felony for a male over sixteen to engage in sexual intercourse with a female under sixteen if the offender is at least two years older than the victim. ALA. CODE §§ 13A-6-62 (enacted 1977), 13A-6-61 (enacted 1977). Similarly, it is a felony for a person over sixteen to engage in sodomy with a person under sixteen if the offender is at least two years older than the victim, or for a person sixteen or over to subject a person under twelve to sexual contact. ALA. CODE §§ 13A-6-63 (enacted 1977), 13A-6-64 (enacted 1977), 13A-6-66 (enacted 1977). It is a misdemeanor for a person nineteen or older to engage in sexual contact with a person under sixteen but over twelve. ALA. CODE § 13A-6-67 (enacted 1977).

Both parties must be eighteen to marry without parental consent. A person who is at least fourteen may, however, marry with parental consent. ALA. CODE §§ 30-1-4 (enacted 1977), 30-1-5 (enacted 1977).

ALASKA: It is a felony for a person sixteen years or older to engage in sexual penetration or contact with a person fifteen or younger, and at least three years younger than the offender. ALASKA STAT. §§ 11.41.434 (enacted 1983), 11.41.436 (enacted 1983), 11.41.438 (enacted 1983). It is a misdemeanor for a person under sixteen to engage in sexual penetration or sexual contact with a person under thirteen and at least three years younger than the offender. ALASKA STAT. § 11.41.440 (enacted 1978). It is an affirmative defense to these charges that at the time of the alleged offense, the defendant reasonably believed the victim was of an age to consent, unless the victim was under the age of thirteen. ALASKA STAT. § 11.41.445 (enacted 1983). Indecent exposure before a person under sixteen is a misdemeanor. ALASKA STAT. §§ 11.41.460 (enacted 1983), 11.61.110 (enacted 1978).

Both parties must be eighteen to marry without approval. A sixteen- or seventeen- year-old may marry with judicial or parental approval; a person fourteen or over may marry with judicial approval only. ALASKA STAT. §§ 25.05.111 (enacted 1963), 25.05.171 (enacted 1963).

ARIZONA: It is a felony for a person to engage in sexual intercourse or oral sexual contact with any person who is under eighteen. ARIZ. REV. STAT. ANN. § 13-1405 (enacted 1977). It is a felony for a person over eighteen to touch the private parts of or cause his or her private parts to be touched by a person under fourteen. It is a felony to engage in sexual contact involving the female breast with a person who is under fifteen. ARIZ. REV. STAT. ANN. §§ 13-1404 (enacted 1977), 13-1410 (enacted 1965).

Both parties must be eighteen to marry without parental approval. Sixteen- and seventeen-year-olds may marry with parental approval. People under sixteen require both parental and judicial approval. ARIZ. REV. STAT. ANN. § 25-102 (enacted 1974).

ARKANSAS: It is a felony for a person more than two years older than the victim to engage in sexual intercourse or deviate sexual activity with a person under fourteen. ARK. CODE ANN. §§ 5-14-103 (enacted 1975), 5-14-104 (enacted 1975), 5-14-108 (enacted 1975), 5-14-109 (enacted 1975). It is a misdemeanor for a person over eighteen to solicit a person under eighteen to engage in sexual intercourse, deviate sexual activity, or sexual contact. ARK. CODE ANN. § 5-14-110 (enacted 1975). It is no defense that the offender did not know the age of the victim, or reasonably believed the victim to be fourteen years of age or older. ARK. CODE ANN. § 5-14-102 (enacted 1975). It is a misdemeanor for a person twenty or older to engage in sexual intercourse or deviate sexual intercourse with a person under sixteen. ARK. CODE ANN. § 5-14-106 (enacted 1975). It is an affirmative defense to this charge that the offender reasonably believed the victim to be older than sixteen. ARK. CODE ANN. § 5-14-102 (enacted 1975).

Both parties must be eighteen to marry without approval. Seventeen-year-old males and sixteen- or seventeen-year-old females may marry with parental consent. Where either party is under these ages, they may marry if the female is pregnant or has given birth to a child and the underaged party has parental and judicial consent. ARK. CODE ANN. §§ 9-11-102 (enacted 1941), 9-11-103 (enacted 1941).

CALIFORNIA: It is unlawful to commit an act of sexual intercourse with a person who is under eighteen. If the parties are not more than three years apart in age, the offense is a misdemeanor; otherwise the offense may be either a felony or a misdemeanor. CAL. PENAL CODE § 261.5 (enacted 1970). It is a felony for a person at least twenty-one to commit an act of sexual penetration with a person under sixteen, and a misdemeanor for any person to commit an act of sexual penetration with a person who is under eighteen. CAL. PENAL CODE § 289 (enacted 1978). It is a felony for any person to commit a lewd or lascivious act upon or with a person not yet fourteen with the intent to arouse or gratify the sexual desire of either; the same acts are a felony with a fourteen- or fifteen-year-old if the offender is at least ten years older than the child. CAL. PENAL CODE § 288 (enacted 1988).

Both parties must be eighteen to marry without approval. Individuals under eighteen may marry with the written approval of one parent and the court. CAL. FAM. CODE §§ 301 (enacted 1992), 302 (enacted 1992).

COLORADO: Any person who knowingly subjects another not his or her spouse to any sexual penetration or contact commits sexual assault on a child, a felony, if the victim is under fifteen and the offender is at least four years older than the victim. COLO. REV. STAT. ANN. §§ 18-3-403 (enacted 1975), 18-3-405 (enacted 1975).

Both parties to a marriage must be eighteen to marry without approval. Seventeen- and sixteen-year-olds may marry with parental or judicial consent. A party under sixteen must have judicial or parental consent and satisfactory proof that the marriage is not incestuous or bigamous. COLO. REV. STAT. ANN. §§ 14-2-106 (enacted 1973), 14-2-108 (enacted 1973).

CONNECTICUT: A person commits a felony by engaging in sexual intercourse with someone under sixteen where the offender is more than two years older than the victim. CONN. GEN. STAT. ANN. §§ 53a-70 (enacted 1969), 53a-71 (enacted 1969). A person commits a misdemeanor by intentionally subjecting to sexual contact another person who is under fifteen. CONN. GEN. STAT. ANN. § 53a-73a (enacted 1975).

Both parties must be eighteen to marry without approval. Sixteen- and seventeen-year-olds require parental consent; people under sixteen may marry with parental and judicial consent. CONN. GEN. STAT. ANN. § 46b-30 (enacted 1967).

DELAWARE: It is a felony for any person to engage in sexual intercourse, sexual penetration, or sexual contact with a person under sixteen. DEL. CODE ANN. tit. 11, §§ 768 (enacted 1953), 770 (enacted 1953). It is no defense that the offender did not know the victim's age or believed the victim to be sixteen or older. It is a defense to any action that the offender is no more than four years older than the victim, the victim is over twelve, and the sexual conduct was consensual. DEL. CODE ANN. tit. 11, § 762 (enacted 1953). A person is guilty of a felony if he or she permits or advances an exhibition, display, or performance of a child engaging in a prohibited sexual act or the simulation of such an act. DEL. CODE ANN. tit. 11, § 1108 (enacted 1961). Prohibited sexual acts include: anal intercourse, fellatio, and cunnilingus. DEL. CODE ANN. tit. 11, § 1103 (enacted 1953).

Both parties must be eighteen to marry without approval. Sixteen- and seventeen-year-old females may marry with parental consent; males may not. These age restrictions do not apply to couples who wish to marry and are parents or prospective parents of a child. DEL. CODE ANN. tit. 13, § 123 (enacted 1915).

DISTRICT OF COLUMBIA: It is a felony for any person to take, or attempt to take, any immoral, improper, or indecent liberties with any child under sixteen, or to entice, alllure, or persuade such child to any place with the intent of taking any such liberties. Lack of knowledge of the age of the child is not a defense. D.C. CODE ANN. § 22-3501 (enacted 1948). Whoever carnally knows and abuses a female under sixteen is guilty of a felony. D.C. CODE § 22-2801 (enacted 1901).

Both parties must be eighteen to marry without approval, or sixteen to marry with parental or judicial consent. D.C. CODE ANN. §§ 30-103 (enacted 1901), 30-111 (enacted 1901).

FLORIDA: It is a felony to have unlawful carnal intercourse with any unmarried person, of previous chaste character, who at the time of the intercourse was under eighteen. FLA. STAT. ANN. § 794.05 (enacted 1892). A person who is eighteen or older commits a capital felony by engaging in oral, anal, or vaginal penetration, including with an object, or union with the sexual organ, of a person under twelve, or by injuring the sexual organs of a person under twelve in an attempt to do the same. If the offender is under eighteen, that person is guilty of a life felony. FLA. STAT. ANN. § 794.011 (enacted 1992). It is a felony to commit any of the above actions, or handle or fondle in a lewd manner, or commit actual or simulated intercourse, bestiality, masturbation, or sadomasochistic abuse, on or in the presence of any child under the age of sixteen. Neither the victim's lack of chastity nor the victim's consent is a defense under this section. FLA. STAT. ANN. § 800.04 (enacted 1993).

A person must be eighteen to marry without consent, or between sixteen and eighteen to marry with parental consent. A judge may issue a license to marry to a person under eighteen if both parties swear under oath that they are the parents of a child or are expecting a child, and the judge may issue a license to a female under eighteen and a male over eighteen upon the female's sworn oath that she is an expecting parent. FLA. STAT. ANN. § 741.0405 (enacted 1978).

GEORGIA: Statutory rape and child molestation are felonies. A person commits statutory rape when he engages in sexual intercourse with any female under fourteen not his spouse, but no conviction can be had for this offense on the unsupported testimony of the female. GA. CODE ANN. § 16-6-3 (enacted 1918). A person is guilty of child molestation when that person does any immoral or indecent act to, with, or in the presence of a child under fourteen with the intent to arouse or satisfy the sexual desires of either the child or the person. GA. CODE ANN. § 16-6-4 (enacted 1950). It is a felony to solicit, entice, or take any child under fourteen to any place whatsoever for the purpose of child molestation or indecent acts. GA. CODE ANN. § 16-6-5 (enacted 1950).

Both parties must be at least eighteen to marry without approval. Sixteen- and seventeen-year-olds may marry with parental consent.

No age limitations or parental consent requirements apply where the female is pregnant or where both parties are the parents of a living child born out of wedlock. GA. CODE ANN. §§ 19-3-2 (enacted 1863), 19-3-37 (enacted 1863).

HAWAII: A person commits a felony by knowingly subjecting another person under fourteen to sexual penetration or sexual contact or causing such a child to have sexual contact with the person. HAW. REV. STAT. §§ 707-730 (enacted 1986), 707-732 (enacted 1986).

Both parties must be eighteen to marry without approval. Sixteen- and seventeen-year-olds may marry with parental consent. Fifteen-year-olds may marry with both parental and judicial consent. HAW. REV. STAT. §§ 572-1 (enacted 1872), 572-2 (enacted 1859).

IDAHO: It is a felony to engage in sexual intercourse with a female who is under eighteen. IDAHO CODE § 18-6101 (enacted 1972). It is a felony for any person eighteen or older to solicit a minor under sixteen to participate in a sexual act or sexual conduct. IDAHO CODE §18-1506 (enacted 1982). It is a felony to commit any lewd or lascivious act or acts on a child under the age of sixteen. IDAHO CODE § 18-1508 (enacted 1973).

Both parties must be eighteen to marry without approval. Sixteen- and seventeen-year-olds may be married with parental consent. Individuals under sixteen may marry with parental and judicial consent. IDAHO CODE § 32-202 (enacted 1864).

ILLINOIS: It is a felony to commit an act of sexual conduct or sexual penetration with a person who is seventeen or younger. ILL. ANN. STAT. ch. 720, paras. 5/12-13 (enacted 1961), 5/12-14 (enacted 1961), 5/12-16 (enacted 1961). If the offender is seventeen or younger and the victim is between nine and seventeen, or if the offender is no more than five years older than the victim who is between nine and seventeen, then the crime is a misdemeanor. ILL. ANN. STAT. ch. 720, para. 5/12-15 (enacted 1961). It is a misdemeanor for a person over seventeen to solicit a child under sixteen to do any act of sexual contact. It is a felony for a person over seventeen to solicit a child under thirteen to do any act of sexual penetration. ILL. ANN. STAT. ch. 720, para. 5/11-6 (enacted 1961). It is a defense to these charges that the offender reasonably believed the victim to be seventeen or older. ILL. ANN. STAT. ch. 720, para. 5/12-17 (enacted 1961). A person commits sexual exploitation of a child if, in the presence of a child under seventeen and with intent or knowledge that a child under seventeen would view his or her acts, that person engages in a sexual act or exposes his or her sex organs, anus, or breast for the purpose of sexual arousal or gratification of such person or child. Sexual act means masturbation, sexual conduct, or sexual penetration. The first offense is a misdemeanor; each subsequent offense is a felony. ILL. ANN. STAT. ch. 720, para. 5/11-9.1 (enacted 1961).

Both parties must be eighteen to marry without approval. Sixteen- and seventeen-year-olds may marry with parental or judicial approval. ILL. ANN. STAT. ch. 750, paras. 5/203 (enacted 1977), 5/208 (enacted 1977).

INDIANA: It is a felony for a person who is sixteen or older to perform or submit to sexual intercourse, deviate sexual conduct, or any fondling or touching of either a child under sixteen or of the offender with intent to arouse or satisfy the sexual desire of either. It is a defense that the offender reasonably believed the child was sixteen or older. IND. CODE ANN. §§ 35-42-4-3 (enacted 1976), 35-42-4-5 (enacted 1984), 35-42-4-9 (enacted 1994). It is a felony for a person eighteen or older to knowingly or intentionally solicit a child under fourteen to engage in sexual intercourse, deviate sexual conduct, or any fondling or touching intended to arouse or satisfy the sexual desires of either the victim or the offender. IND. CODE ANN. § 35-42-4-6 (enacted 1984).

Both parties must be at least eighteen to marry without approval. IND. CODE ANN. § 31-7-1-5 (enacted 1986). Individuals who are at least seventeen may marry with written parental consent. A court may authorize the marriage of a female who is at least fifteen and is pregnant or a mother to a male who is at least fifteen and who is the putative father of the child or expected child. IND. CODE ANN. §§ 31-7-1-6 (enacted 1986), 31-7-1-7 (enacted 1986), 31-7-2-2 (enacted 1986). A judge may authorize a person under eighteen to marry. IND. CODE ANN. § 31-7-2-3 (enacted 1986).

IOWA: Any sex act with a person under fourteen is a felony. Any sex act with a person who is fourteen or fifteen is a felony if the offender is at least six years older than the victim. IOWA CODE ANN. §§ 702.17 (enacted 1976), 709.1 (enacted 1976), 709.3 (enacted 1976), 709.4 (enacted 1976). It is a felony for a person eighteen or older to fondle or touch the genitals or pubes of a child, or permit or cause the child to fondle the offender's genitals or pubes; solicit a child to engage in a sex act; or engage in the infliction of pain or discomfort on the child. IOWA CODE ANN. § 709.8 (enacted 1976). It is an aggravated misdemeanor for a person eighteen or older to fondle or touch a child or solicit a child to fondle or touch the offender for the purpose of gratifying sexual desire. This section also applies to persons sixteen or seventeen who commit the offense with a child at least five years their junior. IOWA CODE ANN. § 709.12 (enacted 1981).

Both parties must be eighteen to marry without approval. A sixteen- or seventeen-year-old may marry with parental or judicial consent. IOWA CODE ANN. § 595.2 (enacted 1961).

KANSAS: It is a felony to engage in sexual intercourse, or any lewd fondling or touching with the intent to arouse or satisfy the sexual desires of the offender or the victim, with a child under sixteen. KAN. STAT. ANN. § 21-3503 (enacted 1969). It is a felony to entice or solicit any child under the age of sixteen to commit or submit to an unlawful sexual act. KAN. STAT. ANN. § 21-3510 (enacted 1969).

Both parties must be eighteen to marry without parental and judicial consent. KAN. STAT. ANN. § 23-106 (enacted 1867).

KENTUCKY: It is a felony for any person to engage in sexual intercourse with a person under twelve, or for a person at least eighteen to engage in sexual intercourse with a person under fourteen. KY. REV. STAT. ANN. §§ 510.040 (enacted 1974), 510.050 (enacted 1974). It is a felony for a person at least twenty-one to engage in sexual intercourse with a person under sixteen. KY. REV. STAT. ANN. § 510.060 (enacted 1974). It is a felony to subject a person under twelve to sexual contact, and a misdemeanor to engage in sexual contact with a person under fourteen, or with a person over fourteen but under sixteen if the offender is at least five years older than the victim. KY. REV. STAT. ANN. §§ 510.110 (enacted 1974), 510.120 (enacted 1974), 510.130 (enacted 1974). But it is a defense that the offender was unaware of the victim's inability to consent. KY. REV. STAT. ANN. § 510.030 (enacted 1974).

Both parties must be eighteen to marry without approval. A person under eighteen may be married with parental consent. If the female is pregnant, a person under eighteen may marry with judicial consent. KY. REV. STAT. ANN. § 402.020 (enacted 1960).

LOUISIANA: A male over seventeen commits a felony when he has sexual intercourse with any unmarried female over eleven and under seventeen if there is an age difference of greater than two years between the two people. A person over seventeen commits a felony by having anal or oral intercourse with a person over eleven and under seventeen when there is an age difference of more than two years between the two people. LA. REV. STAT. ANN. §§ 14:80 (enacted 1942), 14:81 (enacted 1942). It is also a felony to touch the anus or genitals, using the mouth or any other instrumentality, when the victim is not the offender's spouse, is under fifteen, and is at least three years younger than the offender. LA. REV. STAT. ANN. §§ 14:43.1 (enacted 1978), 14:43.3 (enacted 1985). It is a felony for any person over seventeen to commit any lewd or lascivious act on the person of or in the presence of a person under seventeen where the victim is more than two years younger than the offender. LA. REV. STAT. ANN. § 14:81 (enacted 1942). It is a felony for someone over seventeen to commit any lewd or lascivious act upon the person, or in the presence of, any child under seventeen, where there is an age difference of more than two years between the two persons, with the intention of arousing or gratifying the sexual desires of either person. Lack of knowledge of the child's age is not a defense. LA. REV. STAT. ANN. § 14:106 (enacted 1950).

Both parties must be eighteen to marry without written judicial or parental approval. A person under sixteen must obtain the authorization of a judge. LA. REV. STAT. ANN. art. 1545 (enacted 1991).

MAINE: It is a felony for any person to engage in a sexual act with a person who is under fourteen, and for a person who is at least nineteen and five years older than the victim to engage in a sexual act with a person who is under sixteen but over fourteen. ME. REV. STAT. ANN. tit. 17A, §§ 253 (enacted 1975), 254 (enacted 1975). It is a felony for a person to engage in sexual contact with a person under fourteen where the offender is at least three years older than the victim. ME. REV. STAT. ANN. tit. 17A, § 255 (enacted 1975).

Both parties must be eighteen to marry without approval. A person who is at least sixteen may be married with parental consent. A person under sixteen may marry with parental and judicial consent. ME. REV. STAT. ANN. tit. 19, § 62 (enacted 1954).

MARYLAND: A person commits a felony by engaging in vaginal intercourse, a sexual act, or sexual contact with a victim under fourteen if the offender is at least four years older. MD. CRIM. LAW CODE ANN. §§ 463 (enacted 1976), 464A (enacted 1976), 464B (enacted 1976). The same acts are a misdemeanor where the victim is fourteen or fifteen and the offender is at least four years older. MD. CRIM. LAW CODE ANN. § 464C (enacted 1976).

Both parties must be eighteen to marry without any approval.

People who are sixteen or seventeen require either parental consent or a certificate from a physician saying that the woman is pregnant or has given birth to a child. People under sixteen require both parental consent and the physician's certificate. MD. CRIM. LAW CODE ANN. § 2-301 (enacted 1957).

MASSACHUSETTS: It is a felony to engage in sexual intercourse or unnatural sexual intercourse with a child under sixteen. MASS. GEN. LAWS ch. 265, § 23 (enacted 1697). It is a felony to commit any unnatural and lascivious act with a child under sixteen. MASS. GEN. LAWS ch. 272, § 35A (enacted 1955).

Both parties must be eighteen to marry without approval. MASS. GEN. LAWS ch. 207, § 7 (enacted 1941). A person under eighteen may marry with parental and judicial approval. MASS. GEN. LAWS ch. 207, § 25 (enacted 1987).

MICHIGAN: It is a felony for any person to engage in sexual penetration with a person who is under sixteen. MICH. COMP. LAWS ANN. §§ 750.520d (enacted 1931), 750.520b (enacted 1931). It is a felony for any person to engage in sexual contact with a person who is under thirteen. MICH. COMP. LAWS ANN. § 750.520c (enacted 1931). It is a felony to entice any female under the age of sixteen for the purpose of concubinage, sexual intercourse, or marriage. MICH. COMP. LAWS ANN. § 750.13 (enacted 1931). It is a misdemeanor for a person to accost, entice, or solicit a child under sixteen with the intent to induce the child to commit or submit to an act of sexual intercourse, gross indecency, or any other act of depravity. MICH. COMP. LAWS ANN. § 750.145a (enacted 1931).

Both parties must be eighteen to marry without any approval. Persons who are sixteen or seventeen may marry with the consent of one parent. MICH. COMP. LAWS ANN. § 551.103 (enacted 1980).

MINNESOTA: It is a felony to engage in sexual penetration with a person under thirteen, or under sixteen when the accused is more than twenty-four months older than the victim. MINN. STAT. ANN. §§ 609.342 (enacted 1975), 609.344 (enacted 1975). It is a felony to engage in sexual contact with a minor under thirteen, or with a minor under sixteen when the actor is more than forty-eight months older than the victim. MINN. STAT. ANN. §§ 609.343 (enacted 1975), 609.345 (enacted 1975). It is a felony for a person eighteen or older to solicit a person under fifteen to engage in sexual conduct. MINN. STAT. ANN. § 609.352 (enacted 1986).

Both parties must be eighteen to marry without approval. A person who is at least sixteen may be married with the consent of the person's parents or the court. MINN. STAT. ANN. § 517.02 (enacted 1927).

MISSISSIPPI: It is a felony to carnally and unlawfully know a child under fourteen. MISS. CODE ANN. § 97-3-65 (enacted 1848). It is a felony to have carnal knowledge of or seduce and have illicit connection with a child under eighteen of previously chaste character where the offender is older than the victim. MISS. CODE ANN. §§ 97-3-67 (enacted 1917), 97-5-21 (enacted 1857). It is a felony for a person over eighteen to indulge in his or her depraved licentious sexual desires by handling, touching, or rubbing with the hands or any part of his or her body for the purpose of gratifying his or her lust any person under fourteen. MISS. CODE ANN. § 97-5-23 (enacted 1921).

Males must be at least seventeen and females must be at least fifteen to marry without approval. Underaged applicants may marry with both parental and judicial approval. If either applicant is under twenty-one, the parents of both applicants will be notified of the license application. MISS. CODE ANN. § 93-1-5 (enacted 1930).

MISSOURI: Sexual intercourse or deviate sexual intercourse with a person under seventeen is a felony, as is sexual contact with a person who is thirteen or younger, except as follows: if the defendant is under seventeen and the victim is fourteen or fifteen, the crime is a misdemeanor. Sexual intercourse between a seventeen-year-old and sixteen-year-old is not prohibited. A seventeen-year-old is guilty of a misdemeanor for engaging in opposite-sex deviate sexual intercourse with a sixteen-year-old. MO. ANN. STAT. §§ 566.030 (enacted 1977), 566.040 (enacted 1977), 566.050 (enacted 1977), 566.060 (enacted 1977), 566.070 (enacted 1977), 566.100 (enacted 1977), 566.090 (enacted 1977). If the victim is fourteen or fifteen, it is a defense that the offender believed the victim was sixteen or older. If the victim was under fourteen, it is no defense that the offender believed the victim was fourteen or older. MO. ANN. STAT. § 566.020 (enacted 1977).

Both parties must be eighteen to marry without approval. Individuals at least fifteen and under eighteen may marry with parental approval. Individuals under fifteen may marry for good cause with parental and judicial approval. MO. ANN. STAT. § 451.090 (enacted 1939).

MONTANA: It is a felony to engage in sexual intercourse or sexual contact with a person under sixteen. MONT. CODE ANN. §§ 45-5-501 (enacted 1973), 45-5-502 (enacted 1973), 45-5-503 (enacted 1973). If the victim is fifteen or sixteen, it is a defense that the offender reasonably believed the victim was older than sixteen. If the victim was fourteen or younger, such beliefs shall be deemed unreasonable. MONT. CODE ANN. § 45-5-511 (enacted 1973).

Both parties must be eighteen to marry without approval. Individuals who are sixteen or seventeen may marry with judicial or parental approval. MONT. CODE ANN. § 40-1-402 (enacted 1975).

NEBRASKA: It is a felony for a person who is at least nineteen to engage in sexual penetration with a person who is under sixteen. NEB. REV. STAT. § 28-319 (enacted 1977). It is a felony for a person at least nineteen to subject a person under fourteen to sexual contact. NEB. REV. STAT. § 28-320.01 (enacted 1984).

Both parties must be seventeen to marry without approval. NEB. REV. STAT. § 42-102 (enacted 1866). Persons under seventeen may marry with parental consent. NEB. REV. STAT. § 42-105 (enacted 1866).

NEVADA: A person who is at least twenty-one commits a felony by engaging in sexual intercourse, anal intercourse, oral sex, or other sexual penetration with a person under sixteen. If the defendant is between eighteen and twenty-one, the offense is a misdemeanor. NEV. REV. STAT. §§ 200.364 (enacted 1977), 200.368 (enacted 1977). It is a felony to commit any lewd or lascivious act with a child under fourteen with the intent of arousing, appealing to, or gratifying the sexual desires of the offender or the child. NEV. REV. STAT. § 201.230 (enacted 1911). The crime of pandering includes: as a spouse, parent, or guardian of a person under eighteen permitting, conniving at, or consenting to the minor's being or remaining in a house of prostitution; or decoying, enticing, procuring, or in any manner inducing a person under twenty-one, to go into or visit, upon any pretext or for any reason whatever, any house of ill fame or prostitution, or any room or place inhabited or frequented by any prostitute, or used for purposes of prostitution. NEV. REV. STAT. §§ 201.300 (enacted 1913), 201.310 (enacted 1913), 201.330 (enacted 1913), 201.340 (enacted 1913), 201.360 (enacted 1913).

Both parties must be eighteen to marry without approval. Sixteen- and seventeen-year-olds may marry with the consent of either parent; younger people require both a parent's and judicial consent. NEV. REV. STAT. §§ 122.020 (enacted 1861), 122.025 (enacted 1957).

NEW HAMPSHIRE: It is a felony to engage in sexual penetration with a person under sixteen, or sexual contact with a person under thirteen. N.H. REV. STAT. ANN. § 632-A:3 (enacted 1975). A person is guilty of indecent exposure if that person purposely performs any act of sexual penetration or sexual contact alone or with another person in the presence of a child under sixteen. The first offense is a misdemeanor. If an individual has previously been convicted of indecent exposure in any jurisdiction, the offense is a felony. N.H. REV. STAT. ANN. § 645:1 (enacted 1971).

Both parties must be eighteen to marry without approval. N.H. REV. STAT. ANN. § 457:5. Males who are fourteen or over and females who are thirteen or over may marry with parental consent. N.H. REV. STAT. ANN. §§ 457:4 (enacted 1907), 457:6 (enacted 1907).

NEW JERSEY: It is a felony to commit an act of sexual penetration or sexual contact with a person under thirteen, or a person under sixteen if the actor is at least four years older than the victim. N.J. STAT. ANN. §§ 2C:14-2 (enacted 1978), 2C:14-3 (enacted 1978).

Both parties must be eighteen to marry without approval. Sixteen- and seventeen-year-olds may marry with the consent of either parent; younger persons require both a parent's and judicial consent. An exception is made for a male under eighteen who has been arrested on a charge of sexual intercourse with a single, widowed, or divorced female of good repute for chastity who has thereby become pregnant; he does not need parental or judicial approval to marry her. N.J. STAT. ANN. § 37:1-6 (enacted 1977).

NEW MEXICO: It is a felony to engage in sexual penetration or sexual contact with a person between thirteen and sixteen where the actor is over eighteen and at least four years older than the victim. It is a felony for anyone to engage in sexual penetration or sexual contact with a person thirteen or under. N.M. STAT ANN. §§ 30-9-11 (enacted 1975), 30-9-13 (enacted 1975).

Both parties must be eighteen to marry without approval. Sixteen- and seventeen-year-olds may marry with the consent of either parent; younger persons require both a parent's and judicial consent. N.M. STAT ANN. §§ 40-1-5 (enacted 1862–63), 40-1-6 (enacted 1876).

NEW YORK: A person is deemed incapable of consenting to a sexual act if he is under seventeen. N.Y. PENAL LAW § 130.05 (enacted 1965). A person who engages in sexual intercourse or sodomy commits a felony under the following circumstances: the offender is at least twenty-one and the victim is under seventeen; the offender is at least eighteen and the victim is under fourteen; or the victim is under eleven. If the victim is under eleven, sexual contact is also a felony. N.Y. PENAL

LAW §§ 130.25 (enacted 1965), 130.30 (enacted 1965), 130.35 (enacted 1965), 130.40 (enacted 1965), 130.45 (enacted 1965), 130.50 (enacted 1965), 130.65 (enacted 1965). The same person commits a misdemeanor under the following circumstances: by engaging in sexual contact with a person between fourteen and seventeen where the offender is at least five years older than the victim, or where the victim is under fourteen. N.Y. PENAL LAW §§ 130.55 (enacted 1965), 130.60 (enacted 1965).

A marriage is voidable by a court if one party is under eighteen. N.Y. DOM. REL. LAW § 7 (enacted 1909). A marriage of any person under fourteen is prohibited. N.Y. DOM. REL. LAW § 15a (enacted 1926).

NORTH CAROLINA: It is a felony to engage in vaginal intercourse or commit other sexual acts with a person under thirteen where the actor is both over twelve and at least four years older than the victim. N.C. GEN. STAT. §§ 14-27.2 (enacted 1979), 14-27.4 (enacted 1979). It is a felony to take or attempt to take any immoral, improper, or indecent liberties, or to commit or attempt to commit any lewd or lascivious act upon or with the body of any child of either sex under sixteen if the offender is at least sixteen and five years older than the victim. N.C. GEN. STAT. § 14-202.1 (enacted 1955).

Both parties must be eighteen to marry without approval. Sixteen- and seventeen-year-olds may marry with the consent of one parent. An unmarried female over twelve but under eighteen who is pregnant or has given birth may marry the putative father of that child with his agreement and either parental consent or the consent of the director of social services for the county in which either resides. N.C. GEN. STAT. § 51-2 (enacted 1985).

NORTH DAKOTA: It is a felony to engage in a sexual act or sexual contact with a person who is under fifteen. N.D. CENT. CODE § 12.1-20-03 (enacted 1973). It is a misdemeanor to engage in a sexual act or sexual contact with a person who is a minor and at least fifteen where the offender is an adult. N.D. CENT. CODE §§ 12.1-20-05 (enacted 1973), 12.1-20-07 (enacted 1973). It is not a defense to this charge that the offender did not know the victim's age, or believed the victim to be older than fourteen. N.D. CENT. CODE § 12.1-20-01 (enacted 1973).

Both parties must be eighteen to marry without approval. Sixteen- and seventeen-year-olds may marry with the consent of the parents.

No person under sixteen may marry. N.D. CENT. CODE § 14-03-02 (enacted 1890).

OHIO: It is a felony for a person eighteen or older to knowingly engage in sexual conduct with a person at least thirteen but not yet sixteen if the offender is at least four years older than the victim. OHIO REV. CODE ANN. §§ 2907.04 (enacted 1972), 2907.06 (enacted 1972). It is a felony for any person to engage in sexual contact or conduct with a person who is under thirteen. OHIO REV. CODE ANN. §§ 2907.02 (enacted 1972), 2907.05 (enacted 1972). It is a misdemeanor for a person eighteen or older to engage in sexual contact with a person at least thirteen but not yet sixteen if the offender is at least four years older than the victim. OHIO REV. CODE ANN. § 2907.06 (enacted 1972). It is a misdemeanor to solicit a person under the age of fifteen to engage in any sexual activity if the offender is at least eighteen and four years older than the victim, whether or not the offender knows the age of the victim. It is a misdemeanor to solicit a person under thirteen to engage in sexual activity. OHIO REV. CODE ANN. § 2907.07 (enacted 1972).

Males at least eighteen and females at least sixteen may marry; below these ages parental consent is required. OHIO REV. CODE ANN. § 3105.01 (enacted 1953).

OKLAHOMA: It is a felony for any person to engage in sexual penetration with a person under fourteen. It is a felony for any person over eighteen to engage in sexual penetration with a person under sixteen. OKLA. STAT. ANN. tit. 21, §§ 1111 (enacted 1981), 1112 (enacted 1981), 1114 (enacted 1981). It is a felony to make any oral or written lewd or indecent proposal to any child under sixteen, for the child to have unlawful sexual relations or intercourse with any person, or to look upon, touch, maul, or feel the body or private parts of any child under sixteen in any lewd or lascivious manner by any acts against public decency or morality as defined by law. OKLA. STAT. ANN. tit. 21, § 1123 (enacted 1945). Soliciting or aiding a child to expose her or himself is a felony. OKLA. STAT. ANN. tit. 21, § 1021 (enacted 1910).

Both parties must be eighteen to marry without approval. Sixteen- and seventeen-year-olds may marry with parental consent. When the female is pregnant the parties may marry with judicial consent as long as the parents are given an opportunity to be heard. OKLA. STAT. ANN. tit. 43, § 3 (enacted 1910).

OREGON: It is a felony to engage in sexual intercourse with a person under sixteen, or to engage in sexual penetration or sexual contact with a person under fourteen. OR. REV. STAT. §§ 163.355 (enacted 1971), 163.408 (enacted 1981), 163.427 (enacted 1991). It is no defense that the offender did not know the age of the victim, or reasonably believed the victim to be older than sixteen. OR. REV. STAT. § 163.25 (enacted 1971). It is a misdemeanor to engage in sexual contact with a person under eighteen. OR. REV. STAT. § 163.415 (enacted 1971). It is a defense that the offender reasonably believed the victim to be eighteen or older. OR. REV. STAT. § 163.25 (enacted 1971). It is a felony to intentionally cause a person under eighteen to touch or contact the mouth, anus, or sex organs of an animal for the purpose of arousing or gratifying the sexual desire of a person. OR. REV. STAT. § 163.427 (enacted 1991).

Both parties must be eighteen to marry without approval. Seventeen-year-olds may marry with parental consent. OR. REV. STAT. §§ 106.010 (enacted 1965), 106.060 (enacted 1965).

PENNSYLVANIA: It is a felony for a person to engage in sexual intercourse or deviate sexual intercourse with a complainant who is under thirteen; or under sixteen if the person is four or more years older than the complainant, and the complainant and the person are not married to each other. 18 PA. CONS. STAT. ANN. §§ 3121 (enacted 1995), 3122.1 (enacted 1995), 3123 (enacted 1995), 3125 (enacted 1990). It is a misdemeanor for a person to engage in sexual contact with a person under the circumstances defined above. 18 PA. CONS. STAT. ANN. § 3126 (enacted 1972). It is no defense that the offender did not know the age of the child, or reasonably believed the child to be at least fourteen. 18 PA. CONS. STAT. ANN. § 3102 (enacted 1972). It is a more serious misdemeanor to expose ones genitals to someone under sixteen. 18 PA. CONS. STAT. ANN. § 3127 (enacted 1995). It is a felony to seduce any female of good repute, under eighteen, with promise of marriage. 18 PA. CONS. STAT. ANN. § 4510 (enacted 1939).

Both parties must be eighteen to marry without approval. Sixteen- and seventeen-year-olds may marry with parental consent. Individuals under sixteen may marry with parental and judicial consent. 23 PA. CONS. STAT. ANN. § 1304 (enacted 1990).

RHODE ISLAND: It is a felony to engage in sexual penetration with a person under sixteen where the offender is over eighteen. R.I. GEN. LAWS § 11-37-6. It is a felony for any person to engage in sexual penetration or sexual contact with a person under fifteen. R.I. GEN. LAWS §§ 11-37-8.1 (enacted 1984), 11-37-8.3 (enacted 1984).

Both parties must be eighteen to marry without approval. Sixteen- and seventeen-year-old females may marry with parental consent. Males under eighteen and females under sixteen may marry with both parental and judicial approval R.I. GEN. LAWS §§ 15-2-11 (enacted 1896).

SOUTH CAROLINA: It is a felony to engage in sexual intercourse or sexual penetration with a person who is under fifteen. S.C. CODE ANN. § 16-3-655 (enacted 1977). It is a felony for a person over fourteen to willfully and lewdly commit or attempt to commit any lewd or lascivious act on a child under the age of fourteen. S.C. CODE ANN. § 16-15-140 (enacted 1962).

Both parties must be eighteen to marry without approval. Males at least sixteen and females at least fourteen may marry with parental approval. S.C. CODE ANN. § 20-1-250 (enacted 1911).

SOUTH DAKOTA: It is a felony for a person to engage in sexual penetration with a person under sixteen if the offender is at least three years older than the victim, or to engage in sexual penetration with a child under ten. S.D. CODIFIED LAWS ANN. § 22-22-1 (enacted 1877). It is a felony for a person sixteen years or older to engage in sexual contact with a person under sixteen if the offender is three or more years older than the victim. If the offender is less than three years older, the crime is a misdemeanor. S.D. CODIFIED LAWS ANN. § 22-22-7 (enacted 1950). It is a misdemeanor for a person under sixteen to engage in sexual contact with another person under sixteen. S.D. CODIFIED LAWS ANN. § 22-22-7.3 (enacted 1989).

Both parties must be eighteen to marry without approval. Sixteen- and seventeen-year-olds may marry with parental consent. S.D. CODIFIED LAWS ANN. § 25-1-9 (enacted 1877).

TENNESSEE: It is a felony to engage in sexual penetration with a person under eighteen where the defendant is at least four years older than the victim. TENN. CODE ANN. § 39-13-506 (enacted 1989). It is a felony for anyone to engage in sexual penetration or sexual contact with a person under thirteen. TENN. CODE ANN. §§ 39-13-504 (enacted 1989), 39-13-522 (enacted 1992).

Both parties must be eighteen to marry without approval. Sixteen- and seventeen-year-olds may marry with parental consent. TENN. CODE ANN. §§ 36-3-105 (enacted 1937), 36-3-106 (enacted 1937). Courts have the power to waive the age requirements. TENN. CODE ANN. § 36-3-107 (enacted 1937).

TEXAS: A person is guilty of a felony if that person engages in sexual contact with a child under seventeen and not the offender's spouse. It is an affirmative defense that the actor was not more than three years older than the victim and of the opposite sex and did not use duress, force, or a threat against the victim at the time of the offense. TEX. PENAL CODE ANN. § 21.11 (enacted 1973).

Both parties must be eighteen to marry without approval. Individuals who are at least fourteen but not yet eighteen may marry with either parental or judicial approval. TEX. FAM. CODE ANN. §§ 1.51 (enacted 1969), 1.52 (enacted 1969), 1.53 (enacted 1973).

UTAH: It is a felony to engage in any sexual act with a person under fourteen. UTAH CODE ANN. §§ 76-5-402.1 (enacted 1953), 76-5-403.1 (enacted 1953), 76-5-404.1 (enacted 1953). If the victim is over fourteen but not over seventeen and the offender is at least three years older than the victim and entices the victim to submit, the offense is a felony. UTAH CODE ANN. § 76-5-406 (enacted 1953). It is not a defense that the offender mistakenly believed the victim to be of the age of consent at the time of the offense or was unaware of the victim's true age. UTAH CODE ANN. § 76-2-304.5 (enacted 1953).

Both parties must be eighteen to marry without approval. Sixteen- and seventeen-year-olds may marry with the consent of a parent. Fourteen- and fifteen-year-olds need both parental and judicial consent. No person under fourteen may marry. UTAH CODE ANN. §§ 30-1-2 (enacted 1898), 30-1-9 (enacted 1898).

VERMONT: It is a felony to engage in a sexual act with a person under sixteen. VT. STAT. ANN. tit. 13, § 3252 (enacted 1977).

Both parties must be eighteen to marry without approval. Sixteen- and seventeen-year-olds may marry with parental consent. Fourteen- and fifteen-year-olds may marry with parental and judicial consent. VT. STAT. ANN. tit. 18, § 5142 (enacted 1951).

VIRGINIA: It is a felony to engage in sexual intercourse with a person under fifteen, but a misdemeanor if the victim is at least thirteen and the offender is less than three years older than the victim. VA. CODE ANN. §§ 18.2-61 (enacted 1950), 18.2-63 (enacted 1950). It is a felony for any person over eighteen to knowingly and intentionally propose to any child under fourteen the performance of any sexual conduct. VA. CODE ANN. § 18.2-370 (enacted 1950). A person who is eighteen years of age or over and with lascivious intent exposes his or her sexual or genital parts to any child under fourteen to whom the actor is not legally married, or who proposes that any such child expose his or her sexual or genital parts, is guilty of a felony. VA. CODE ANN. § 18.2-370 (enacted 1950).

Both parties must be eighteen to marry without approval. A person over sixteen and under eighteen may marry with parental approval. A person under sixteen may marry when the female is pregnant, with parental and judicial consent. VA. CODE ANN. §§ 20-45.1 (enacted 1975), 20-48 (enacted 1919).

WASHINGTON: It is a felony to engage in sexual intercourse or sexual contact with a person under sixteen where the offender is at least forty-eight months older than the victim. If the victim is under fourteen, the offender must be at least thirty-six months older than the victim. WASH. REV. CODE ANN. §§ 9A.44.073 (enacted 1988), 9A.44.076 (enacted 1988), 9A.44.079 (enacted 1988), 9A.44.083 (enacted 1988), 9A.44.086 (enacted 1988), 9A.44.089 (enacted 1988).

A person must be eighteen to marry without approval. The marriage of a person under seventeen is void unless judicial waiver is obtained. WASH. REV. CODE ANN. § 26.04.010 (enacted 1881).

WEST VIRGINIA: It is a felony for a person sixteen or older to engage in sexual intercourse with another person under sixteen and at least four years younger than the offender. W. VA. CODE § 61-8B-5 (enacted 1976). It is a felony for a person at least fourteen to engage in sexual intercourse, sexual intrusion, or sexual contact with a person under twelve. W. VA. CODE §§ 61-8B-3 (enacted 1976). It is a misdemeanor for a person sixteen or over to engage in sexual contact with another person under sixteen and at least four years younger than the offender. W. VA. CODE § 61-8B-9 (enacted 1976).

A person must be eighteen to marry without approval. A person under eighteen requires parental approval. A person under sixteen requires judicial approval. W. VA. CODE § 48-1-1 (enacted 1849).

WISCONSIN: Sexual intercourse with a person under fifteen is a felony. A person at least fifteen but under eighteen is rebuttably presumed to be incapable of consent, thus rendering sexual intercourse with that person a felony. Sexual contact with a person under fifteen is a misdemeanor. A person at least fifteen but under eighteen is rebuttably presumed to be incapable of consent, thus rendering sexual contact with that person a misdemeanor. WIS. STAT. ANN. §§ 940.225 (enacted 1987), 948.09 (enacted 1987). It is a felony to cause any child under eighteen to go into any vehicle, building, room, or secluded place with the intent of having sexual contact with the child. WIS. STAT. ANN. § 948.07 (enacted 1987). If, for the purposes of sexual arousal or gratification, a person exposes genitals or pubic area to a child or causes a child to expose genitals or pubic area, that person is guilty of a misdemeanor. WIS. STAT. ANN. § 948.10 (enacted 1987).

Persons must be eighteen to marry without approval. Sixteen- and seventeen-year-olds may marry with parental consent. WIS. STAT. ANN. § 765.02 (enacted 1917).

WYOMING: It is a felony to subject a person under twelve to sexual intrusion or sexual contact if the actor is at least four years older than the victim. WYO. STAT. § 6-2-303 (enacted 1982). It is a felony to subject a person under sixteen to sexual intrusion if the actor is at least four years older than the victim. WYO. STAT. § 6-2-304 (enacted 1982). It is a felony for any person to take immodest, immoral, or indecent liberties with any person under eighteen. WYO. STAT. § 14-3-105 (enacted 1957).

Both parties must be eighteen to marry without approval. Sixteen- and seventeen-year-olds may marry with parental consent. Persons under sixteen may marry with parental and judicial approval. WYO. STAT. § 20-1-102 (enacted 1876).

UNITED STATES: It is a felony for any person in the special maritime and territorial jurisdiction of the United States, or in a Federal prison, to knowingly engage in a sexual act or sexual contact with another person under sixteen, and at least four years younger than the offender. It is a defense that the offender reasonably believed the victim to be at least sixteen, or that the defendant and victim were married at the time. 18 U.S.C.A. §§ 2243(a) (enacted 1986), 2244 (enacted 1986). It is an aggravated felony to engage in a sexual act or sexual contact with anyone under twelve. 18 U.S.C.A. §§ 2241 (enacted 1986), 2244 (enacted 1986).

There is no federal minimum age for marriage.

4
Sodomy

This chapter summarizes statutes that apply to consensual sodomy in private between adults. In most states sodomy is prohibited in public places, without the consent of one party, or with a person under the age of consent. Those crimes are not unique to sodomy, and are covered in the chapters on public nudity (chap. 6), sexual assault (chap. 1), and the age of consent (chap. 3). If sodomy is not prohibited in private between consenting adults, we have said "no statute" even if it is prohibited under other circumstances. There is no uniform definition that specifies which acts constitute "sodomy."

Sodomy was first prohibited by the English common law in the sixteenth century under the rule of Henry VIII, and was prohibited under church law even earlier. The early prohibitions, which used the term "crime against nature," were limited to anal intercourse. Most American jurisdictions have expanded the definition of sodomy to include contact between mouth and genitals. Sometimes this expansion of the definition is done by statutory language, but sometimes it occurs instead through a long history of judicial construction of an apparently nonspecific statute. The Model Penal Code uses far more specific language: "deviate sexual intercourse" used in conjunction with language specifically describing the acts prohibited. A few states have explicitly limited the prohibition to same-sex conduct, and others have created exceptions for married people by judicial construction.

Constitutional challenges to sodomy statutes have proceeded on two grounds, privacy and vagueness, with varying degrees of success. In 1986 the Supreme Court held that the federal right to privacy does not extend to sodomy. *Bowers v. Hardwick*, 478 U.S. 186 (1986). Nearly half the state constitutions also confer a right to privacy, and a number of sodomy statutes have been successfully challenged as infringing that right. The Supreme Court has also held that the nonspecific statutory language of the sodomy statutes is not unconstitutionally vague when judicial decisions have interpreted the language as applying to the particular acts in question or even when, in a case involving new facts, the statute can reasonably be interpreted as covering the acts in question. *Rose v. Locke*, 423 U.S. 48 (1975).

Prosecutions for sodomy are today almost entirely limited either to sexual conduct in a public place, such as a public restroom or a night club, or sexual conduct involving force or lack of consent, where a sexual assault charge would be difficult to prove or the public nudity statute carries a sentence that is judged too light by prosecutors. Though extremely rare, prosecution for consensual sodomy between adults in private is not unheard of. In the *Bowers* case, the plaintiff was charged with sodomy after police gained entrance to his home on an unrelated matter and witnessed the defendant engaged in oral sex through a bedroom door left partially ajar, but the charges were dropped before trial.

ALABAMA: A person commits sexual misconduct, a misdemeanor, by engaging in deviate sexual intercourse with another person. ALA. CODE § 13A-6-65 (enacted 1977). Deviate sexual intercourse is any act of sexual gratification between persons not married to each other involving the sex organs of one person and the mouth or anus of another. ALA. CODE § 13A-6-60 (enacted 1977).

ALASKA: No statute.

ARIZONA: A person who knowingly and without force commits the infamous crime against nature with an adult is guilty of a misdemeanor. ARIZ. REV. STAT. ANN. § 13-1411 (enacted 1965). A person who knowingly and without force commits, in any unnatural manner, any lewd or lascivious act upon or with the body or any part or member thereof of a male or female adult, with the intent of arousing, appealing to, or gratifying the lust, passion, or sexual desires of either of such persons, is guilty of a misdemeanor. ARIZ. REV. STAT. ANN. § 13-1412 (enacted 1965).

ARKANSAS: Sodomy is any act of sexual gratification involving the penetration, however slight, of the anus or mouth of a male by the penis of another male; or the penetration, however slight, of the anus or vagina of a female by any body member of another female. Sodomy is a misdemeanor. ARK. CODE ANN. § 5-14-122 (enacted 1977).

CALIFORNIA: It is a misdemeanor for any person to participate in an act of sodomy or oral copulation with any other person while confined in any state prison. Sodomy means sexual conduct involving contact between the penis of one person and the anus of another; oral copulation is the act of connecting the mouth of one person with the sexual organ or anus of another person. CAL. PENAL CODE §§ 286 (enacted 1872), 288a (enacted 1921), 289 (enacted 1978).

COLORADO: No statute.

CONNECTICUT: No statute.

DELAWARE: No statute.

DISTRICT OF COLUMBIA: It is a felony to take the sexual organ of another person into one's mouth or anus or to place one's sexual organ in the mouth or anus of another or to have carnal copulation in an opening of the body other than the sexual parts with another person. D.C. CODE ANN. § 22-3502 (enacted 1948). It is a violation to commit a lewd or indecent act. D.C. CODE ANN. § 22-1112 (enacted 1892).

FLORIDA: Whoever commits any unnatural and lascivious act with another person is guilty of a misdemeanor. A mother's breast feeding of her baby does not violate this section. FLA. STAT. ANN. § 800.02 (enacted 1993).

GEORGIA: Sodomy consists of performing or submitting to any sexual act involving the sex organs of one person and the mouth or anus of another. It is a felony. GA. CODE ANN. § 16-6-2 (enacted 1833). It is unlawful to perform sodomy or oral copulation on premises licensed for alcholic beverages. GA. STAT. ANN. § 3-3-41. Solicitation of sodomy means soliciting another to perform or submit to an act of sodomy. It is a misdemeanor except when the person being solicited is under seventeen, in which case it is a felony. GA. CODE ANN. § 16-6-15 (enacted 1933).

HAWAII: No statute.

IDAHO: The infamous crime against nature is a felony. IDAHO CODE § 18-6605 (enacted 1972). Any penetration, however slight, is sufficient to complete the crime. IDAHO CODE § 18-6606 (enacted 1972).

ILLINOIS: No statute.

INDIANA: No statute.

IOWA: No statute.

KANSAS: Sodomy means oral or anal copulation; or any penetration of the anal opening by any body part or object. Sodomy between persons of the same sex is a misdemeanor. KAN. CRIM. CODE ANN. §§ 21-3501 (enacted 1969), 21-3505 (enacted 1969).

KENTUCKY: It is a misdemeanor to engage in deviate sexual intercourse with another person of the same sex. KY. REV. STAT. ANN. § 510.100 (enacted 1974). Deviate sexual intercourse means any act of sexual gratification involving the sex organs of one person and the mouth or anus of another. KY. REV. STAT. ANN. § 510.010 (enacted 1974).

LOUISIANA: The unnatural carnal copulation by a human being with another of the same or opposite sex is a crime against nature and is a felony. Emission is not necessary and the use of the genital organ of one of the offenders of whatever sex is sufficient to constitute the crime. LA. REV. STAT. ANN. § 14:89 (enacted 1975).

MAINE: No statute.

MARYLAND: Sodomy is a felony. MD. ANN. CODE, art. 27, § 553 (enacted 1793). Taking another person's sexual organ into one's mouth or placing one's sexual organ into another person's mouth, or committing any other unnatural or perverted sexual practice with any other person, is also a felony. In an indictment under this section, it is not necessary to set forth the particular manner in which such unnatural or perverted sexual practice was committed. MD. ANN. CODE, art. 27, § 554 (enacted 1916).

MASSACHUSETTS: Whoever commits the abominable and detestable crime against nature is guilty of a felony. MASS. GEN. LAWS ch. 272, § 34 (enacted 1784). Whoever commits any unnatural and lascivious act with another person commits a felony. MASS. GEN. LAWS ch. 272, § 35 (enacted 1887).

MICHIGAN: It is a felony to commit the abominable and detestable crime against nature. MICH. COMP. LAWS ANN. § 750.158 (enacted 1931). Any person who, in public or in private, commits or is party to the comission of or procures or attempts to procure the commission by any person of any act of gross indecency with another person shall be guilty of a felony. MICH. COMP. LAWS ANN. §§ 750.338 (enacted 1931), 750.338a (enacted 1931), 750.338b (enacted 1931).

MINNESOTA: Any person who voluntarily engages in or submits to sodomy commits a misdemeanor. Sodomy means carnally knowing any person by the anus or with the mouth. MINN. STAT. ANN. § 609.293 (enacted 1967).

MISSISSIPPI: Every person convicted of the detestable and abominable crime against nature is guilty of a felony. MISS. CODE. ANN. § 97-29-59 (enacted 1848).

MISSOURI: A person who has deviate sexual intercourse with another person of the same sex is guilty of sexual misconduct, a misdemeanor. MO. ANN. STAT. § 566.090 (enacted 1977). Deviate sexual intercourse means any act involving the genitals of one person and the mouth, tongue, or anus of another person, or a sexual act involving the penetration, however slight, of the male or female sex organs by a finger, instrument, or object done for the purpose of arousing or gratifying the sexual desire of any person. MO. ANN. STAT. § 566.010 (enacted 1977).

MONTANA: Deviate sexual relations between two persons is a felony. MONT. CODE ANN. § 45-5-505 (enacted 1973).

NEBRASKA: No statute.

NEVADA: No statute.

NEW HAMPSHIRE: No statute.

NEW JERSEY: No statute.

NEW MEXICO: No statute.

NEW YORK: Deviate sexual intercourse is a misdemeanor. N.Y. PENAL LAW § 130.38 (enacted 1965). Deviate sexual intercourse means sexual conduct between persons not married to each other consisting of contact between the penis and the anus, the mouth and penis, or the mouth and the vulva. N.Y. PENAL LAW § 130.00 (enacted 1965).

NORTH CAROLINA: It is a felony to commit the crime against nature. N.C. GEN. STAT. § 14-177 (enacted 1868–69).

NORTH DAKOTA: No statute.

OHIO: No statute.

OKLAHOMA: It is a felony to commit the detestable and abominable crime against nature. Any sexual penetration, however slight, is sufficient to complete the crime against nature. OKLA. STAT. ANN. tit. 21, §§ 886 (enacted 1910), 887 (enacted 1910).

OREGON: No statute.

PENNSYLVANIA: A person who engages in deviate sexual intercourse per os or per anus is guilty of a misdemeanor. Married couples are exempt. 18 PA. CONS. STAT. ANN. §§ 3101 (enacted 1972), 3124 (enacted 1972).

RHODE ISLAND: Anyone who commits the abominable and detestable crime against nature with another person commits a felony carrying a seven-year minimum sentence. R.I. GEN. LAWS § 11-10-1 (enacted 1896).

SOUTH CAROLINA: Buggery is a felony. S.C. CODE ANN. § 16-15-120 (enacted 1902).

SOUTH DAKOTA: No statute.

TENNESSEE: It is a misdemeanor to engage in consensual sexual penetration with a person of the same gender. TENN. CODE ANN. § 39-13-510 (enacted 1989). Sexual penetration means sexual intercourse, cunnilingus, fellatio, anal intercourse, or any other intrusion, however slight, of any part of a person's body or any object into the genital or anal openings of the victim's, the defendant's, or any other person's body; the emission of semen is not required. TENN. CODE ANN. § 39-13-501 (enacted 1989).

TEXAS: Deviate sexual intercourse with another individual of the same sex is a misdemeanor. TEXAS PENAL CODE ANN. § 21.06 (enacted 1973). Deviate sexual intercourse means any contact between the genitals of one person and the mouth or anus of another person, or the penetration of the genitals or the anus of another person with an object. TEXAS PENAL CODE ANN. § 21.06 (enacted 1973).

UTAH: It is a misdemeanor called sodomy to engage in any sexual act involving the genitals of one person and mouth or anus of another person, regardless of the gender of either participant. UTAH CODE ANN. § 76-5-403 (enacted 1953). Any sexual penetration or any sexual touching, however slight, is sufficient to constitute the relevant element of the offense. UTAH CODE ANN. § 76-5-407 (enacted 1953).

VERMONT: No statute.

VIRGINIA: It is a felony designated as a crime against nature to carnally know any male or female person by or with the anus or mouth or to submit to such carnal knowledge. VA. CODE ANN. § 18.2-361 (enacted 1950).

Washington: No statute.

West Virginia: No statute.

Wisconsin: No statute.

Wyoming: No statute.

United States: Whoever knowingly transports, or knowingly persuades, induces, entices, or coerces any individual to travel in interstate or foreign commerce, or in any territory or possession of the United States, with intent that such individual engage in any sexual activity for which any person can be charged with a criminal offense, shall be guilty of a felony. 18 U.S.C.A. §§ 2421 (enacted 1948), 2422 (enacted 1948).

5

Transmission of Disease

This chapter covers criminal acts that a person having a sexually transmitted disease (STD) may be convicted for committing because the acts place another person at risk of becoming infected. It does not cover the general public health regulations of STDs found in almost every state: testing requirements for marriage licenses; registration of the names of HIV-infected persons with health officials; discretionary police powers given to health officials to control disease; testing prison inmates for disease; or health regulations for restaurants that may include reporting or testing for disease. Where prostitution is an element of the offense, the reader should consult chapter 12.

Even where there is no explicit provision criminalizing the transmission of an STD, some states punish the conduct under more general laws—manslaughter, reckless endangerment, attempted murder, or murder. For example, in 1992, the state of Texas convicted a man who was HIV-positive for attempted murder, and sentenced him to life in prison, for spitting on a prison guard. *Weeks v. State*, 834 S.W.2d 559 (Tex. Ct. App. 1992).

In 1990, Congress passed the Ryan White Comprehensive AIDS Resources Emergency Act of 1990, Pub. L. No. 101-381, which conditions the grant of some federal aid to states on a finding that the state has criminalized exposure to HIV, either explicitly or through general criminal assault statutes. This gave state legislatures an incentive to pass criminal transmission statutes. Because many of the statutes are new, their application raises questions for which there are not as yet any ready answers. For example, some of the statutes provide that if the defendant obtained the victim's consent after disclosing his or her HIV status, no crime occurs. Other states do not recognize such a defense, thus making consensual sexual relations between an HIV-positive and an HIV-negative person a crime, even if a condom is used to protect against transmission. In this connection, it should be noted that in some states that criminalize behavior that "exposes" another person to infection, the status of sexual acts that are low-risk but not zero-risk is unclear. Some statutes prohibit all sexual intercourse when a person is infected with a communicable disease, without any defense for taking precautions that reduce the risk of transmission.

Many states do not explicitly require that the defendant know he or she is HIV-positive as a result of having tested positive for the disease. In these states, it may be possible to punish a person who has not been tested for HIV but knows, based on past repeated conduct or a single high-risk act with an infected person, that he or she has a high probability of being infected. See, for example, *Cooper v. State*, 539 So. 2d 508 (Fla. Dist. Ct. App. 1989).

The statutes do not generally require any actual injury to or infection in the victim, or that the defendant intend to injure the victim. Ordinary criminal assault statutes usually require one or the other.

We have used the term "HIV" to refer to the human immunodeficiency virus, and "AIDS" to refer to acquired immunodeficiency syndrome.

ALABAMA: No statute.

ALASKA: No statute.

ARIZONA: No statute.

ARKANSAS: A person who knows he or she has tested positive for HIV commits the offense of exposing another to HIV if that person exposes another person to such viral infection through the injected transfer of blood or blood products or engages in sexual penetration with another person without first having informed the other person of the presence of HIV. Sexual penetration includes sexual intercourse, cunnilingus, fellatio, anal intercourse, or any other intrusion, however slight, of any part of a person's body or of any object into the genital or anal openings of another person's body. Exposing another to HIV is a felony. ARK. CODE ANN. § 5-14-123 (enacted 1989).

CALIFORNIA: Any person who exposes another person to or infects another person with any venereal disease is guilty of a misdemeanor. It is also a misdemeanor for any person infected with a venereal disease who knows of such condition to marry or have sexual intercourse. CAL. HEALTH & SAFETY CODE § 3198 (enacted 1957).

A person also receives a three-year sentence enhancement for the commission of certain specified crimes, such as rape and sodomy, when the offender commits such offenses with the knowledge that he or she has AIDS or the HIV virus at the time of commission. CAL. PENAL CODE § 12022.85 (enacted 1988).

COLORADO: It is a misdemeanor for any person who knows or has reasonable grounds to suspect that he or she is infected with a venereal disease, defined as syphilis, gonorrhea, chancroid, granuloma inguinale, and lymphogranuloma venereum, to willfully expose to or infect another person with such disease or to knowingly perform an act which exposes to or infects another person with a venereal disease. COLO. REV. STAT. ANN. §§ 25-4-401 (enacted 1919), 25-4-407 (enacted 1919). It is a felony to engage in prostitution or to patronize a prostitute with knowledge of being infected with AIDS. COLO. REV. STAT. ANN. §§ 18-7-201.7 (enacted 1990), 18-7-205.7 (enacted 1990).

CONNECTICUT: No statute.

DELAWARE: No statute.

DISTRICT OF COLUMBIA: No statute.

FLORIDA: It is unlawful for any person who has chancroid, gonorrhea, granuloma inguinale, lymphogranuloma venereum, genital herpes simplex, chlamydia, nongonococcal urethritis, pelvic inflammatory disease, acute salpingitis, syphilis, or HIV infection, when such person knows he or she is infected with one or more of these diseases and when such person has been informed that he or she may communicate the disease to another person through sexual intercourse, to have sexual intercourse with any other person unless the other person has been informed of the presence of the disease and has consented to the sexual intercourse. FLA. STAT. ANN. § 384.24 (enacted 1988).

Persons convicted of sexual crimes are required by the court to undergo HIV testing. If such an offender, after testing positive for HIV, commits a second or subsequent sexual crime, he or she commits criminal transmission of HIV, a felony. It is not necessary for the offender to actually infect the victim with HIV to be found guilty of criminal transmission of HIV. The court may require the offender, if convicted, to serve a term of criminal quarantine community control, in addition to any other penalty provided for the underlying sexual crime. FLA. STAT. ANN. § 775.0877 (enacted 1993).

A person who knows he or she has tested positive for a sexually transmissible disease other than HIV and could possibly communicate such disease to another person through sexual activity and who still commits prostitution or procures another for prostitution is guilty of a misdemeanor. If the sexually transmissible disease is HIV, the crime is a felony. The offender can also be convicted and sentenced separately for the underlying crime of prostitution or procurement of prostitution. FLA. STAT. ANN. § 796.08 (enacted 1993).

GEORGIA: A person who does any of the following after obtaining knowledge of being infected with HIV commits a felony: (1) knowingly engages in sexual intercourse or performs or submits to any act involving the sex organs of one person and the mouth or anus of another person and the HIV-infected person does not disclose to the other person the presence of the infection prior to the sexual conduct; (2) knowingly allows another person to use a hypodermic needle, syringe, or both for the introduction of drugs or any other substance into or for the withdrawal of body fluids from the other person's body and the needle or syringe so used had been previously used by the HIV-infected person for the same purpose and where the infected person does not disclose to the other person the presence of the HIV infection before such use; (3) offers or consents to perform with another person an act of sexual intercourse for money without disclosing to that other person the presence of the HIV infection prior to such act; (4) solicits another person to perform or submit to sodomy for money without disclosing to that person the presence of the HIV infection prior to such act; or (5) donates blood, blood products, other bodily fluids, or any body organ or body part without previously disclosing the presence of the HIV infection to the person drawing the blood or blood products or the person or entity collecting or storing the other bodily fluids, body organ, or body part. GA. CODE ANN. § 16-5-60 (enacted 1988).

HAWAII: No statute.

IDAHO: It is unlawful for anyone infected with syphilis, gonorrhea, AIDS, AIDS-related complexes, other manifestations of HIV infections, chancroid, or hepatitis B virus to knowingly expose another person to the infection of such diseases. Where the offender is infected with syphilis, gonorrhea, or chancroid, the crime is a misdemeanor. IDAHO CODE §§ 39-601 (enacted 1921), 39-607 (enacted 1921). Any person who exposes another in any manner with the intent to infect or, knowing that he or she has been afflicted with AIDS, AIDS-related complexes, or other manifestations of HIV infection, transfers or attempts to transfer any of his or her body fluids, body tissues, or organs to another person is guilty of a felony. Transfer means engaging in any sexual activity by genital-genital contact, oral-genital contact, anal-genital contact; permitting the use of a hypodermic syringe, needle, or similar device without sterilization; or giving, whether or not for value, blood, semen, body tissues, or organs to a person, blood bank, hospital, or other medical care facility for purposes of transfer to another person. IDAHO CODE § 39-608 (enacted 1988).

ILLINOIS: A person commits criminal transmission of HIV by, knowing that he or she is infected with HIV, (1) exposing the body of another person to a bodily fluid in a manner that could result in the transmission of HIV; (2) transfering, donating, or providing his or her blood, tissue, organs, semen, or other potentially infectious body fluids for transfusion, transplantation, insemination, or administration to another; or (3) dispenses, delivers, exchanges, sells or in any other way transfers to another person any nonsterile intravenous or intramuscular drug paraphernalia. It is an affirmative defense that the person exposed knew that the infected person was infected with HIV, knew that the action could result in infection with HIV, and consented to the action with that knowledge. The victim need not become infected with HIV for the offender to be convicted of criminal transmission of HIV. ILL. ANN. STAT. ch. 720, para. 5/12-16.2 (enacted 1961, amended for HIV 1989).

INDIANA: A person who recklessly, knowingly, or intentionally donates, sells, or transfers blood, a blood component, or semen for artificial insemination that contains the human immunodeficiency virus commits transferring contaminated body fluids, a felony. This section does not apply to blood donated for research purposes. IND. CODE ANN. § 35-42-1-7 (enacted 1988).

IOWA: No statute.

KANSAS: No statute.

KENTUCKY: It is a felony for a person to donate or sell blood if the person is at high risk for infection with the HIV virus, or has AIDS, or has tested confirmatory positive for HIV or any other known causative agent of a blood-borne communicable disease. KY. REV. STAT. ANN. §§ 214.452(3)(d) (enacted 1994), 214.454(1) (enacted 1994). It is a felony to commit, offer or agree to commit, or procure another to commit prostitution by engaging in sexual activity in a manner likely to transmit HIV if the offender knew, prior to the commission of the crime, that he or she had tested positive for HIV and that the sexual activity could transmit HIV. A person who commits prostitution and who, prior to the commission of the crime, knew that he or she had tested positive for a sexually transmitted disease and knew that the sexual activity might transmit the disease to another person is guilty of a misdemeanor. Note that a person may be convicted and sentenced separately for this crime and for the underlying crime of prostitution. KY. REV. STAT. ANN. § 529.090 (enacted 1992).

LOUISIANA: It is a felony to intentionally expose another person or a police officer to any AIDS virus through sexual contact or through any means or contact, including spitting, biting, stabbing with an AIDS-contaminated object, and throwing of blood or other bodily substances, without the knowing and lawful consent of the victim. LA. REV. STAT. ANN. § 14:43.5 (enacted 1987).

MAINE: No statute.

MARYLAND: It is a misdemeanor for any individual who has HIV to knowingly transfer or attempt to transfer the virus to another person. MD. HEALTH-GEN. CODE ANN. § 18-601.1 (enacted 1989).

MASSACHUSETTS: No statute.

MICHIGAN: It is a felony for a person who knows that he or she has acquired or has been diagnosed as having acquired AIDS, AIDS-related complex, or an HIV infection to engage in sexual intercourse, cunnilingus, fellatio, anal intercourse, or any intrusion of any part of that person's body or of any object into the genital or anal openings of another person's body without first having informed the other person of his or her condition. MICH. STAT. ANN. § 333.5210 (enacted 1988).

MINNESOTA: No statute.

MISSISSIPPI: It is a felony for a person afflicted with a life-threatening communicable disease or the causative agent thereof to knowingly and willfully violate the lawful order of a health officer. MISS. CODE ANN. § 41-23-2 (enacted 1988).

MISSOURI: It is a felony for any individual knowingly infected with HIV to be or attempt to be a blood, organ, sperm, or tissue donor except as deemed necessary for medical research. It is unlawful, but not a felony, for any individual knowingly infected with HIV to deliberately create a grave and unjustifiable risk of infecting another with HIV through sexual or other contact when the individual knows that he or she is creating that risk. MO. STAT. ANN. § 191.677 (enacted 1988).

MONTANA: A person infected with a sexually transmitted disease who knowingly exposes another person to infection is guilty of a misdemeanor. MONT. CODE ANN. §§ 50-18-112 (enacted 1967), 50-18-113 (enacted 1967).

NEBRASKA: No statute.

NEVADA: Any person who, after testing positive for HIV and receiving actual notice of that fact, intentionally, knowingly, or willfully engages in conduct in a manner that is intended or likely to transmit the disease to another person is guilty of a felony. It is an affirmative defense that the person exposed to HIV (1) knew of the defendant's condition; (2) knew the conduct could result in exposure to HIV; and (3) consented to the conduct with this knowledge. NEV. REV. STAT. § 201.205 (enacted 1993). Any person who works as a prostitute after testing positive for HIV and receiving notice of that fact is guilty of a felony. NEV. REV. STAT. § 201.358 (enacted 1987).

NEW HAMPSHIRE: No statute.

NEW JERSEY: Any person who commits an act of sexual penetration, knowing that he or she is infected with a venereal disease such as chancroid, gonorrhea, syphilis, herpes virus, or any of the varieties or stages of such diseases, is a petty disorderly person. N.J. STAT. ANN. § 2C:34-5 (enacted 1978).

NEW MEXICO: No statute.

NEW YORK: Any person who, knowing himself or herself to be infected with an infectious venereal disease, has sexual intercourse with another is guilty of a misdemeanor. N.Y. PUB. HEALTH LAW § 2307 (enacted 1953).

NORTH CAROLINA: No statute.

NORTH DAKOTA: A person who knows himself or herself to be afflicted with AIDS, AIDS-related complexes, or HIV, and who willfully transfers any of that person's body fluid to another person, is guilty of a felony. Transfer means to engage in sexual activity by genital-genital contact, oral-genital contact, or anal-genital contact, or to permit the reuse of a hypodermic syringe, needle, or similar device without sterilization; body fluid means semen, blood, or vaginal secretion. It is an affirmative defense that the sexual activity took place between consenting adults after full disclosure of the risk of such activity and with the use of an appropriate prophylactic device. N.D. CENT. CODE § 12.1-20-17 (enacted 1989).

OHIO: Any person who, with knowledge that he or she is a carrier of an AIDS virus, sells or donates blood, plasma, or blood products for the known purpose of transfusion to another individual is guilty of selling or donating contaminated blood, a felony. OHIO REV. CODE ANN. § 2927.13 (enacted 1988). Any person knowing or having reason to believe that he or she is suffering from a dangerous contagious disease must take reasonable measures to prevent exposing others to the disease, except when the actor is seeking medical aid. OHIO REV. CODE ANN. § 3701.81 (enacted 1972).

OKLAHOMA: It is a felony to inoculate oneself or any other person or allow oneself to be inoculated with smallpox, syphilis, or gonorrhea and then intentionally or recklessly spread or cause to be spread to any other persons such infectious disease. OKLA. STAT. ANN. tit. 21, § 1192 (enacted 1910). It is a felony for any person knowing that he or she has AIDS or is a carrier of HIV to, with intent to infect another, engage in conduct reasonably likely to result in the transfer of the person's own blood, bodily fluids containing visible blood, semen, or vaginal secretions into the bloodstream of another or through the skin or other membranes of another person. These acts do not constitute a crime if the other person consented to the transfer of blood or other fluids after being informed by the actor that the actor had AIDS or was a carrier of HIV. Transmission in utero does not fall within this section. OKLA. STAT. ANN. tit. 21, § 1192.1 (enacted 1988). Every person who, being affected with any contagious disease, willfully exposes himself or another person in any public place or thoroughfare, is guilty of a misdemeanor, except in the person's necessary removal in a manner not dangerous to the public health. OKLA. STAT. ANN. tit. 21, § 1199 (enacted 1910). It is a felony for any person, after becoming infected with a venereal disease and before being discharged and pronounced cured by a physician in writing, to marry any other person, or to expose any other person by the act of copulation or sexual intercourse to such venereal disease or to liability to contract the same. OKLA. STAT. ANN.

tit. 63, § 1-519 (enacted 1913). Any person who engages in an act of prostitution with knowledge that he or she is infected with HIV is guilty of a felony. OKLA. STAT. ANN. tit. 21, § 1031 (enacted 1943, amended for HIV 1991).

OREGON: It is a misdemeanor for a person to donate semen for use in artificial insemination if he knows or has reason to know that he has a venereal disease. OR. REV. STAT. §§ 677.370 (enacted 1977), 677.990 (enacted 1967).

PENNSYLVANIA: No statute.

RHODE ISLAND: It is a misdemeanor to knowingly expose another person to infection while in an infectious condition with a sexually transmitted disease. Sexually transmitted diseases include but are not limited to syphilis, gonorrhea, chancroid, granuloma inguinale, and lymphogranuloma venereum, and any other disease the director of health determines by regulation to be a sexually transmitted disease. R.I. GEN LAWS § 23-11-1 (enacted 1921).

SOUTH CAROLINA: It is a misdemeanor for anyone infected with a sexually transmitted disease to knowingly expose another person to infection. For this section, sexually transmitted diseases are those that are included in the annual Department of Health and Environmental Control List of Reportable Diseases. S.C. CODE ANN. §§ 44-29-60 (enacted 1962), 44-29-140 (enacted 1962). No person imprisoned under § 44-29-60 may be discharged from confinement unless he is pronounced cured of the disease by a state, county, or municipal health officer or, if no cure is available, upon the recommendation of the Department of Health and Environmental Control. S.C. CODE ANN. § 44-29-110 (enacted 1962).

There is a separate provision for HIV. It is a felony for a person who knows that he or she is infected with HIV to (1) knowingly engage in vaginal, anal, or oral intercourse with another person without first informing that person of the HIV infection; (2) knowingly commit an act of prostitution with another person; (3) knowingly sell or donate blood, blood products, semen, tissue, organs, or other bodily fluids; (4) forcibly engage in vaginal, anal, or oral intercourse without the consent of the other person, including one's legal spouse; or (5) knowingly share with another person a hypodermic needle, syringe, or both, for the introduction of drugs or any other substance into or for withdrawal of blood or body fluids from the other person's body without first informing that person that the item has been used by someone infected with HIV. S.C. CODE ANN. § 44-29-145 (enacted 1988).

SOUTH DAKOTA: It is a misdemeanor for any person infected with syphilis, gonorrhea, or chancroid to expose another person to infection. S.D. CODIFIED LAWS ANN. § 34-23-1 (enacted 1919).

TENNESSEE: A person commits the offense of criminal exposure of another to HIV when, knowing that he or she is infected with HIV or any other identified causative agent of AIDS, the person knowingly (1) engages in intimate contact with another; (2) transfers, donates, or provides blood, tissue, semen, organs, or other potentially infectious body fluids or parts for transfusion, transplantation, insemination, or other administration to another in any manner that presents a significant risk of HIV transmission; or (3) dispenses, delivers, exchanges, sells, or in any other way transfers to another any nonsterile intravenous or intramuscular drug paraphernalia. Intimate contact with another means the exposure of the body of one person to a bodily fluid of another person in any manner that presents a significant risk of HIV transmission. Criminal exposure of another to HIV is a felony. Actual transmission of HIV is not required under this section. It is an affirmative defense that the person exposed to HIV (a) knew that the offender was infected with HIV; (b) knew that the action could result in HIV infection; and (c) gave advance consent to the action with that knowledge. This defense must be proven by a preponderance of the evidence. TENN. ANN. CODE § 39-13-109 (enacted 1994).

It is a felony called aggravated prostitution for a person to engage in sexual activity as a business or to be an inmate of a house of prostitution or to loiter in a public place for the purpose of being hired to engage in sexual activity if that person knows that he or she is infected with HIV or any other identified causative agent of AIDS. It is not necessary for an HIV infection to have been transmitted for the person to be found guilty of aggravated prostitution. TENN. ANN. CODE § 39-13-516 (enacted 1991).

TEXAS: No statute.

UTAH: Any person who willfully or knowingly introduces any communicable or infectious disease into any county, municipality, or community is guilty of a misdemeanor. UTAH CODE ANN. § 26-6-5 (enacted 1981). An HIV-positive individual wih actual knowledge of his or her infection suffers enhanced penalties for other sexual crimes. UTAH CODE ANN. § 76-10-1309 (enacted 1993).

VERMONT: A person who has sexual intercourse while knowingly infected with gonorrhea or syphilis in a communicable stage commits a felony. VT. STAT. ANN. tit. 18, § 1106 (enacted 1947). It is a felony for a person infected with gonorrhea or syphilis in an infectious stage or in a stage which may become infectious to a marital partner to marry. VT. STAT. ANN. tit. 18, § 1105 (enacted 1947).

VIRGINIA: Any person who attempts to donate or sell, does donate or sell, or who consents to the donation or sale of blood, other bodily fluids, organs, or tissues knowing that the donor is or was infected with HIV and having been instructed that the item may transmit the infection, is guilty of a felony. The donation of these items for use in medical or scientific research is not prohibited. VA. CODE ANN. § 32.1-289.2 (enacted 1989).

WASHINGTON: It is a civil offense for a person who knows that he or she is infected with a sexually transmitted disease other than HIV infection and has been informed that he or she may communicate the disease to have sexual intercourse with any other person unless the other person has been informed of the presence of the disease. WASH. REV. CODE ANN. §§ 70.24.084 (enacted 1988), 70.24.140 (enacted 1988).

A person is guilty of assault in the second degree if he or she, with the intent to inflict bodily harm, administers to or causes to be taken by another the human immunodeficiency virus or exposes to or transmits HIV. Assault in the second degree is a felony. WASH. REV. CODE ANN. § 9A.36.021 (enacted 1986).

WEST VIRGINIA: It is unlawful for a person suffering with an infectious venereal disease to perform any act which exposes another person to infection with such disease. W. VA. CODE § 16-4-20 (enacted 1921).

WISCONSIN: No statute.

WYOMING: No statute.

UNITED STATES: No statute.

6

Public Nudity and Indecency

Public nudity is a misdemeanor for first-time offenders in almost every state; we have noted the states where it is a felony. Before the legal reforms that followed the Model Penal Code, public nudity usually was prohibited under statutes barring lewd and lascivious conduct or public indecency. The precise acts prohibited were not specified in the statute, though public nudity was routinely prosecuted under these statutes. Some courts viewed the requirement that the conduct be "lewd" as a limitation on some public nudity prosecutions; a New York court held that a woman who sunbathed nude on a public beach did not conduct herself "lewdly" and was therefore not guilty of a lewd act. *People v. Gilbert*, 338 NYS2d 457 (1972). The New York legislature later added a provision to the statute that barred all nudity in public, whether lewd or not, in order to prohibit nude sunbathing. Many statutes still require lewdness, and their applicability to nudist camps and nude beaches remains in flux. Nudist camps have been allowed by some state courts on a theory of consent and prohibited by other state courts as plainly indecent.

The Model Penal Code clarifies the traditional public indecency statutes in two ways. First, it requires that the exposure be for the purpose of arousing or gratifying the offender's sexual desire or the sexual desire of someone else. This provision seeks to separate nude sunbathing and prank activity such as streaking from acts of sexual aggression, prohibiting only the latter. Many states have adopted this aspect of the Model Penal Code, leaving the question of nude sunbathing to local ordinances that prohibit disorderly conduct.

Second, the Model Penal Code clarifies the exposure required for an act of public nudity: exposure of a person's genitals. Those states that have adopted the Model Penal Code language do not prohibit exposure of the female breast. A few states, on the other hand, have added exposure of the female breast to the Model Penal Code language. One court has hinted without deciding that these provisions unconstitutionally deny women the equal protection of the laws. *New York v. Santorelli*, 80 NY2d 875 (1992).

The Supreme Court has decided that nude erotic dancing, though it may be in some sense expressive conduct, can be prohibited under public nudity statutes without violating the right of free speech. *Barnes v. Glen Theatre, Inc.*, 501 U.S. 560 (1991). One court held that public nudity is protected expression in a case involving a group of women who appeared in public topless to protest the different treatment of men's and women's breasts under the statute; the activity there was protected expression because it was an explicitly political objection to the statute. *New York v. Craft*, 564 N.Y.S.2d 695 (1991).

We have included prohibitions on indecency without a "public" requirement because indecency may imply a public situation; generally, courts have held that the acts are indecent only when they are or can be viewed by third parties. Some states include exposure on private property within view of people who may be offended. Other states forbid exposure to nonconsenting people without explicit limitation on the places that the statute covers; in such cases, there is sometimes an apparent exception for nonconsenting spouses. The definitions in the Glossary may be helpful in understanding these statutes.

ALABAMA: A county commissioner of any county in which is located a municipality with a population of not less than 100,000 and not more than 174,999 may prohibit topless, bottomless, or nude dancing for monetary consideration within the boundaries of the county. A violation of this ordinance is a misdemeanor. ALA. CODE § 11-3-27 (enacted 1994). A person commits a misdemeanor if, with the intent to sexually arouse or gratify any person other than the offender's spouse and with knowledge that the conduct is likely to cause affront or alarm, he or she exposes his or her genitals in a public place or on private premises that can be viewed from other private premises. ALA. CODE § 13A-6-68 (enacted 1977). A person who makes an obscene gesture in a public place is guilty of disorderly conduct. ALA. CODE § 13A-11-7 (enacted 1977). A person commits a misdemeanor if he or she exposes his or her anus or genitals in a public place and is reckless about whether another may be present who will be offended or alarmed by the act; or does any lewd act in a public place which the offender knows is likely to be observed by others who would be affronted or alarmed. ALA. CODE § 13A-12-130 (enacted 1977).

ALASKA: It is a misdemeanor to expose one's genitals with reckless disregard for the offensive, insulting, or frightening effect of the conduct. Indecent exposure before a person under sixteen is a misdemeanor, as is intentionally exposing one's buttocks or anus to another with reckless disregard for the offensive or insulting effect the act may have on that person. ALASKA STAT. §§ 11.41.460 (enacted 1983), 11.61.110 (enacted 1978).

ARIZONA: If a man exposes his genitals or anus, or a woman exposes her genitals, anus, or the areola or nipple of her breast, when another person is present, and the offender is reckless about whether the witness, as a reasonable person, would be offended or alarmed by the act, the offender has committed a misdemeanor. If the witness is under fifteen, indecent exposure is a felony. ARIZ. REV. STAT. ANN. § 13-1402 (enacted 1977). A person commits public sexual indecency by intentionally or knowingly engaging in any of the following acts if another person is present and the offender is reckless about whether the witness, being a reasonable person, would be offended or alarmed by the act: sexual contact; oral sexual contact; sexual intercourse; or contact between the offender's mouth, vulva, or genitals and the anus or genitals of an animal. Public sexual indecency is a misdemeanor. If the offender knowingly or intentionally engages in any of the listed acts and such person is reckless as to whether a minor under the age of fifteen is present, the offender has committed a felony. ARIZ. REV. STAT. ANN. § 13-1403 (enacted 1977).

ARKANSAS: A person commits indecent exposure by exposing his or her sex organs with the purpose of arousing or gratifying any person's sexual desire in a public place, in public view, or in circumstances where the offender knows the conduct is likely to cause affront or alarm. Indecent exposure is a misdemeanor. ARK. CODE ANN. § 5-14-112 (enacted 1975). A person also commits a misdemeanor by engaging in any of the following acts in a public place or in public view: an act of sexual intercourse, an act of deviate sexual activity, or an act of sexual contact. ARK. CODE ANN. § 5-14-111 (enacted 1975). A person commits a misdemeanor if, with the purpose of causing public inconvenience, annoyance, or alarm, or if recklessly creating the risk thereof, the offender exposes his or her private parts in a public place or makes an obscene gesture in a public place. ARK. CODE ANN. § 5-71-207 (enacted 1975). It is unlawful for any person or organization to advocate, demonstrate, or promote nudism. ARK. CODE ANN. § 5-68-204 (enacted 1957).

CALIFORNIA: It is a misdemeanor to willfully and lewdly expose one's person, or the private parts thereof, either in a public place or where there are people likely to be offended or annoyed. It is also a misdemeanor to procure, counsel, or assist any persons to expose themselves or take part in any model artist exhibition, or to make any other exhibition of themselves to public view such as is offensive to decency, or is adapted to excite vicious or lewd thoughts or acts. CAL. PENAL CODE § 314 (enacted 1961).

COLORADO: A person commits a petty offense by performing any of the following acts in a public place or where the conduct may reasonably be expected to be viewed by members of the public: an act of sexual or deviate sexual intercourse; a lewd exposure of the body done with the intent to arouse or gratify the sexual desire of any person; or a lewd fondling or caress of the body of another person. COLO. REV. STAT. § 18-7-301 (enacted 1971). A person commits indecent exposure by knowingly exposing his or her genitals to the view of any person in circumstances in which such conduct is likely to cause affront or alarm to the other person. Indecent exposure is a misdemeanor. Indecent exposure to a child under fourteen is a misdemeanor. COLO. REV. STAT. § 18-7-302 (enacted 1972).

CONNECTICUT: A person commits a misdemeanor by performing one of the following acts in a public place, or where it may reasonably be expected to be seen: sexual intercourse, oral or anal sex, any object manipulation into a genital or anal opening, a lewd exposure of the body with intent to sexually arouse or gratify the offender, or a lewd fondling of the body of another, limited to persons not married to each other. CONN. GEN. STAT. ANN. §§ 53a-186 (enacted 1969), 53a-65 (enacted 1969). A person commits a misdemeanor if, with intent to cause inconvenience, annoyance, or alarm, or recklessly creating a risk therof, the person makes an obscene gesture. CONN. GEN. STAT. ANN. § 53a-181 (enacted 1969).

DELAWARE: A male may not expose his genitals or buttocks and a female may not expose her genitals, breast, or buttocks where the actor knows that the conduct is likely to cause affront or alarm to another person. If the actor does so, he or she has committed a misdemeanor. DEL. CODE ANN. tit. 11, §§ 764 (enacted 1953), 765 (enacted 1953). A person is guilty of lewdness when he or she does any lewd act in any public place or any lewd act knowing that it is likely to be observed by others who would be affronted or alarmed. DEL. CODE ANN. tit. 11, § 1341 (enacted 1953). A person is guilty of a felony if he or she permits or advances an exhibition, display, or performance of a child engaging in a prohibited sexual act or the simulation of such an act. DEL. CODE ANN. tit. 11, § 1108 (enacted 1961). Prohibited sexual acts include sexual intercourse, anal intercourse, masturbation, bestiality, sadism, masochism, fellatio, cunnilingus, sexual contact, and nudity, if such nudity is depicted for the purpose of the sexual stimulation or the sexual gratification of any individual who may view such depiction. DEL. CODE ANN. tit. 11, § 1103 (enacted 1953).

DISTRICT OF COLUMBIA: It is a misdemeanor to make any obscene or indecent exposure of one's person or to commit any other lewd, obscene, or indecent act. Any person who commits this offense, knowing that he or she is in the presence of a child under sixteen, is guilty of a misdemeanor. D.C. CODE ANN. § 22-1112 (enacted 1892).

FLORIDA: Open and gross lewdness and lascivious behavior is a misdemeanor. FLA. STAT. ANN. § 798.02 (enacted 1971). It is a misdemeanor to expose or exhibit one's sexual organs in any public place or on the private premises of another, or so near thereto as to be seen from the private premises, in a vulgar or indecent manner; or to be naked in public except in any place provided or set apart for that purpose. FLA. STAT. ANN. § 800.03 (enacted 1993). A person commits a felony by knowingly committing any lewd or lascivious act in the presence of any child under sixteen. FLA. STAT. ANN. § 800.04 (enacted 1990). It is a misdemeanor to commit such acts as are of a nature to corrupt the public morals, or outrage the sense of public decency, or affect the peace and quiet of persons who might witness them. FLA. STAT. ANN. § 877.03 (enacted 1971).

GEORGIA: Exposure of the sexual organs or appearance in a state of partial or complete nudity in a public place is a misdemeanor if it is lewd. Sexual intercourse or a lewd fondling of the body of another person in a public place is also a misdemeanor. The third conviction for public indecency is a felony. GA. CODE ANN. § 16-6-8 (enacted 1833). It is unlawful to perform the following acts on premises licensed for alcholic beverages: sexual intercourse, masturbation, sodomy, bestiality, oral copulation, flagellation, or any sexual acts which are prohibited by law; the touching, caressing, or fondling of the breast, buttocks, anus, or genitals; or the displaying of any portion of the female breast below the top of the areola or the displaying of any portion of any person's pubic hair, anus, cleft of the buttocks, vulva, or genitals. GA. STAT. ANN. § 3-3-41 (enacted 1988).

HAWAII: It is a misdemeanor to expose oneself to any person to whom the offender is not married in circumstances likely to cause affront. This section applies only to the exposure of genitals and without any apparent restriction on where this act takes place. HAW. REV. STAT. § 707-734 (enacted 1986). It is also a misdemeanor to commit any lewd act in public if it is likely to be observed by others who would be affronted or alarmed. HAW. REV. STAT. § 712-1217 (enacted 1972).

IDAHO: It is a misdemeanor for a person to knowingly exhibit or display, or permit to be displayed, any of the following in such a manner as to be easily visible from any public area, or from any residence when the person knows that the owner or occupant objects to such exhibit or display: human genitals or pubic area without a full opaque covering; an actual or simulated sex act or sexual contact between humans and animals; or masturbation. IDAHO CODE § 18-4105 (enacted 1973).

ILLINOIS: It is a misdemeanor to engage in a lewd exposure of the body with the intent to sexually arouse or satisfy the offender's desire or to commit an act of sexual penetration or conduct, including touching sex organs through clothing, in any place in which the conduct may reasonably be expected to be viewed. A person must be at least seventeen to be convicted of public indecency. ILL. ANN. STAT. ch. 720, para. 5/11-9 (enacted 1961). A person commits sexual exploitation of a child if, in the presence of a child under seventeen and with intent or knowledge that a child under seventeen would view his or her acts, that person engages in a sexual act or exposes his or her sex organs, anus, or breast for the purpose of sexual arousal or gratification of such person or child. Sexual act means masturbation, sexual conduct, or sexual penetration. The first offense is a misdemeanor; each subsequent offense is a felony. ILL. ANN. STAT. ch. 720, para. 5/11-9.1 (enacted 1961).

INDIANA: A person who, knowingly or intentionally, in a public place or in a place other than a public place with the intent to be seen by persons other than invitees and occupants, engages in sexual intercourse or deviate sexual conduct; or fondles his or her genitals or those of another person is guilty of public indecency. A person who appears in a public place in a state of nudity is guilty of public indecency. Nudity means the showing of the human male or female genitals, pubic area, or buttocks with less than a fully opaque covering, the showing of the female breast with less than a fully opaque covering of any part of the nipple, or the showing of covered male genitals in a discernibly turgid state. IND. CODE ANN. § 35-45-4-1 (enacted 1976).

IOWA: It is a misdemeanor to expose genitals or pubes to another person, not including the offender's spouse, or to commit a sex act (enacted intercourse, oral sex, or anal sex) in view of a third person with the intent to arouse or satisfy someone's sexual desire and with the knowledge that the act may be offensive to the viewer. IOWA CODE ANN. § 709.9 (enacted 1976).

KANSAS: It is a misdemeanor to engage in sexual intercourse or sodomy with knowledge or reasonable anticipation that the participants are being viewed by others, or to expose a sex organ either publicly or to a nonconsenting person who is not the offender's spouse with the intent to sexually gratify or arouse someone. KAN. CODE ANN. § 21-3508 (enacted 1969).

KENTUCKY: A person is guilty of a misdemeanor when that person intentionally exposes his or her genitals in circumstances in which he or she knows or should know that such conduct is likely to cause affront or alarm. It is a violation designated as harassment to make an offensively coarse gesture or display. KY. REV. STAT. ANN. § 510.150 (enacted 1974).

LOUISIANA: It is a misdemeanor to intentionally expose the genitals, pubic hair, anus, vulva, or female breast nipples in a public place or in public view with the intent to arouse sexual desire or with an appeal to prurient interests or in a way that is patently offensive. It is also a misdemeanor to participate in or to promote hard-core sexual conduct when the trier of fact determines that the conduct appeals to prurient interests, is presented in a patently offensive manner, and lacks serious literary, artistic, political, or scientific value. Hard-core sexual conduct is the public portrayal, for its own sake, and for ensuing commercial gain, of ultimate sexual acts, masturbation, excretory functions, lewd exhibition, sexual touching, or sadomasochistic abuse. It is a felony for someone over seventeen to commit any lewd or lascivious act in the presence of any child under seventeen where there is an age difference of more than two years between the two persons, with the intention of arousing or gratifying the sexual desires of either person. Lack of knowledge of the child's age is not a defense. LA. REV. STAT. ANN. § 14:106 (enacted 1950).

MAINE: A person commits public indecency by, in a public place, engaging in a sexual act or knowingly exposing his or her genitals under circumstances which are likely to cause affront or alarm; or, in a private place, exposing his or her genitals with the intention of being seen from a public place or from another private place. Public place includes, but is not limited to, motor vehicles on a public way. ME. REV. STAT. ANN. tit. 17-A, § 854 (enacted 1975).

MARYLAND: The Maryland Code simply prescribes the punishment for the common law crime of indecent exposure. MD. ANN. CODE art. 27, § 335A (enacted 1977).

MASSACHUSETTS: Persons who with offensive or disorderly acts accost or annoy persons of the opposite sex; lewd, wanton, and lascivious persons in speech or behavior, and persons guilty of indecent exposure, commit a misdemeanor. MASS. GEN. LAWS ch. 272, § 53 (enacted 1943). A man and a woman, married or unmarried, guilty of open and gross lewdness and lascivious behavior commit a felony. MASS. GEN. LAWS ch. 272, § 16 (enacted 1784).

MICHIGAN: A person who knowingly makes any open or indecent exposure of his or her person or of the person of another is guilty of a misdemeanor. MICH. COMP. LAWS ANN. § 750.335a (enacted 1931). Any person who is guilty of open and gross lewdness and lascivious behavior is guilty of a misdemeanor. MICH. COMP. LAWS ANN. § 750.335 (enacted 1931). Any person who commits or is party to the commission of or procures or attempts to procure the commission of an act of gross indecency with another person is guilty of a felony. MICH. COMP. LAWS ANN. §§ 750.338 (enacted 1931), 750.338a (enacted 1931), 750.338b (enacted 1931).

MINNESOTA: It is a misdemeanor for a person to expose his or her body, or the private parts thereof, to another person, in any place, if done willfully and lewdly. The statute also prohibits any open or gross lewdness or lascivious behavior or any public indecency. MINN. STAT. ANN. § 617.23 (enacted 1994).

MISSISSIPPI: A person who willfully and lewdly exposes his or her person, or private parts thereof, in any public place or in any place where others are present, or procures another to do the same, is guilty of a misdemeanor. MISS. CODE ANN. § 97-29-31 (enacted 1892). It is a misdemeanor to be guilty of any indecent exposure of one's person in the dwelling house or yard of another or upon the public highway or any other place near such premises and in the presence or hearing of the family or the possessor or occupant thereof. MISS. CODE ANN. § 97-35-11 (enacted 1880). It is a misdemeanor to disturb the peace by indecent or offensive conduct. MISS. CODE ANN. § 97-35-15 (enacted 1942).

MISSOURI: No statute.

MONTANA: A person commits a misdemeanor by exposing his or her genitals for the purpose of arousing or gratifying any person's sexual desire in circumstances where the offender knows the conduct is likely to cause affront or alarm. The third conviction is a felony. MONT. CODE ANN. § 45-5-504 (enacted 1973).

NEBRASKA: A person who is at least eighteen commits a misdemeanor by, in a public place and where the conduct may reasonably be expected to be viewed by members of the public, performing, procuring, or assisting another person in performing an act of sexual penetration; an exposure of the genitals of the body done with the intent to affront or alarm any person; or a lewd fondling or caressing of the body of another person. NEB. REV. STAT. § 28-806 (enacted 1943).

NEVADA: It is a felony to commit anal intercourse, cunnilingus, or fellatio in public. A person who commits an act of open or gross lewdness is guilty of a gross misdemeanor for the first offense and a felony for any subsequent offense. NEV. REV. STAT. § 201.210 (enacted 1911). A person who makes any open and indecent or obscene exposure of his or her person or of the person of another is guilty of a gross misdemeanor for the first offense and a felony for the second offense. NEV. REV. STAT. § 201.220 (enacted 1911).

NEW HAMPSHIRE: A person is guilty of indecent exposure if that person fornicates, exposes his or her genitals, or performs any other act of gross lewdness in circumstances that the offender should know will likely cause affront or alarm, or if a person purposely performs any act of sexual penetration or sexual contact alone or with another person in the presence of a child under sixteen years of age. The first offense is a misdemeanor. If an individual has previously been convicted of indecent exposure in any jurisdiction, the offense is a felony. N.H. REV. STAT. ANN. § 645.1 (enacted 1971).

NEW JERSEY: A person commits a disorderly person offense by doing any flagrantly lewd or offensive act which the offender knows or reasonably expects is likely to be observed by nonconsenting persons who would be affronted or alarmed. A lewd act includes exposing the genitals for the purpose of arousing or gratifying the sexual desire of the offender or of any other person. N.J. STAT. ANN. § 2C:14-4 (enacted 1978).

NEW MEXICO: Indecent exposure consists of knowingly and intentionally exposing the primary genital area, including mons pubis, penis, testicles, mons veneris, vulva, or vagina. N.M. STAT ANN. § 30-9-14 (enacted 1975). Indecent dancing consists of knowingly and intentionally exposing the primary genital area or female areola to public view while dancing or performing in a licensed liquor establishment. N.M. STAT ANN. § 30-9-14.1 (enacted 1979). Indecent waitering consists of knowingly and intentionally exposing the primary genital area or female areola while serving beverage or food in a licensed liquor establishment. N.M. STAT ANN. § 30-9-14.2 (enacted 1979). They are all misdemeanors. It is a petty misdemeanor to engage in indecent conduct which tends to disturb the peace. N.M. STAT ANN. § 30-20-1 (enacted 1963).

NEW YORK: A person is guilty of a violation when, with the intent to cause public inconvenience, annoyance, or alarm, or recklessly creating a risk thereof, that person makes an obscene gesture or creates a physically offensive condition by any act which serves no legitimate purpose. N.Y. PENAL LAW § 240.20 (enacted 1905). It is a misdemeanor to intentionally expose the private or intimate parts of the body in a lewd manner or to commit any other lewd act in a public place, or in private premises under circumstances in which one may readily be observed from either a public place or from other private premises, and with intent that one be so observed. N.Y. PENAL LAW § 245.00 (enacted 1905). A person is guilty of a misdemeanor for appearing in a public place in such a manner that the private or intimate parts of the actor's body are unclothed or exposed, including the portion of the breast which is below the top of the areola for females. This section does not apply to the breast feeding of infants or to any person entertaining or performing in a play, exhibition, show, or entertainment. N.Y. PENAL LAW § 245.01 (enacted 1983).

NORTH CAROLINA: A person who willfully exposes the private parts of his or her person in any public place and in the presence of any other person or persons of the opposite sex, or aids or abets in any such act, or procures another to perform such an act; or any person who knowingly permits premises over which he or she has control to be used for such an act, is guilty of a misdemeanor. A mother's breast feeding is not a violation. N.C. GEN. STAT. § 14-190.9 (enacted 1971).

NORTH DAKOTA: A person is guilty of a misdemeanor for the knowing exposure of penis, vulva, or anus in a public place with the intent to annoy or harass another person. Masturbating in a public place is also a misdemeanor under the statute. N.D. CENT. CODE § 12.1-20-12.1 (enacted 1979). It is a misdemeanor to engage in a sexual act in a public place. N.D. CENT. CODE § 12.1-20-08 (enacted 1973).

OHIO: It is a misdemeanor to trespass or otherwise invade the privacy of another for the purpose of sexually arousing or gratifying oneself. OHIO REV. CODE ANN. § 2907.08 (enacted 1972). No person shall recklessly do any of the following if it is likely to be viewed by and affront others who are not members of the offender's household: expose his or her private parts or engage in masturbation; engage in sexual conduct; or engage in conduct which to an ordinary observer would appear to be sexual conduct or masturbation. OHIO REV. CODE ANN. § 2907.09 (enacted 1990).

OKLAHOMA: Every person who willfully exposes his or her person or genitals in any public place or in any place where there are other people present to be offended or annoyed commits a felony. Assisting another to expose her- or himself, or to make any other exhibition in the view of any number of persons for the purpose of sexual stimulation of the viewer is a felony. Soliciting or aiding a child to expose her- or himself is a felony carrying a more severe penalty. OKLA. STAT. ANN. tit. 21, § 1021 (enacted 1910).

OREGON: A person commits a misdemeanor if while in or in view of a public place the person performs an act of sexual or deviate sexual intercourse or exposes his or her genitals with the intent of arousing the sexual desire of the actor or of another person. It is a violation for a student organization to require, encourage, authorize, or permit a person to be totally or substantially nude. OR. REV. STAT. § 163.465 (enacted 1971).

PENNSYLVANIA: It is a violation to engage in indecent or unbecoming conduct tending to disturb the peace and good order in the county court house, jail, or other county building. 16 PA. CONST. STAT. ANN. §§ 2329 (enacted 1959), 5529 (enacted 1953). A person commits a misdemeanor if that person exposes his or her genitals in any public place or in any place where there are present other persons under circumstances in which he or she knows or should know that this conduct is likely to offend, affront, or alarm. 18 PA. CONST. STAT. ANN. § 3127 (enacted 1972). A person is guilty of disorderly conduct if, with the intent to cause public inconvenience, annoyance, or alarm, or recklessly creating a risk thereof, that person makes an obscene gesture or creates a hazardous or physically offensive condition by any act which serves no legitimate purpose. If the intent of the actor is to cause substantial harm or serious inconvenience, or if the offender persists after a reasonable warning or request to desist, the offense is a misdemeanor. If not, the offense is a summary offense. 18 PA. CONST. STAT. ANN. § 5503 (enacted 1972). A person commits a misdemeanor by doing any lewd act which he or she knows is likely to be observed by others who would be alarmed or affronted. 18 PA. CONST. STAT. ANN. § 5901 (enacted 1972).

RHODE ISLAND: A person commits a misdemeanor if he or she intentionally, knowingly, or recklessly enters onto another person's property and for a lascivious purpose looks into an occupied dwelling through an opening or window; or exposes his or her genitals to the view of others in circumstances in which the conduct is likely to cause affront, distress, or alarm to the other person. R.I. GEN. LAWS § 11-45-1 (enacted 1979).

SOUTH CAROLINA: It is a misdemeanor to willfully and maliciously expose the offender's person in any public place or on property of others or to the view of any person on the street or highway. S.C. CODE ANN. § 16-15-130 (enacted 1962). A person who willfully and knowingly exposes his private parts in a lewd and lascivious manner and in the presence of any other person, or aids and abets any such act, is guilty of a misdemeanor. S.C. CODE ANN. § 16-15-365 (enacted 1987).

SOUTH DAKOTA: Any person who intentionally and with an immoral purpose exposes his or her genitalia in any place where there is present a person to be offended or annoyed is guilty of a misdemeanor for the first two convictions and a felony for all subsequent convictions. S.D. CODIFIED LAWS ANN. § 22-24-1 (enacted 1877).

TENNESSEE: It is a misdemeanor for a person, in a public place or in the view of another's private premises, to intentionally expose the offender's genitals or buttocks to one or more persons or engage in sexual contact or sexual penetration and reasonably expect that the act will be viewed by another and that the act will offend an ordinary viewing person or is for the purpose of sexual arousal and gratification of the offender. TENN. CODE ANN. § 39-13-511 (enacted 1989).

TEXAS: A person commits a misdemeanor by exposing the offender's anus or any parts of the offender's genitals with the intent to arouse or gratify the sexual desire of any person, if the offender is reckless about whether another person is present who will be offended or alarmed by the act. TEX. PENAL CODE ANN. § 21.08 (enacted 1973). A person commits a misdemeanor if that person knowingly engages in any of the following acts in a public place or in a private place where the offender is reckless about whether another person is present who will be offended or alarmed by the act: an act of sexual intercourse or deviate sexual intercourse; an act of sexual contact; or an act involving contact between the offender's mouth or genitals and the anus or genitals of an animal or fowl. TEX. PENAL CODE ANN. § 21.07 (enacted 1973). A person is guilty of a felony if, with a child younger than seventeen and not the offender's spouse, that person exposes any part of his or her gentials or anus, knowing the child is present, with intent to arouse or gratify the sexual desire of any person. It is an affirmative defense that the actor was not more than two years older than the victim and of the opposite sex and did not use duress, force, or a threat against the victim at the time of the offense. TEX. PENAL CODE ANN. § 21.11 (enacted 1973). A person is guilty of a misdemeanor if the offender intentionally or knowingly exposes his or her anus or genitals in a public place or near a private residence and is reckless about whether any person may be present who would be offended or alarmed by the act; or if the person intentionally or knowingly makes an offensive gesture or display in a public place and the gesture or display tends to incite an immediate breach of the peace. TEX. PENAL CODE ANN. § 42.01 (enacted 1973).

UTAH: A person is guilty of a misdemeanor if the person performs an act of sexual intercourse or sodomy, exposes his or her genitals or private parts, masturbates, engages in trespassory voyeurism, or performs any other act of lewdness in a public place or in circumstances which the person should know will likely cause affront or alarm. UTAH CODE ANN. §§ 76-9-702 (enacted 1973), 76-9-702.5 (enacted 1983).

VERMONT: Open and gross lewdness and lascivious behaviour is a felony. VT. STAT. ANN. tit. 13, § 2601 (enacted 1947). It is a misdemeanor to engage in or aid lewdness. VT. STAT. ANN. tit. 13, § 2632 (enacted 1947).

VIRGINIA: Every person who intentionally makes an obscene display or exposure of his or her person or the private parts thereof in any public place or in any place where others are present, or procures any person to be so exposed, is guilty of a misdemeanor. VA. CODE ANN. § 18.2-387 (enacted 1950). The offender is guilty of a felony if he has been convicted within the ten-year period immediately preceding the offense charged of two or more of the following offenses: sexual battery, attempted sexual battery, consensual intercourse with a child, indecent exposure, or procuring another to expose himself. VA. CODE ANN. § 18.2-67.5:1 (enacted 1994). Open and gross lewdness and lasciviousness is a misdemeanor. VA. CODE ANN. § 18.2-345 (enacted 1950). A person who is eighteen years of age or over and with lascivious intent exposes his or her sexual or genital parts to any child under fourteen to whom the actor is not legally married, or who proposes that any such child expose his or her sexual or genital parts, is guilty of a felony. VA. CODE ANN. § 18.2-370 (enacted 1950).

WASHINGTON: A person is guilty of a misdemeanor if he or she intentionally makes any open and obscene exposure of his or her person or the person of another knowing that such conduct is likely to cause reasonable affront or alarm. The offense is a felony if the exposure is to a child under fourteen and the offender has previously been convicted under this statute or of a sex offense. WASH. REV. CODE. ANN. § 9A.88.010 (enacted 1975).

WEST VIRGINIA: A person is guilty of a misdemeanor when that person intentionally exposes his or her sex organs or anus or the sex organs or anus of another person, or intentionally causes such exposure by another person, or engages in any act of overt sexual gratification, and does so under circumstances in which the person knows that the conduct is likely to cause affront or alarm. W. VA. CODE § 61-8-9 (enacted 1992). It is a violation to engage in indecent conduct in the presence of a magistrate. W. VA. CODE § 50-5-11 (enacted 1976). It is a misdemeanor to engage in indecent conduct in a public place, mobile home park, public parking area, common area of an apartment building or dormitory, or a common area of a privately owned commercial shopping center, mall, or other group of commercial retail establishments. W. VA. CODE § 61-6-1b (enacted 1987). It is a misdemeanor for any person to engage in open or gross lewdness or lasciviousness. W. VA. CODE § 61-6-4 (enacted 1849).

WISCONSIN: Sexual intercourse and sexual gratification, defined as oral or anal sex or bestiality, where a person might be viewed or in the presence of a third party, is a misdemeanor. WIS. STAT. ANN. §§ 944.15 (enacted 1983), 944.17 (enacted 1983). Public and indecent exposure of genitals or pubic area is also a misdemeanor. WIS. STAT. ANN. § 944.20 (enacted 1983). It is a misdemeanor to engage in indecent or profane conduct in a public or private place. WIS. STAT. ANN. § 947.01 (enacted 1863). If, for the purposes of sexual arousal or gratification, a person exposes genitals or pubic area to a child or causes a child to expose genitals or pubic area, that person is guilty of a misdemeanor. WIS. STAT. ANN. § 948.10 (enacted 1987).

WYOMING: A person is guilty of a misdemeanor if, while in a public place where that person may reasonably be expected to be viewed by others, that person exposes intimate parts including breasts for women or engages in intercourse or intimate touching including touching clothing covering genitals with the intent to arouse someone. WYO. STAT. § 6-4-201 (enacted 1982).

UNITED STATES: No statute.

7
Fornication

This chapter covers consensual heterosexual acts performed in private between unmarried adults and heterosexual cohabitation. It does not cover acts that are prohibited because they are performed in public or with children, or acts that traditionally have been covered by another statute (e.g., sodomy).

It is commonly thought that fornication charges are never prosecuted. This is true to a great extent, but exceptions persist. See, for example, *Commonwealth v. Sager*, 277 Pa. Super. 555 (1980). Fornication charges may be brought along with sexual assault or public nudity charges when it appears that a conviction on the primary charge is not certain. See, for example, *State v. Spanbauer*, 108 Wis. 2d 548 (1982).

The United States Supreme Court has never had occasion to consider whether fornication statutes are a violation of the constitutional right to privacy. However, in *Griswold v. Connecticut,* 381 U.S. 479 (1965), Justice Goldberg wrote in his concurrence that the constitutionality of fornication and adultery laws is "beyond doubt." Some state courts have held that fornication laws violate the state constitution. See, for example, *State v. Saunders*, 75 N.J. 200 (1977).

Fornication statutes can retain significance even where they are no longer directly enforced. For example, in *Cooper v. French*, 460 N.W.2d 2 (Minn. 1990), a landlord was charged with marital status discrimination for refusing to rent to an unmarried couple in violation of a state civil rights statute. The landlord successfully argued that he was not required to rent to the couple because the couple intended to violate a criminal fornication statute. The Minnesota Supreme Court said that the fornication statute was not, in fact, in complete disuse, citing a 1986 fornication prosecution in Minnesota that did not end in a conviction. The court said that the fornication prohibition still expressed Minnesota's public policy. The Illinois Supreme Court used the fornication statute to divest a mother of child custody, arguing that because the mother disregarded a criminal law she was an unfit role model to her children. *Jarrett v. Jarrett*, 400 N.E.2d 421 (Ill. 1979). Similarly, fornication statutes may be cited in a range of unexpected legal actions including civil defamation suits, alienation of affection suits, and medical malpractice actions.

ALABAMA: No statute.

ALASKA: No statute.

ARIZONA: A person who lives in a state of open and notorious cohabitation is guilty of a misdemeanor. ARIZ. REV. STAT. ANN. § 13-1409 (enacted 1977).

ARKANSAS: No statute.

CALIFORNIA: No statute.

COLORADO: No statute.

CONNECTICUT: No statute.

DELAWARE: No statute.

DISTRICT OF COLUMBIA: It is a misdemeanor for any unmarried man or woman to commit fornication. D.C. CODE § 22-1002 (enacted 1953).

FLORIDA: It is a misdemeanor for any man and woman, not being married to each other, to lewdly and lasciviously associate and cohabit together. Open and gross lewdness and lascivious behavior is a misdemeanor. FLA. STAT. ANN. § 798.02 (enacted 1868).

GEORGIA: It is a misdemeanor for an unmarried person to voluntarily engage in sexual intercourse with another person. GA. CODE ANN. § 16-6-18 (enacted 1833).

HAWAII: No statute.

IDAHO: It is a misdemeanor for any unmarried person to engage in sexual intercourse with an unmarried person of the opposite sex. IDAHO CODE § 18-6603 (enacted 1972).

ILLINOIS: It is a misdemeanor to engage in sexual intercourse with a person to whom the offender is not married if the behavior is open and notorious. ILL. ANN. STAT. ch. 720, para. 5/11-8 (enacted 1961).

INDIANA: No statute.

IOWA: No statute.

KANSAS: No statute.

KENTUCKY: No statute.

LOUISIANA: No statute.

MAINE: No statute.

MARYLAND: No statute.

MASSACHUSETTS: It is a misdemeanor to engage in fornication. MASS. GEN. LAWS ch. 272, § 18 (enacted 1692). Persons divorced from each other but cohabiting are considered guilty of adultery. MASS. GEN. LAWS ch. 208, § 40 (enacted 1785).

MICHIGAN: It is a misdemeanor for any man and woman, not being married to each other, to lewdly and lasciviously associate and cohabit together. MICH. COMP. LAWS ANN. § 750.335 (enacted 1931). Persons divorced from each other but cohabiting are liable for penalties against adultery. MICH. COMP. LAWS ANN. § 750.32 (enacted 1931).

MINNESOTA: When any man and single woman have sexual intercourse with each other, they are both guilty of fornication, a misdemeanor. MINN. STAT. § 609.34 (enacted 1967).

MISSISSIPPI: It is a misdemeanor for a man and a woman to unlawfully cohabit in fornication. It is not necessary to show that the parties dwell together publicly as husband and wife; offense can be proved by circumstances which show habitual sexual intercourse. MISS. CODE ANN. § 97-29-1 (enacted 1848). If any persons divorced from each other cohabit, they shall be liable to all the pains provided by law against adultery. MISS. CODE ANN. § 93-5-29 (enacted 1848).

MISSOURI: No statute.

MONTANA: No statute.

NEBRASKA: No statute.

NEVADA: No statute.

NEW HAMPSHIRE: No statute.

NEW JERSEY: No statute.

New Mexico: It is unlawful for persons who are not married to one another to cohabit as husband and wife. Upon the first conviction, the offenders will only be warned by the judge to cease and desist the unlawful cohabitation. It is a misdemeanor to persist in committing the crime after being warned. N.M. Stat Ann. § 30-10-2 (enacted 1953).

New York: No statute.

North Carolina: It is a misdemeanor for any man and woman, not being married to each other, to lewdly and lasciviously associate, bed, and cohabit together. N.C. Gen. Stat. § 14-184 (enacted 1805). It is a misdemeanor for any man and woman to be found occupying the same bedroom in any hotel, public inn, or boardinghouse for any immoral purpose, or for any man and woman to falsely register as, or otherwise represent themselves to be, husband and wife in any hotel, public inn, or boardinghouse. N.C. Gen. Stat. § 14-186 (enacted 1917).

North Dakota: It is a misdemeanor to live openly and notoriously with a person of the opposite sex as a married couple where the cohabitants are not married. N.D. Cent. Code § 12.1-20-10 (enacted 1973).

Ohio: No statute.

Oklahoma: It is a felony to seduce and have illicit connection with any unmarried female of previous chaste character under promise of marriage; later marriage is a defense. Okla. Stat. Ann. tit. 21, §§ 1120 (enacted 1910), 1121 (enacted 1910).

Oregon: No statute.

Pennsylvania: No statute.

Rhode Island: No statute.

South Carolina: It is a misdemeanor for any man and woman, both being unmarried, to live together and engage in carnal intercourse with one another or to engage in habitual carnal intercourse without living together. S.C. Code Ann. §§ 16-15-60 (enacted 1880), 16-15-80 (enacted 1880).

South Dakota: No statute.

Tennessee: No statute.

Texas: No statute.

UTAH: It is a misdemeanor for any unmarried person to voluntarily engage in sexual intercourse. UTAH CODE ANN. § 76-7-104 (enacted 1973).

VERMONT: No statute.

VIRGINIA: Any unmarried person who voluntarily engages in sexual intercourse with any other person is guilty of a misdemeanor. VA. CODE ANN. § 18.2-344 (enacted 1950). It is a misdemeanor for any persons, not being married to each other, to lewdly and lasciviously associate and cohabit together. VA. CODE ANN. § 18.2-345 (enacted 1950).

WASHINGTON: No statute.

WEST VIRGINIA: It is a misdemeanor to engage in fornication. W. Va. Code § 61-8-3 (enacted 1849). It is a misdemeanor for any persons, presumed not to be married to each other, to lewdly and lasciviously associate and cohabit together. W. Va. Code § 61-8-4 (enacted 1849).

WISCONSIN: No statute.

WYOMING: No statute.

UNITED STATES: Whoever knowingly transports, or knowingly persuades, induces, entices, or coerces any individual to travel in interstate or foreign commerce, or in any territory or possession of the United States, with intent that such individual engage in any sexual activity for which any person can be charged with a criminal offense, shall be guilty of a felony. 18 U.S.C.A. §§ 2421 (enacted 1948), 2422 (enacted 1948).

8

Adultery

Some states criminalize adultery by name without defining it. Two issues arise in the definition of adultery. The first is whether only a married person can be guilty of adultery or whether an unmarried person is also guilty of adultery for engaging in sex with a married person; states differ. The second issue is what acts constitute adultery; some states require habitual relations, cohabitation, or open adultery, while others prohibit adultery of any kind. If the statute defines adultery, we have provided the definition. In some states, only the nonparticipating spouse may initiate a prosecution. At least one state court has held that this is not an unconstitutional delegation of government authority. *State v. Ronek*, 176 N.W.2d 153 (Iowa 1970).

As with fornication, it is commonly thought that adultery charges are never prosecuted. This is true to a great extent, but exceptions persist. See, for example, *State v. Mangon*, 603 So. 2d 1131 (Ala. App. 1992); *Commonwealth v. Papariella*, 439 A.2d 827 (1982); *Commonwealth v. Stowell*, 449 N.E.2d 357 171 (1983).

Not all adultery statutes are criminal, and we have mixed the criminal with the civil here. In many states, adultery is grounds for divorce only. In an era of no-fault divorce this may appear inconsequential; however, in some states proof of adultery will enable a person seeking a divorce to forgo waiting periods, and in many states fault-based grounds for divorce influence the property distribution or child custody. In some states, adultery requires the forfeit of any interest in the estate of a deceased spouse.

Alabama: Adultery is committed when a person engages in sexual intercourse and cohabits with another person not his spouse. It is a misdemeanor, and both parties are guilty where either is married. Ala. Code § 13A-13-2 (enacted 1977). A person does not commit adultery, however, if he reasonably believes that he and the other person are unmarried persons. ALA. CODE §13A-13-2(b) (enacted 1977). Adultery also provides grounds for divorce. ALA. CODE § 30-2-1(a)(2) (enacted 1852).

ALASKA: Adultery provides grounds for divorce only. ALASKA STAT. § 25.24.050(2) (enacted 1962).

ARIZONA: Adultery is sexual intercourse between a married person and another person not his or her spouse. Both are guilty of a misdemeanor even if only one is married. A prosecution for adultery may only be commenced upon the complaint of the other spouse. ARIZ. REV. STAT. ANN. § 13-1408 (enacted 1977).

ARKANSAS: Adultery provides grounds for divorce, unless it is the product of collusion or done with an intent to procure a divorce. ARK. CODE ANN. §§ 9-12-301(5) (enacted 1873), 9-12-308 (enacted 1947).

CALIFORNIA: No statute.

COLORADO: Adultery is sexual intercourse by a married person with another not his spouse, but is prohibited for the married party only. COLO. REV. STAT. § 18-6-501 (enacted 1971).

CONNECTICUT: Adultery is voluntary sexual intercourse between a married person and a person other than such person's spouse. CONN. GEN. STAT. § 46b-40(f) (enacted 1973). Adultery provides grounds for divorce only. CONN. GEN. STAT. § 46b-40(c)(3) (enacted 1973).

DELAWARE: A man forfeits all demands on his wife's estate by leaving his wife to be with an adulteress or by living in adultery separated from his wife if the conduct is not occasioned by the wife's fault and the wife does not permit the husband to dwell with her after the offense. DEL. CODE ANN. tit. 25, § 744 (enacted 1935).

DISTRICT OF COLUMBIA: Adultery is a misdemeanor. When the act is between a married woman and an unmarried man, both parties are guilty; when between a married man and an unmarried woman, only the man is deemed guilty. D.C. CODE ANN. § 22-301 (enacted 1901). Adultery is grounds for legal separation. D.C. CODE ANN. § 16-904(b)(3) (enacted 1963). A person who leaves his or her spouse and is convicted of living with another in adultery forfeits the right to his or her dower, unless the aggrieved spouse pardons the offending spouse and they resume cohabitation. D.C. CODE ANN. § 19-103 (enacted 1965).

FLORIDA: Both parties to sexual intercourse are guilty of a misdemeanor for living in an open state of adultery if either party is married. FLA. STAT. ANN. § 798.01 (enacted 1874).

GEORGIA: Adultery is voluntary sexual intercourse with a person other than one's spouse. It is a misdemeanor, but only for the married party. GA. CODE ANN. § 16-6-19 (enacted 1833). It is also grounds for divorce, unless (1) the adultery complained of was occasioned by the collusion of the parties with the intention of causing a divorce; (2) the complaining party consented to the adultery; or (3) there was voluntary cohabitation after knowledge of the adultery. GA. CODE ANN. §§ 19-5-3(6) (enacted 1850), 19-5-4 (enacted 1850).

HAWAII: No statute.

IDAHO: Adultery is voluntary sexual intercourse between two people, one or both of whom is married to a third person. Both are guilty of a felony. IDAHO CODE § 18-6601 (enacted 1972). Adultery also is grounds for divorce. IDAHO CODE § 32-603 (enacted 1864).

ILLINOIS: Any person who has open and notorious sexual intercourse with another not his spouse commits adultery. It is a misdemeanor, and both parties are guilty if either one is married, provided that the unmarried person knew that the other was married. ILL. ANN. STAT. ch. 720, para. 5/11-7 (enacted 1961). Adultery is also grounds for the dissolution of marriage. ILL. ANN. STAT. ch. 750, para. 5/401(1) (enacted 1977).

INDIANA: A person living in adultery receives no part of a deceased spouse's estate. IND. CODE. § 29-1-2-14 (enacted 1953).

IOWA: No statute.

KANSAS: Adultery is defined as sexual intercourse or sodomy with a person who is not married to the offender. It is a misdemeanor for both parties where one is married, provided that the unmarried offender knows that the other is married. KAN. STAT. ANN. § 21-3507 (enacted 1969).

KENTUCKY: If a person leaves his or her spouse and lives in adultery, that person forfeits all right and interest in and to the property and estate of the spouse, unless the two afterward become reconciled and live together again as husband and wife. KY. REV. STAT. ANN. § 392.090(2) (enacted 1942). An accusation of adultery is actionable as a tort and the plaintiff is not required to allege or prove special damages. KY. REV. STAT. ANN. § 411.040 (enacted 1974).

LOUISIANA: Adultery provides grounds for divorce only. LA. CIV. CODE ANN. art. 103(2) (enacted 1990).

MAINE: Adultery provides grounds for divorce only. ME. REV. STAT. ANN. tit. 19, § 691 (enacted 1954).

MARYLAND: Adultery is a misdemeanor, but punishable only by a $10 fine. MD. ANN. CODE art. 27, § 3 (enacted 1749). Adultery provides grounds for absolute divorce. MD. FAM. LAW CODE ANN. § 7-103(a)(1) (enacted 1957).

MASSACHUSETTS: Adultery, a felony, occurs when a married person has sexual intercourse with a person who is not his or her spouse; both are guilty of adultery where either one or both is married. MASS. GEN. LAWS ch. 272, § 14 (enacted 1978). Persons divorced from each other yet cohabiting as husband and wife or living together in the same house are guilty of adultery. MASS. GEN. LAWS ch. 208, § 40 (enacted 1785). Adultery is also cause for divorce. MASS. GEN. LAWS ch. 208, § 1 (enacted 1967).

MICHIGAN: Adultery is sexual intercourse between two persons either of whom is married to a third person. MICH. COMP. LAWS § 750.29 (enacted 1931). Adultery is a felony, and both parties are guilty if the woman is married and the man is not; only the man is guilty if he is married and the woman is not. MICH. COMP. LAWS § 750.30 (enacted 1931). Prosecutions for adultery may only be commenced by a complaint of the aggrieved spouse. MICH. COMP. LAWS § 750.31 (enacted 1931). People who cohabit together after being divorced are guilty of adultery. MICH. COMP. LAWS § 750.32 (enacted 1931).

MINNESOTA: Adultery occurs when a married woman has sexual intercourse with a man other than her husband, whether the man is married or not. Both parties are guilty of a misdemeanor. A prosecution for adultery requires a complaint by a spouse of one of the offenders, unless those spouses are insane. It is a defense to adultery that the man did not know the marital status of the woman. There is no prohibition against sex between a married man and an unmarried woman. MINN. STAT. § 609.36 (enacted 1963).

MISSISSIPPI: A man and woman are guilty of adultery if they unlawfully cohabit, which may be proved by evidence of habitual sexual intercourse. Adultery is a misdemeanor, and also cause for divorce. MISS. CODE ANN. §§ 97-29-1 (enacted 1848), 93-5-1 (enacted 1848). Divorced people who later cohabit are guilty of adultery. MISS. CODE ANN. § 93-5-29 (enacted 1848).

MISSOURI: By continuing in an adulterous relationship after leaving home a spouse forfeits any inheritance rights and statutory rights to an elective share in the nonparticipating spouse's estate. The rights may be restored by a reconciliation if the spouses resume cohabitation. MO. ANN. STAT. § 474.140 (enacted 1955). Adultery is also grounds for divorce. MO. ANN. STAT. § 452.320(2)(1)(a) (enacted 1973).

MONTANA: No statute.

NEBRASKA: Any married person who deserts his or her spouse and lives, cohabits, and engages in sexual penetration with another person commits adultery, a misdemeanor. NEB. REV. STAT. § 28-704 (enacted 1977).

NEVADA: No statute.

NEW HAMPSHIRE: Adultery is sexual intercourse between two persons where either is married to a third person. Both people are guilty, so long as the unmarried party knows his or her partner is married. Adultery is a misdemeanor, and also cause for divorce. N.H. REV. STAT. ANN. §§ 645:3 (enacted 1971), 458:7 (enacted 1938).

NEW JERSEY: Adultery is grounds for divorce, and a married person who leaves his or her spouse to live in adultery with another is barred from having jointure, dower, or curtesy, unless there is a reconciliation. N.J. REV. STAT. §§ 2A:34-2(a) (enacted 1971), 3A:37-2 (enacted 1877).

NEW MEXICO: Adultery is grounds for divorce only. N.M. STAT. ANN. § 40-4-1(C) (enacted 1953).

NEW YORK: Adultery is defined as one person having sexual intercourse with another person, where one of the parties has a living spouse. Both parties are guilty of a misdemeanor. N.Y. PENAL LAW § 255.17 (enacted 1965). A person cannot be convicted solely on the testimony of the other party to the adulterous conduct, however. N.Y. PENAL LAW § 255.30(1) (enacted 1965). It is an affirmative defense that the defendant thought the other party was unmarried. N.Y. PENAL LAW § 255.20 (enacted 1965).

Adultery provides grounds for divorce unless (1) it is procured by or committed with the connivance of the plaintiff; (2) the offense has been forgiven (which may be proved by voluntary cohabitation); (3) suit was not brought within five years of discovery of the adultery; or (4) the plaintiff was also guilty of adultery. N.Y. DOM. REL. LAW §§ 170 (enacted 1966), 171 (enacted 1962).

NORTH CAROLINA: Adultery is a misdemeanor, prohibited jointly with fornication: adultery/fornication takes place when a man and a woman, not married to each other, lewdly and lasciviously associate, bed, and cohabit together. The admission or confessions of one party cannot be received in evidence against the other. N.C. GEN. STAT. § 14-184 (enacted 1805). Adultery is grounds for divorce, and a person who voluntarily separates from his or her spouse and lives in adultery loses all rights to the property of the spouse. N.C. GEN. STAT. §§ 50-7(6) (enacted 1871), 31A-1 (enacted 1961).

NORTH DAKOTA: Adultery is defined as the voluntary sexual intercourse of a married person with a person other than the offender's husband or wife. N.D. CENT. CODE § 14-05-04 (enacted 1877). Only the married party is guilty of adultery, which is a misdemeanor, and only the spouse of the alleged offender may initiate prosecution. N.D. CENT. CODE § 12.1-20-09 (enacted 1973). Adultery is also cause for divorce. N.D. CENT. CODE § 14-05-03(1) (enacted 1877).

OHIO: A spouse who dwells in adultery will be barred from dower in the real property of the nonparticipating spouse, unless the conduct is condoned by the nonparticipating spouse. OHIO REV. CODE ANN. § 2103.05 (enacted 1953). Adultery provides grounds for divorce and for legal separation. OHIO REV. CODE ANN. §§ 3105.01 (enacted 1953), 3105.17 (enacted 1953).

OKLAHOMA: Adultery, a felony, is defined as the unlawful voluntary sexual intercourse of a married person with one of the opposite sex. Both parties are guilty of adultery where either party is married to someone else. Prosecution can be pursued by anyone if the parties are openly living together in adultery; otherwise only the nonparticipating spouse of either party can pursue prosecution against either party. OKLA. STAT. ANN. tit. 21, §§ 871 (enacted 1910), 872 (enacted 1910). Adultery also provides grounds for divorce. OKLA. STAT. ANN. tit. 43, §101 (enacted 1910).

OREGON: No statute.

Pennsylvania: No statute.

Rhode Island: Adultery is sexual intercourse between any two persons, where either of them is married to someone else. Both parties are guilty of adultery, which is a misdemeanor and carries a maximum fine of $500. R.I. Gen. Laws § 11-6-2 (enacted 1896). Adultery provides grounds for divorce, unless the adultery was the result of collusion with the intention to procure the divorce. R.I. Gen. Laws §§ 15-5-2 (enacted 1896), 15-5-4 (enacted 1896).

South Carolina: Adultery is carnal intercourse while living together, or habitual carnal intercourse, between a man and a woman while either is lawfully married to some other person. S.C. Code Ann. § 16-15-70 (enacted 1880). It is a misdemeanor and carries a mandatory fine or prison sentence. S.C. Code Ann. § 16-15-60 (enacted 1880). Adultery is also grounds for divorce. S.C. Code Ann. § 20-3-10(1) (enacted 1949).

South Dakota: Adultery is the voluntary sexual intercourse of a married person with one of the opposite sex to whom he or she is not married. S.D. Codified Laws Ann. § 25-4-3 (enacted 1877). Adultery provides grounds for divorce only. S.D. Codified Laws Ann. § 25-4-2(1) (enacted 1877).

Tennessee: Adultery provides grounds for divorce only. Tenn. Code Ann. §§ 36-4-101(3) (enacted 1858), 36-4-112 (enacted 1858).

Texas: Adultery provides grounds for divorce only. Tex. Fam. Code Ann. § 3.03 (enacted 1969).

Utah: Adultery occurs when a married person voluntarily has sexual intercourse with a person other than his or her spouse. It is a misdemeanor, but only for the married party. Utah Code Ann. § 76-7-103 (enacted 1953). It is also grounds for divorce. Utah Code Ann. § 30-3-1(3)(b) (enacted 1898).

Vermont: Adultery is grounds for divorce only. Vt. Stat. Ann. tit. 15, § 551 (enacted 1969).

Virginia: Adultery, defined as voluntary sexual intercourse by any married person with any other person not his or her spouse, is a misdemeanor for the married party only. Va. Code Ann. § 18.2-365 (enacted 1950). Conspiracy between a married person and a third party to cause the married person's spouse to commit adultery is a felony. Va.

CODE ANN. § 18.2-367 (enacted 1950). Adultery is also grounds for divorce, unless the married parties voluntarily cohabited after knowledge of the adultery, or the adultery occurred more than five years before the institution of the suit, or it was committed by the procurement or connivance of the party alleging adultery. VA. CODE ANN. §§ 20-91 (enacted 1919), 20-94 (enacted 1919).

WASHINGTON: No statute.

WEST VIRGINIA: Adultery is a misdemeanor carrying a mandatory fine. W. VA. CODE § 61-8-3 (enacted 1849). Adultery is also grounds for divorce, but only if one of the two parties is a resident of the state. W. VA. CODE §§ 48-2-4(1) (enacted 1849), 48-2-7(a) (enacted 1849). There are other statutory defenses to divorce for adultery. W. VA. CODE § 48-2-14 (enacted 1849).

WISCONSIN: Adultery means sexual intercourse between a married person and a third party; it is a felony for both parties. WIS. STAT. ANN. § 944.16 (enacted 1849).

WYOMING: No statute.

UNITED STATES: Whoever knowingly transports, or knowingly persuades, induces, entices, or coerces any individual to travel in interstate or foreign commerce, or in any territory or possession of the United States, with intent that such individual engage in any sexual activity for which any person can be charged with a criminal offense, shall be guilty of a felony. 18 U.S.C.A. §§ 2421 (enacted 1948), 2422 (enacted 1948).

9

Abuse of Position of Trust or Authority

This chapter covers acts that carry criminal penalties because of the relationship between the parties. It should be read in conjunction with several others. A number of terms are defined in the chapter on sexual assault (chap. 1); reference to that chapter will also provide insight into the nature of the offense. Laws prohibiting incest (see next chapter) are often aimed in part at the abuse of a relationship of trust, as in parent-child incest. Finally, many states make conduct by a person in a position of authority unlawful only where the victim is under a certain age. The age of consent chapter (chap. 3) should be consulted to see how the victim's age of consent differs depending on whether the offender has a special relationship to the victim.

Many states do not classify sexual conduct between stepparents and young adult children as incest; some do, however, either explicitly or by punishing sexual intercourse between guardian and ward.

The language of the statutes is so varied that generalizations are difficult. In some cases, the state is adding a criminal overlap to behavior it already regulates through licensing. So, for example, a state court may hear a disciplinary action to revoke a physician's license based on sexual conduct with a patient; the same state may prosecute the physician criminally for that conduct. In these cases, the criminal law tracks the ethical constraints within the regulated activity.

Some states are very specific about who is covered by the statute, naming professionals such as teachers, acupuncturists, and psychiatrists. Some states use catch-all language, for example, "position of trust or supervision." In one Illinois case, that language was construed to cover conduct between a seventeen-year-old woman and her brother-in-law, when the brother-in-law was a onetime overnight guest. The court labeled him a "temporary caretaker" who fell within the statutory prohibition. *People v. Kaminski*, 615 N.E.2d 808 (Ill. App. 1993).

ALABAMA: No statutes.

ALASKA: It is a felony to engage in sexual penetration or sexual contact with a person who the offender knows is mentally incapable and who is entrusted to the offender's care by authority of law or in a facility or program that is required by law to be licensed by the Department of Health and Social Services; or where the offender knows that the victim is mentally incapable, incapacitated, or unaware that a sexual act is being committed and the offender is a health care worker and the offense takes place during the course of professional treatment of the victim. ALASKA STAT. §§ 11.41.410 (enacted 1978), 11.41.420 (enacted 1978). It is a felony to engage in sexual penetration or sexual contact where, being eighteen or older, the offender engages in sexual penetration or sexual contact with a person who is under eighteen and the offender is the victim's legal guardian; or, being eighteen or older, the offender engages in sexual penetration or sexual contact with a person who is under sixteen and the victim at the time of the offense is residing in the same household as the offender and the offender has authority over the victim, or the offender occupies a position of authority in relation to the victim. ALASKA STAT. §§ 11.41.434 (enacted 1983), 11.41.436 (enacted 1983). It is a felony for a person eighteen or over to engage in sexual penetration and a misdemeanor to engage in sexual contact with a person who is sixteen or seventeen and at least three years younger than the offender, where the offender occupies a position of authority in relation to the victim. ALASKA STAT. §§ 11.41.438 (enacted 1983), 11.41.440 (enacted 1983). Health care worker includes a person who is or purports to be an acupuncturist, anesthesiologist, chiropractor, dentist, health aide, hypnotist, massage therapist, mental health counselor, midwife, naturopath, nurse practitioner, osteopath, physical therapist, physical therapy assistant, physician, physician's assistant, psychiatrist, psychologist, psychological associate, radiologist, religious healing practitioner, surgeon, x-ray technician, or occupies a substantially similar position. Legal guardian means a person who is under a duty to exercise general supervision over a minor as a result of a court order, statute, or regulation, and includes foster parents and staff members and other employees of group homes or youth correctional facilities where a child is placed as a result of a court order or the action of the Division of Family and Youth Services, and police officers and probation officers when those officers are exercising custodial control over a minor. Position of authority denotes an employer, youth leader, scout leader, coach, teacher, counselor, school administrator, religious leader, doctor, nurse, psychologist, guardian ad litem, babysitter, or a substantially similar position, or a police officer or probation officer other than when the officer is exercising custodial control over a minor. ALASKA STAT. § 11.41.420 (enacted 1978). It is a felony, acting other than as a prostitute or patron, to induce or cause a person in the offender's legal custody to engage in prostitution. ALASKA STAT. § 11.66.110 (enacted 1978).

ARIZONA: No statute.

ARKANSAS: It is a felony to engage in sexual intercourse, deviate sexual intercourse, or sexual contact with a person under eighteen where the offender is the victim's guardian, an employee in the victim's school or school district, a temporary caretaker, or a person in a position of trust or authority over the minor. ARK. CODE ANN. §§ 5-14-120 (enacted 1947), 5-14-121 (enacted 1947).

CALIFORNIA: It is a misdemeanor for any physician, surgeon, psychotherapist, or anyone holding himself or herself out to be a physician and surgeon, or psychotherapist to engage in an act of sexual intercourse, sodomy, oral copulation, or sexual contact with a patient or client, or with a former patient or client when that relationship was terminated primarily for the purpose of engaging in those acts, unless the physician and surgeon or psychotherapist has referred the patient or client to an independent and objective physician and surgeon or psychotherapist, recommended by a third-party physician, surgeon, or psychotherapist for treatment. In no instance shall consent of the patient or client be a defense. This section shall not apply to sexual contact between a physician and surgeon and his spouse or person in an equivalent domestic relationship. CAL. BUS. & PROF. CODE § 729 (enacted 1989).

It is a felony for a person to engage in sexual penetration against the victim's will by threatening to use the authority of a public official to incarcerate, arrest, or deport the victim or another, where the victim has a reasonable belief that the offender is a public official whether or not the offender is in fact one. Public official means a person employed by a governmental agency who has authority, as part of the position, to incarcerate, arrest, or deport another person. It is a misdemeanor to engage in sodomy, oral copulation, or object penetration where the victim is incapable, because of a mental disorder or developmental or physical disability, of giving legal consent and this should reasonably be known or is known to the offender and both the offender and victim are at the time confined in a state hospital for the care and treatment of the mentally disordered or in any other public or private facility for the same treatment approved by a county mental health director. It is a misdemeanor for any person to participate in an act of sodomy or oral copulation with any other person while confined in any state prison. Sodomy means sexual conduct involving contact between the penis of one person and the anus of another; oral copulation is the act of connecting the mouth of one person with the sexual organ or anus of another person; object penetration means penetration of the genital or anal openings of any person, for the purpose of sexual arousal, gratification, or abuse, by any foreign object. CAL. PENAL CODE §§ 261 (enacted 1872), 286 (enacted 1872), 288a (enacted 1921), 289 (enacted 1978).

COLORADO: It is a misdemeanor for an acupuncturist to engage in sexual contact, and a felony to engage in sexual intrusion or penetration, with a patient during the course of patient care. COLO. REV. STAT. § 12-29.5-108 (enacted 1989).

It is a felony to engage in sexual penetration or sexual contact with a person if the victim is in custody of law or detained in a hospital or other institution and the offender has supervisory or disciplinary authority over the victim and uses this position of authority to coerce the victim to submit unless the intrusion is incident to a lawful search; or the offender engages in treatment or examination of a victim for other than bona fide medical purposes or in a manner substantially inconsistent with reasonable medical practices. COLO. REV. STAT. §§ 18-3-403 (enacted 1975), 18-3-404 (enacted 1975). It is a felony for a person in a position of trust with respect to another person under eighteen to engage in any sexual contact with that child. COLO. REV. STAT. § 18-3-405.3 (enacted 1990). A person in a position of trust includes, but is not limited to, any person who is acting in the place of a parent and charged with any of a parent's rights, duties, or responsibilities concerning a child, including a guardian or someone otherwise responsible for the general supervision of a child's welfare, or a person who is charged with any duty or responsibility for the health, education, welfare, or supervision of a child, including foster care, child care, family care, or institutional care, either independently or through another, no matter how brief, at the time of the offense. COLO. REV. STAT.

§ 18-3-401 (enacted 1975). A psychotherapist who engages in sexual penetration commits a felony, or who engages in sexual contact commits a misdemeanor, where the victim is a client of the psychotherapist, whether or not the contact occurred by means of therapeutic deception. Consent by the client to the sexual penetration, intrusion, or contact shall not constitute a defense. Psychotherapist means any person who performs or purports to perform psychotherapy. Psychotherapy means treatment, diagnosis, or counseling in a professional relationship to assist individuals or groups to alleviate mental disorders, understand unconscious or conscious motivation, resolve emotional, relationship, or attitudinal conflicts, or modify behaviors which interfere with effective emotional, social, or intellectual functioning. COLO. REV. STAT. § 18-3-405.5 (enacted 1988).

CONNECTICUT: It is a felony to engage in sexual penetration and a misdemeanor to engage in sexual contact under the following circumstances: where the victim is less than eighteen and the offender is the victim's guardian or otherwise responsible for general supervision of the victim's welfare; where the victim is in custody of law or detained in a hospital or other institution and the offender has supervisory or disciplinary authority over the victim; or where the offender is a psychotherapist and the victim is a patient and the contact occurs during the psychotherapy session, the victim is a patient or former patient and emotionally dependent on the offender or the victim is a patient or former patient and the contact occurs by means of a therapeutic deception, or the offender accomplishes the contact by means of a false representation that the contact is for a bona fide medical purpose by a health care professional. CONN. GEN. STAT. ANN. §§ 53a-65 (enacted 1969), 53a-71 (enacted 1969), 53a-73a (enacted 1975).

DELAWARE: It is a felony for an employee at a detention facility to engage in sexual intercourse or deviate sexual intercourse on the premises of the facility. It is no defense that such conduct was consensual. DEL. CODE ANN. tit. 11, § 1259 (enacted 1980).

DISTRICT OF COLUMBIA: It is a felony for any person over twenty-one, who is a superintendent, tutor, or teacher in any public or private school, seminary, or other institution, to have sexual intercourse with any student between sixteen and twenty-one, with the student's consent, while under the person's instruction during the term of his or her engagement as superintendent, tutor, or teacher. D.C. CODE ANN. § 22-3002 (enacted 1901).

FLORIDA: It is a felony to falsely imprison a child under the age of thirteen and, during the course of imprisonment, commit sexual battery on the child, or a lewd, lascivious, or indecent assault upon or in the presence of the child. FLA. STAT. ANN. § 787.02 (enacted 1993). It is a felony for a person who is in a position of familial or custodial authority over a person under eighteen to solicit or engage that person in an act which would constitute sexual battery. Willingness or consent of the victim is not a defense. FLA. STAT. ANN. § 794.011 (enacted 1992).

GEORGIA: It is a felony for a probation or parole officer or other custodian or supervisor to engage in sexual contact with a probationer or parolee under the supervision of the offender or a victim who is in the custody of law or enrolled in a school or who is detained in or is a patient in a hospital or other institution and the offender has supervisory or disciplinary authority over the victim. It is a felony for an actual or purported practitioner of psychotherapy to engage in sexual contact with a victim who the offender knew or should have known is the subject of the offender's actual or purported treatment or counseling or where the treatment or counseling relationship was used to facilitate sexual contact between the offender and the victim. Consent of the victim shall not be a defense to a prosecution. Psychotherapy means the professional treatment or counseling of a mental illness, symptom, or condition. GA. CODE ANN. § 16-6-5.1 (enacted 1981).

HAWAII: It is a felony for a person employed in a state correctional facility to engage in sexual penetration or sexual contact with an imprisoned person. HAW. REV. STAT. §§ 707-731 (enacted 1986), 707-732 (enacted 1986).

IDAHO: It is a felony for any officer, employee, or agent of a jail or correctional facility to engage in sexual penetration or sexual contact with an inmate of such facility. IDAHO CODE § 18-6110 (enacted 1993).

ILLINOIS: It is a felony to engage in sexual penetration or sexual contact with a person under eighteen where the offender has resided in the houshold with the victim for at least one year. It is a felony to engage in sexual penetration or sexual contact with a person who is under eighteen but at least thirteen where the offender held a position of trust, authority, or supervision in relation to the victim. ILL. REV. STAT. ch. 720, paras. 5/12-12 (enacted 1961), 5/12-13 (enacted 1961), 5/12-16 (enacted 1983).

INDIANA: It is a felony to engage in sexual penetration with a person who is under eighteen where the offender is the guardian or custodian of the victim. Custodian includes any person responsible for a child's welfare who is employed by a public or private residential school or foster care facility. IND. CODE ANN. § 35-42-4-7 (enacted 1987). A service provider, meaning a public servant or other person employed by a governmental entity or another person who provides goods or services to a person who is subject to lawful detention, commits a felony by engaging in sexual intercourse or deviate sexual conduct with a person who is subject to lawful detention. It is not a defense that the act was consensual. IND. CODE ANN. § 35-44-1-5 (enacted 1987).

IOWA: It is a felony to engage in a sex act with a person who is under sixteen years old under any of the following circumstances: the offender is a member of the same household as the victim; or the offender is in a position of authority over the victim and uses that authority to coerce the victim to submit. IOWA CODE ANN. § 709.4 (enacted 1976). It is a misdemeanor for a counselor or therapist to engage in any sexual conduct with an emotionally dependent patient, client, former patient, or former client, for the purpose of arousing or satisfying the sexual desires of either party. It is a felony for a counselor or therapist to engage in a pattern or practice or scheme of conduct to engage in sexual conduct with an emotionally dependent patient, client, former patient, or former client. Counselor or therapist means a physician, psychologist, nurse, professional counselor, social worker, marriage or family therapist, alcohol or drug counselor, member of the clergy, or any other person, whether or not licensed or registered by the state, who provides or purports to provide mental health services. IOWA CODE ANN. § 709.15 (enacted 1991).

It is a misdemeanor for an officer, employee, contractor, vendor, volunteer, or agent of the Department of Corrections or Juvenile District Department of Correctional Services to engage in a sex act with an individual committed to the custody of the Department of Corrections or Juvenile District Department of Correctional Services. IOWA CODE ANN. § 709.16 (enacted 1991).

KANSAS: It is an aggravated felony to engage in any penetration of the female sex organ or sexual contact with a person under sixteen where the offender is any guardian, proprietor, or employee of any foster home, orphanage, or other public or private institution for the care and custody of minor children, to whose charge the victim has been committed or entrusted by a court, court services officer, department of social and rehabilitation services, or other agency acting under color of law. KAN. STAT. ANN. § 21-3501 (enacted 1969).

It is a felony for an employee of the Department of Corrections or an employee of a contractor under contract to provide services in a correctional institution to engage in consensual sexual intercourse or sodomy with an inmate; or for a parole officer to engage in consensual sexual intercourse or sodomy with an inmate who has been released on parole or conditional release or postrelease supervison under the direct supervision and control of the offender. KAN. STAT. ANN. § 21-3520 (enacted 1991).

KENTUCKY: No statute.

LOUISIANA: It is a felony for anyone, by virtue of a position of control or supervision over a juvenile, to commit any lewd or lascivious act upon or in the presence of a child under the age of seventeen with the intention of arousing or gratifying the sexual desires of either person. Lack of knowledge of the juvenile's age is not a defense. LA. REV. STAT. § 14:81.2 (enacted 1984).

It is a felony for any law enforcement officer, officer of the Department of Corrections, or employee of a prison, jail, or correctional institution, to engage in sexual intercourse or any other sexual conduct with a person confined in a prison, jail, or correctional institution. LA. REV. STAT. § 14:134.1 (enacted 1981).

MAINE: It is a felony for a person to engage in contact between the genitals of one person or an animal or object being manipulated by that person and the anus, genitals, or mouth of another where the victim is not the offender's spouse and the victim is in official custody as a probationer or a parolee or is detained in a hospital, prison, or other institution and the offender has supervisory or disciplinary authority over the victim; the victim is under eighteen and is a student in an elementary, secondary, or special education school, facility, or institution and the offender is a teacher, employee, or other official having instructional, supervisory, or disciplinary authority over the student; the victim is under eighteen and a resident in or attending a children's home, day care facility, residential child care facility, drug treatment center, camp, or similar school, facility, or institution regularly providing care or services for children, and the offender is a teacher, employee, or other person having instructional, supervisory, or disciplinary authority over the victim; the victim is under eighteen and the offender is a foster parent, guardian, or other similar person responsible for the long-term care and welfare of that person; or the offender is a psychiatrist, psychologist, or licensed social worker or purports to be any of those things to the victim and the victim is a patient or client for mental health therapy, meaning psychotherapy or other treatment modalities intended to change behavior, emotions, or attitudes, such therapy being based upon an intimate relationship involving trust and dependency with a substantial potential for vulnerability and abuse. ME. REV. STAT. ANN. tit. 17-A, §§ 251 (enacted 1975), 253 (enacted 1975). Sexual contact is a felony under the same circumstances, excluding contact stemming from the professional relationship of mental health professional and patient or client. ME. REV. STAT. ANN. tit. 17-A, §§ 251 (enacted 1975), 255 (enacted 1975).

MARYLAND: No statute.

MASSACHUSETTS: No statute.

MICHIGAN: It is a felony to engage in sexual penetration or sexual contact with a person under sixteen who is a member of the same household as the offender, or where the victim is under sixteen or mentally incapacitated and the offender is in a position of authority over the victim and used this authority to coerce the victim to submit. MICH. COMP. LAWS ANN. §§ 750.520b (enacted 1984), 750.520c (enacted 1984). It is a misdemeanor for a person who is an employee, a contractual employee, or a volunteer with the Department of Corrections and has knowledge that the victim is under the jurisdiction of the Department of Corrections to engage in sexual contact with the victim. MICH. COMP. LAWS ANN. § 750.520e (enacted 1983).

MINNESOTA: It is a felony for a person to engage in sexual penetration or sexual contact in the following circumstances: where the victim is under sixteen and the offender is more than forty-eight months older than the victim and in a position of authority over the victim, and uses the position to cause the victim to submit; the offender has a significant relationship to the victim and the victim is under sixteen; the offender has a significant relationship to the victim, the victim is under eighteen, and the abuse involves multiple acts committed over an extended period of time; the offender is a psychotherapist and the victim is a patient of the psychotherapist and the act occurred during a psychotherapy session; the offender is a psychotherapist and the victim is a patient or former patient of the psychotherapist and is emotionally dependent upon the psychotherapist; the offender is a psychotherapist and the victim is a patient or former patient and the act occurred by means of therapeutic deception; the offender accomplishes the act by means of a false representation that the act is for a bona fide medical purpose by a health care professional; or the offender is or purports to be a member of the clergy, the victim is not the offender's spouse, and the offense occurred during the course of a meeting in which the victim sought or received religious or spiritual advice, aid, or comfort from the offender in private, or the offense occurred during a period of time in which the complainant was meeting on an ongoing basis with the offender to seek or receive religious or spiritual advice, aid, or comfort in private. All of these offenses are without regard to consent. MINN. STAT. ANN. §§ 609.342 (enacted 1975), 609.343 (enacted 1975), 609.344 (enacted 1975), 609.345 (enacted 1975).

Position of authority includes but is not limited to any person who is a parent or acting in the place of a parent and charged with any of a parent's rights, duties, or responsibilities to a child; or a person who is charged with any duty of responsibility for the health, welfare, or supervision of a child, either independently or through another, no matter how brief, at the time of the act. Significant relationship means a situation in which the offender is the victim's parent, stepparent, or guardian; brother, sister, stepbrother, stepsister, first cousin, aunt, uncle, nephew, niece, grandparent, great-grandparent, great-uncle, or great-aunt, by blood, marriage, or adoption; or an adult who jointly resides intermittently or regularly in the same dwelling as the victim and who is not the victim's spouse. Psychotherapist means a physician, psychologist, nurse, chemical dependency counselor, social worker, clergy, marriage and family therapist, mental health service provider, or other person, whether or not licensed by the state, who performs or purports to perform psychotherapy. Psychotherapy means the professional treatment, assessment, or counseling of a mental or emotional illness, symptom, or condition. Emotionally dependent means that the nature of the patient's or former patient's emotional condition and the nature of the treatment provided by the psychotherapist are such that the psychotherapist knows or has reason to know that the patient or former patient is unable to withhold consent to the sexual act with the therapist. Therapeutic deception means a representation by a psychotherapist that the sexual act with the psychotherapist is consistent with or part of the patient's treatment. MINN. STAT. ANN. § 609.341 (enacted 1975).

MISSISSIPPI: It is a felony to engage in sexual penetration with a child under eighteen if the offender is in a position of trust or authority over the child, including without limitation the child's teacher, counselor, physician, psychiatrist, psychologist, minister, priest, physical therapist, chiropractor, legal guardian, parent, stepparent, aunt, uncle, scout leader, or coach. MISS. CODE ANN. § 97-3-95 (enacted 1980). It is a felony to handle, touch, or rub with hands or any other part of the offender's body a child under the age of eighteen years who is not the offender's spouse, if the offender is in a position of trust or authority over the victim. MISS. CODE ANN. § 97-5-23 (enacted 1920). It is a misdemeanor for a guardian and ward, not being married to each other, to engage in sexual intercourse. MISS. CODE ANN. § 97-29-7 (enacted 1892).

MISSOURI: No statute.

MONTANA: It is a misdemeanor for a guardian or other person supervising the welfare of a child under eighteen to engage in sexual conduct with the child. MONT. CODE. ANN. § 45-5-622 (enacted 1973). It is a felony to promote the prostitution of one's child or ward. Aggravated promotion is a felony. MONT. CODE ANN. § 45-5-603 (enacted 1947).

NEBRASKA: No statute.

NEVADA: It is unlawful for a prisoner in lawful custody or confinement, and a person having custody of a prisoner or an employee of a public institution in which a prisoner is confined, to engage voluntarily in acts of masturbation, homosexuality, sexual intercourse, or physical contact with each other's unclothed genitals or pubic area. NEV. REV. STAT. § 212.187 (enacted 1981). The crime of pandering includes as a spouse, parent, or guardian of a person under age eighteen permitting, conniving at, or consenting to the minor's being or remaining in a house of prostitution; or abuse of any position of confidence or authority, or having legal charge, taking, placing, harboring, inveigling, enticing, persuading, encouraging, or procuring a person to enter any place within this state where prostitution is practiced for the purpose of prostitution or in the same manner causing a person of previous chaste character to enter any place within this state where prostitution is practiced for the purpose of sexual intercourse. NEV. REV. STAT. §§ 201.300 (enacted 1913), 201.310 (enacted 1913), 201.330 (enacted 1913), 201.340 (enacted 1913), 201.360 (enacted 1911).

NEW HAMPSHIRE: It is a felony for a person to engage in sexual penetration with another person when the actor provides therapy, medical treatment, or examination of the victim in a manner or for purposes that are not medically recognized as ethical or acceptable; and when, except as between legally married spouses, the victim is under eighteen and the offender is in a position of authority over the victim and uses this authority to coerce the victim to submit. N.H. REV. STAT. ANN. § 632-A:2 (enacted 1975).

NEW JERSEY: It is a felony to engage in sexual penetration or sexual contact where the victim is less than sixteen but at least thirteen and where the offender has supervisory or disciplinary power over the victim by virtue of the offender's legal, professional, or occupational status, or is a foster parent, a guardian, or stands in loco parentis within the household. N.J. STAT. ANN. §§ 2C:14-1 (enacted 1978), 2C:14-2 (enacted 1978), 2C:14-3 (enacted 1978). It is a felony to engage in sexual penetration and a misdemeanor to engage in sexual contact where the victim is on probation or parole, or is detained in a hospital, prison, or other institution and the offender has supervisory or disciplinary power over the victim by virtue of the offender's legal, professional, or occupational status; or where the victim is at least sixteen but under eighteen and the offender is a foster parent, a guardian, or stands in loco parentis within the household. N.J. STAT. ANN. §§ 2C:14-1 (enacted 1978), 2C:14-2 (enacted 1978), 2C:14-3 (enacted 1978). It is a felony to promote the prostitution of one's child or ward. N.J. STAT. ANN. § 2C:34-1 (enacted 1978).

NEW MEXICO: It is a felony to engage in sexual penetration or contact with a minor under eighteen when the offender is in a position of authority over the child and uses this authority to coerce the child to submit. N.M. STAT ANN. §§ 30-9-11 (enacted 1953), 30-9-13 (enacted 1953).

NEW YORK: No statute.

NORTH CAROLINA: It is a felony to engage in sexual penetration with a minor where the offender has assumed the position of a parent in the home of the minor victim, or where the offender has custody of the victim or the offender is an agent or employee of any person, or institution, whether such institution is private, charitable, or governmental, having custody of the victim. Consent is not a defense. N.C. GEN STAT. § 14-27.7 (enacted 1979). It is a felony for any legal guardian of a child under sixteen to commit or allow the commission of any sexual act on a juvenile. N.C. GEN STAT. § 14-318.4 (enacted 1979).

It is a misdemeanor for a lessor of residential real property or the agent of any lessor of residential property to make unsolicited overt requests for sexual acts when submission to such conduct is made a term of the execution or continuation of the lease agreement, or submission to or rejection of such conduct by an individual is used to determine whether rights under the lease are accorded. N.C. GEN STAT. § 14-395.1 (enacted 1989).

NORTH DAKOTA: It is a felony for a person with supervisory or disciplinary authority over a victim to engage in a sexual act with a victim who is in official custody or detained in a hospital, prison, or other institution. N.D. CENT. CODE § 12.1-20-06 (enacted 1973). It is a felony for a person who purports to be a therapist to engage in sexual contact with a patient or client during any treatment, consultation, interview, or examination. Consent is not a defense. A therapist is a physician, psychologist, psychiatrist, social worker, nurse, chemical dependency counselor, member of the clergy or other person, whether licensed by the state or not, who performs or purports to perform psychotherapy, meaning the diagnosis or treatment of a mental or emotional condition, including alcohol or drug addiction. N.D. CENT. CODE § 12.1-20-06.1 (enacted 1987). It is a misdemeanor to engage in sexual contact where the victim is in official custody or detained in a hospital, prison, or other institution and the offender has supervisory or disciplinary authority over the victim, or the victim is a minor at least fifteen years old and the offender is the victim's parent or guardian or is otherwise responsible for general supervision of the victim's welfare. N.D. CENT. CODE § 12.1-20-07 (enacted 1973). Facilitating prostitution is a felony if the prostitute is the offender's spouse, child, or ward. N.D. CENT. CODE § 12.1-29-02 (enacted 1973).

OHIO: It is a felony to engage in sexual contact where the offender knows that the victim's judgment or control is substantially impaired as a result of the influence of any drug or intoxicant administered to the victim with the victim's consent for the purpose of any kind of medical or dental examination, treatment, or surgery. OHIO REV. CODE ANN. §§ 2907.01 (enacted 1972), 2907.05 (enacted 1972). It is a felony to engage in sexual conduct with another person when the offender is the other person's guardian, custodian, or person in loco parentis; when the victim is in custody of law or a patient in a hospital or other institution, and the offender has supervisory or disciplinary authority over the victim; when the offender is a teacher, administrator, coach, or other person in authority employed by or serving in a school for which the state board of education prescribes minimum standards, which the victim is enrolled in or attends; when the victim is a minor and the offender is a teacher, administrator, coach, or other person in authority in an institution of higher education which the victim is enrolled in or attends; or when the victim is a minor and the offender is the victim's athletic or other type of coach, instructor, leader of a scouting troop, or a person with temporary or occasional disciplinary control over the victim. OHIO REV. CODE ANN. § 2907.03 (enacted 1972).

OKLAHOMA: It is a felony for a state employee to engage in sexual penetration with a person under the legal custody of a state agency where the victim submits in the belief that the conduct will influence the professional responsibility of the employee or if not submitted to will result in a detriment to the victim. OKLA. STAT. ANN. tit. 21, § 1111 (enacted 1910).

OREGON: It is a felony to induce a person's child or stepchild to engage in prostitution. OR. REV. STAT. § 167.017 (enacted 1971).

PENNSYLVANIA: It is a felony for a person to engage in sexual penetration with another person where the victim is in custody of law or detained in a hospital or other institution and the offender has supervisory or disciplinary authority over the victim. 18 PA. CONS. STAT. ANN. § 3125 (enacted 1990). It is a misdemeanor to engage in sexual contact with another person under the same circumstances. 18 PA. CONS. STAT. ANN. § 3126 (enacted 1972). It is a felony to promote the prostitution of a person under sixteen or who is the offender's spouse, child, or dependent. 18 PA. CONS. STAT. ANN. § 5902 (enacted 1972).

RHODE ISLAND: It is a felony to engage in the medical treatment or examination of the victim for the purpose of sexual arousal, gratification, or stimulation. R.I. GEN. LAWS §§ 11-37-4 (enacted 1979), 11-37-5 (enacted 1979). It is unlawful for a mental health professional to engage in voyeurism. A mental health professional commits voyeurism by viewing the patient's or former patient's private anatomy. R.I. GEN. LAWS ANN. § 5-63.1-1 (enacted 1956).

SOUTH CAROLINA: It is a felony to engage in sexual penetration with a person who is under sixteen where the offender is in a position of custodial or official authority to coerce the victim to submit. S.C. CODE ANN. § 16-3-655 (enacted 1977).

SOUTH DAKOTA: It is a felony for a physician, psychologist, nurse, chemical dependency counselor, social worker, member of the clergy, marriage and family therapist, mental health services provider, or other person, without regard to licensing, who performs or purports to perform psychotherapy, to engage in sexual contact with a person who is emotionally dependent on the offender. A person is emotionally dependent when that person's condition or the nature of the treatment provided by the psychotherapist is characterized by significant impairment of the patient's ability to withhold consent to sexual acts or contact with the offender and the offender knows or has reason to know that condition exists. Psychotherapy includes any professional treatment, assessment, or counseling of a mental or emotional illness, symptom, or condition. Consent by the patient is not a defense. S.D. CODIFIED LAWS ANN. §§ 22-22-27 (enacted 1993), 22-22-28 (enacted 1993). It is a felony to promote the prostitution of one's child or ward. S.D. CODIFIED LAWS ANN. § 22-23-2 (enacted 1877).

TENNESSEE: It is a felony to engage in sexual penetration or sexual contact with a person under fifteen by the use of parental, custodial, or official authority. TENN. CODE ANN. §§ 39-13-501 (enacted 1989), 39-13-503 (enacted 1989), 39-13-505 (enacted 1989).

TEXAS: It is a misdemeanor for a public servant acting under the color of his office to make unwelcome sexual advances, requests for sexual favors, or other verbal or physical conduct of a sexual nature, submission to which is made a term or condition of a person's exercise or enjoyment of any right, privilege, power, or immunity, either explicitly or implicitly. TEX. PENAL CODE ANN. § 39.03 (enacted 1973).

UTAH: It is a felony to engage in sexual penetration or sexual contact with a person who is under eighteen where the offender is the victim's parent, stepparent, adoptive parent, or legal guardian, or occupies a position of special trust in relation to the victim. UTAH CODE ANN. § 76-5-406 (enacted 1953). A position of special trust is one occupied by a person in a position of authority who, by reason of that position, is able to exercise undue influence over the victim. It includes but is not limited to a youth leader or recreational leader who is an adult, adult athletic manager, adult coach, teacher, counselor, religious leader, doctor, employer, foster parent, baby-sitter, or adult scout leader. UTAH CODE ANN. § 76-5-404.1 (enacted 1953).

VERMONT: It is a felony to engage in a sexual act where the victim is under eighteen and is entrusted to the care of the offender by authority of law or is the offender's child, grandchild, foster child, adopted child, or stepchild. VT. STAT. ANN. tit. 13, § 3252 (enacted 1977).

VIRGINIA: It is a felony for a person providing services, paid or unpaid, to juveniles under the purview of the Family Court Law, or to juveniles who have been committed to the custody of the State Department of Youth and Family Services, to engage in sexual intercourse, cunnilingus, fellatio, analingus, anal intercourse, or animate or inanimate object sexual penetration, without the use of force, with any minor fifteen years of age or older who has been commited to the custody of the Department of Youth and Family Services. VA. REV. STAT. § 18.2-64.1 (enacted 1977).

It is a felony for any person eighteen years or older who maintains a custodial or supervisory relationship, including but not limited to the parent, stepparent, grandparent, stepgrandparent, or who stands in loco parentis with respect to a child under eighteen, to knowingly and intentionally propose that any such child feel or fondle the sexual or genital parts of such person, or vice versa; propose to such child the performance of an act of sexual intercourse; expose his or her sexual or genital parts to such child; propose that such child expose his or her genital parts to the person; propose to the child that the child engage in sexual intercourse, sodomy, or fondling of sexual or genital parts with another person; or sexually abuse the child. VA. REV. STAT. § 18.2-370.1 (enacted 1982).

WASHINGTON: It is a felony for a person to cause another person not his spouse to have sexual contact with him when the victim is developmentally disabled and the offender has supervisory authority over the victim; the offender is a health care provider, the victim is a client or patient, and the sexual contact occurs during a treatment session, consultation, interview, or examination; or the victim is a resident of a facility for mentally disordered or chemically dependent persons and the offender has supervisory authority over the victim. WASH. REV. CODE ANN. § 9A.44.100 (enacted 1975). It is a felony to engage in sexual penetration with a person where the victim is developmentally disabled, or the victim is a resident of a facility for mentally disordered or chemically dependent persons, and the offender has supervisory authority over the victim. WASH. REV. CODE ANN. § 9A.44.050 (enacted 1975). Supervisory authority means that the offender is a proprietor or employee of any public or private care or treatment facility who directly supervises developmentally disabled persons at the facility. WASH. REV. CODE ANN. § 9A.44.010 (enacted 1975).

It is a felony for a person to engage in sexual penetration with a person under eighteen where the offender is at least sixty months older than the victim, is in a significant relationship to the victim, and abuses a supervisory position within that relationship in order to engage in sexual penetration with the victim. WASH. REV. CODE ANN. § 9A.44.093 (enacted 1988). Sexual contact under the same circumstances is a misdemeanor. WASH. REV. CODE ANN. § 9A.44.096 (enacted 1988). Abuse of a supervisory position means a direct or indirect threat or promise to use authority to the detriment or benefit of the victim. Significant relationship means a situation in which the offender is a person who undertakes the responsibility, professionally or voluntarily, to provide education, health, welfare, or organized recreational activities principally for minors, or who in the course of his or her employment supervises minors. WASH. REV. CODE ANN. § 9A.44.010 (enacted 1975).

WEST VIRGINIA: It is a misdemeanor for any physician, dentist, or other person to administer chloroform, ether, or any anesthetic whatsoever, whereby sleep or total loss of sensation or consciousness may be produced, to any female person, unless in the presence of a third person. W. VA. CODE ANN. § 61-8-10 (enacted 1897).

It is a felony for any parent, guardian, or custodian of a child to engage in or attempt to engage in sexual exploitation of, or sexual intercourse, intrusion, or contact with a child under his or her care, custody, or control, notwithstanding consent or lack of apparent physical, mental, or emotional injury. It is a felony for any parent, guardian, or custodian of a child to procure another person to engage in or attempt to engage in the above actions if the child is under sixteen. It is a misdemeanor if the child is over sixteen. W. VA. CODE ANN. § 61-8D-5 (enacted 1988).

WISCONSIN: It is a felony for a person to engage in sexual penetration or sexual contact where the offender is an employee of an inpatient facility or a state treatment facility and the victim is a patient or resident of the facility. WIS. STAT. ANN. § 940.225 (enacted 1975). It is a felony for any person who is or purports to be a therapist to intentionally engage in sexual contact with a patient or client during any ongoing therapist-patient or therapist-client relationship, regardless of whether it occurs during treatment, consultation, interview, or examination. Consent is not a defense. A therapist includes any physician, psychologist, social worker, marriage and family therapist, professional counselor, nurse, chemical dependency counselor, member of the clergy, or other person, whether or not licensed or certified by the state, who performs or purports to perform psychotherapy. WIS. STAT. ANN. § 940.22 (enacted 1983).

WYOMING: It is a felony to engage in sexual penetration or sexual contact where the offender is in a position of authority over the victim and uses this position of authority to cause the victim to submit. WYO. STAT. §§ 6-2-301 (enacted 1982), 6-2-303 (enacted 1982), 6-2-305 (enacted 1982). It is a felony to inflict sexual penetration on a victim in treatment or examination of a victim for purposes or in a manner substantially inconsistent with reasonable medical practices. WYO. STAT. § 6-2-303 (enacted 1982). A position of authority is a position occupied by a parent, guardian, relative, household member, teacher, employer, custodian, or any other person who, by reason of the position, is able to exercise significant influence over the victim. WYO. STAT. § 6-2-301 (enacted 1982).

UNITED STATES: It is a misdemeanor for anyone in the special maritime and territorial jurisdiction of the United States or in a federal prison to knowingly engage or attempt to engage in a sexual act or sexual contact with a person who is in official detention; and under the custodial, supervisory, or disciplinary authority of the offender. 18 U.S.C.A. §§ 2243(b) (enacted 1986), 2244 (enacted 1986).

10

Incest

Incest is a felony in almost every state. The states take a variety of approaches to the inclusion or exclusion of adoptive, step- and in-law relations. Where the acts constituting the crime are defined by reference to the sexual assault provisions for the state in question, the definitions have been left out here and can be found in chapter 1. Many states do not define the acts in any detail.

This chapter covers only incestuous acts that may be criminally punished. It does not include the limits on legally recognized marriages, though in many cases the relationships in question are the same. If the marriage itself is a crime and not just void or unrecognized, then marriage is included here as criminal incest.

The reasons given for prohibiting apparently consensual incest include consistancy with dominant religious traditions, concern over genetic defects in the offspring of incestuous unions, protection of the family unit from sexual jealousies, reinforcing the deeply held community norm against incestuous relations, and preventing sexual imposition by people in a position of familial power over others. In some cases, the statutory text itself reveals a driving purpose; for example, where prohibited incest includes step- and adoptive relatives, genetic concerns obviously are not an adequate explanation for the prohibition. The strongly held community norms against incest are reason enough, in the minds of most people, to criminalize incest. Yet those very same norms may be to a large extent self-enforcing as there are few reported cases of incestuous relationships between adults.

The Model Penal Code takes a restrictive view of what should be classified as criminal incest, limiting it to sex with biological parents or other ancestors, descendants, and siblings of the whole or half blood, with relations between non–blood relatives only being incestuous as between a parent and child. The Code brackets the relationships of uncle, aunt, niece, or nephew of the whole blood, considering the prudence of criminality of such conduct a close case.

The limited data on incest prosecutions suggest that whatever the legislative purpose behind a given statute, the statutes are used in practice primarily for one reason: preventing sexual imposition by people in a position of familial power over others. Most cases are against a father or stepfather for incestuous relations with a daughter or stepdaughter who is either below or just above the legal age of consent.

ALABAMA: Incest is a felony. A person commits incest by marrying or engaging in sexual intercourse with a person he or she knows to be, either legitimately or illegitimately, an ancestor or descendant by blood or adoption; a brother or sister of the whole or half blood or by adoption; a stepchild or stepparent, while the marriage creating the relationship exists; or an aunt, uncle, nephew, or niece of the whole or half blood. ALA. CODE ANN. § 13A-13-3 (enacted 1971).

ALASKA: Incest is a felony. A person commits incest if, being eighteen years of age or older, that person engages in sexual penetration with another who is related, either legitimately or illegitimately, as an ancestor or descendant of the whole or half blood; a brother or sister of the whole or half blood; or an uncle, aunt, nephew, or niece by blood. ALASKA STAT. § 11.41.450 (enacted 1978).

ARIZONA: Incest is a felony. People who are at least fifteen years of age commit incest if they marry one another or commit fornication or adultery with one another and are in any of the following relationships: parent and child; grandparent and grandchild of every degree; brother and sister of the whole or half blood; uncle and niece; aunt and nephew; or first cousins. First cousins are exempt where both are over sixty-five years old or where one is unable to reproduce. ARIZ. REV. STAT. ANN. §§ 13-3608 (enacted 1977), 25-101 (enacted 1977).

ARKANSAS: Incest is a felony. A person commits incest if, being sixteen years of age or older, he or she purports to marry, has sexual intercourse with, or engages in deviate sexual activity with a person he or she knows to be an ancestor or descendant; a stepchild or adopted child; a brother or sister of the whole or half blood; an uncle, aunt, nephew, or niece; or a step- or adopted grandchild. These relationships include blood relationships without regard to legitimacy. ARK. CODE ANN. § 5-26-202 (enacted 1975).

CALIFORNIA: A person commits incest if he or she marries or commits fornication or adultery with a parent, child, ancestor, descendant, brother, or sister of the half as well as the whole blood, uncle, niece, aunt, or nephew, without regard to legitimacy. CAL. PENAL CODE § 285 (enacted 1872), CAL. FAMILY CODE § 2200 (enacted 1992).

COLORADO: Incest is a felony. Any person who knowingly marries, inflicts sexual penetration or sexual intrusion on, or subjects to sexual contact, an ancestor or descendant, including a natural child, child by adoption, or stepchild; a brother or sister of the whole or half blood; or an uncle, aunt, nephew, or niece of the whole or half blood, commits incest. Descendant includes a child by adoption and a stepchild only if the person is not legally married to the child by adoption or the stepchild. A person commits aggravated incest when the child is under twenty-one years of age. Aggravated incest is a more serious degree of felony. COLO. REV. STAT. §§ 18-6-301 (enacted 1971), 18-6-302 (enacted 1971).

CONNECTICUT: Incest is a felony. A person commits incest when he or she marries a person known to be related within the degrees that make a marriage void. For a man, this means his mother, grandmother, daughter, granddaughter, sister, aunt, niece, stepmother, or stepdaughter. For a woman this means her father, grandfather, son, grandson, brother, uncle, nephew, stepfather, or stepson. CONN. GEN. STAT. §§ 53a-191 (enacted 1969), 466-21 (enacted 1949).

DELAWARE: Incest is a misdemeanor. Incest is sexual intercourse between a man and his child, parent, brother, sister, grandchild, niece or nephew, uncle or aunt by blood, father's wife, wife's child, or wife's grandchild, or between a woman and her parent, child, brother, sister, grandchild, niece or nephew, aunt or uncle by blood, mother's husband, husband's child, or husband's grandchild. These relationships include blood relationships without regard to legitimacy and relationships by adoption. DEL. CODE ANN. tit. 11, § 766 (enacted 1953).

DISTRICT OF COLUMBIA: Incest is a felony. A person commits incest by knowingly marrying, cohabiting, or having sexual intercourse with a person related to but not including the fourth degree of consanguinity. D.C. STAT. § 22-1901 (enacted 1973).

FLORIDA: Incest is a felony. Whoever knowingly marries or has sexual intercourse with a person to whom he or she is related by lineal consanguinity—a brother, sister, uncle, aunt, nephew, or niece—commits incest. FLA. STAT. ANN. § 826.04 (enacted 1975).

GEORGIA: Incest is a felony. A person commits incest by engaging in sexual intercourse with a person who he or she knows is related either by blood or by marriage by one of the following relationships: father and daughter or stepdaughter; mother and son or stepson; brother and sister of the whole or half blood; grandparent and grandchild; aunt and nephew; or uncle and niece. GA. CODE ANN. § 16-6-22 (enacted 1833).

HAWAII: Incest is a felony. A person commits incest by committing an act of sexual penetration with another who is, without regard to legitimacy, an ancestor or descendant of any degree whatsoever; brother or sister of the half as well as the whole blood; uncle or niece; or aunt or nephew. HAW. REV. STAT. §§ 707-741 (enacted 1972), 572-1 (enacted 1994).

IDAHO: Incest is a felony. One commits incest by marrying or committing fornication or adultery with a parent, child, ancestor or descendant of every degree, brother or sister of the half or whole blood, uncle, niece, aunt, or nephew, without regard to legitimacy. IDAHO CODE §§ 18-6602 (enacted 1972), 32-205 (enacted 1867).

ILLINOIS: Sexual relations within families is a felony. A person commits sexual relations within families if he or she commits an act of sexual penetration and the person knows that he or she is related to the other person as follows: brother or sister either of the whole or half blood; father or mother, when the child, regardless of legitimacy and regardless of whether the child was of the whole or half blood or was adopted, was eighteen years of age or over when the act was committed; or stepfather or stepmother, when the stepchild was eighteen years of age or over when the act was committed. ILL. ANN. STAT. ch. 720, para. 5/11-11 (enacted 1961). If the child was under eighteen years of age, the offense is criminal sexual assault. ILL. ANN. STAT. ch. 720, para. 5/12-13 (enacted 1961).

INDIANA: Incest is a felony. A person eighteen years of age or older who engages in sexual intercourse or deviate sexual conduct with another person whom the offender knows is related biologically as a parent, child, grandparent, grandchild, sibling, aunt, uncle, niece, or nephew commits incest. It is a defense that the accused person's otherwise incestuous relation was based on marriage between the two people in question, if it was a valid marriage where it was entered into. IND. CODE 35-46-1-3 (enacted 1971). It is a felony to engage in sexual penetration with a person who is at least sixteen but under eighteen where the offender is the adoptive parent or grandparent of the victim. IND. CODE ANN. § 35-42-4-7 (enacted 1987).

IOWA: Incest is a felony. A person who performs a sex act with another whom the person knows to be related either legitimately or illegitimately, as an ancestor, descendant, brother, or sister of the whole or half blood, aunt, uncle, niece, or nephew commits incest. IOWA CODE ANN. § 726.2 (enacted 1976). It is a felony to engage in a sex act with a person who is fourteen or fifteen years old when the offender is related by blood or affinity to the fourth degree. IOWA CODE ANN. § 709.4 (enacted 1976).

KANSAS: Incest and aggravated incest are both felonies. Incest is marriage to, or engaging in otherwise lawful sexual intercourse or sodomy with a person who is eighteen or older and who is known to the offender to be related to the offender as any of the following biological relatives: parent, child, grandparent of any degree, grandchild of any degree, brother, sister, half brother, half sister, uncle, aunt, nephew, or niece. KAN. STAT. ANN. § 21-3602 (enacted 1969).

Aggravated incest is marriage to, or engaging in sexual intercourse, sodomy, or any unlawful sex act, lewd fondling, or touching of the person of either the child or the offender, done or submitted to with the intent to arouse or to satisfy the sexual desires of either the child or the offender or both, when the child is under eighteen and is known to the offender to be related to the offender as any of the following biological, step- or adoptive relatives: child, grandchild of any degree, brother, sister, half brother, half sister, uncle, aunt, nephew, or niece. KAN. STAT. ANN. § 21-3603 (enacted 1969).

KENTUCKY: Incest is a felony. A person is guilty of incest when he or she has sexual intercourse or deviate sexual intercourse with a person, knowing that person to be an ancestor, descendant, brother, or sister. These relationships include blood relationships of the whole or half blood without regard to legitimacy, the relationship of parent and child by adoption, and the relationship of stepparent and stepchild. KY. REV. STAT. ANN. § 530.020 (enacted 1974).

LOUISIANA: Incest is a felony. Incest is the marriage to, or sexual intercourse with, any descendant or ascendant, brother or sister, uncle or niece, or aunt or nephew, with knowledge of their relationship. The relationship must be by consanguinity, but it is immaterial whether the parties to the act are legitimate or illegitimate or related to one another by the whole or half blood. This section does not apply to anyone who, not a resident of Louisiana at the time of the celebration of his or her marriage, contracted a marriage lawful at the place of celebration and afterwards removed to Louisiana. LA. REV. STAT. ANN. § 14:78 (enacted 1884).

Aggravated incest is also a felony. Aggravated incest is the engaging in of any prohibited act with a person under the age of eighteen whom the offender knows to be related as any of the following biological, step, or adoptive relatives: child, grandchild of any degree, brother, sister, half brother, half sister, uncle, aunt, nephew, or niece. Prohibited acts include sexual intercourse; sexual battery; aggravated sexual battery; carnal knowledge of a juvenile; indecent behavior with juveniles; pornography involving juveniles; crime against nature; cruelty to juveniles; parent enticing a juvenile into prostitution; or any lewd fondling or touching of the person of either the child or the offender, done or submitted to with the intent to arouse or to satisfy the sexual desires of the child, the offender, or both. LA. REV. STAT. ANN. § 14:78.1 (enacted 1993).

MAINE: Incest is a felony. A person is guilty of incest if, being at least eighteen years of age, that person engages in sexual intercourse, meaning any penetration of the female sex organ by the male sex organ, with another person who the actor knows is related within the second degree of consanguinity. It is a defense that the actor was legally married to the other person. ME. REV. STAT. ANN. tit. 17-A, § 556 (enacted 1975). It is a felony for a person to engage in contact between the genitals of one person, or an animal, or an object being manipulated by that person, and the anus, genitals, or mouth of another where the offender is a parent or stepparent. ME. REV. STAT. ANN. tit. 17-A, §§ 251 (enacted 1975), 253 (enacted 1975).

MARYLAND: Incest is a felony. Every person who shall knowingly have carnal knowledge of another person who is within three degrees of direct lineal consanguinity or within first degree of collateral consanguinity commits incest. A man commits incest by knowingly having carnal knowledge of his grandmother, mother, daughter, sister, or granddaughter; or his grandfather's wife, wife's grandmother, father's sister, mother's sister, stepmother, wife's mother, wife's daughter, son's wife, grandson's wife, brother's daughter, or sister's daughter. A woman commits incest by having carnal knowledge of her grandfather, father, son, brother, grandson, grandmother's husband, husband's grandfather, father's brother, mother's brother, stepfather, husband's father, husband's son, daughter's husband, husband's grandson, brother's son, sister's son, or granddaughter's husband. MD.

CRIM. LAW CODE ANN. § 335 (enacted 1951), MD. FAM. LAW CODE ANN. § 2-202 (enacted 1957).

MASSACHUSETTS: Incest is a felony. A man commits incest by intermarrying or engaging in sexual intercourse with his mother, grandmother, daughter, granddaughter, sister, stepmother, grandfather's wife, grandson's wife, wife's mother, wife's grandmother, wife's daughter, wife's granddaughter, brother's daughter, sister's daughter, father's sister, or mother's sister. A woman commits incest by doing the same with her father, grandfather, son, grandson, brother, stepfather, grandmother's husband, daughter's husband, granddaughter's husband, husband's grandfather, husband's son, husband's grandson, brother's son, sister's son, father's brother, or mother's brother. MASS. GEN. LAWS ch. 272, § 17 (enacted 1695), ch. 207, §§ 1 (enacted 1983), 2 (enacted 1785).

MICHIGAN: It is a felony for a person to engage in sexual penetration or sexual contact with a person to whom the actor is related by blood or affinity to the fourth degree. MICH. COMP. LAWS ANN. §§ 750.520b (enacted 1931), 750.520c (enacted 1931).

MINNESOTA: Incest is a felony. Whoever has sexual intercourse with another nearer of kin to the actor than first cousin, computed by rules of the civil law, whether of the half or whole blood, with knowledge of the relationship, is guilty of incest. MINN. STAT. ANN. § 609.365 (enacted 1963). It is a felony for a person to engage in sexual penetration or sexual contact in the following circumstances: where the victim is under sixteen and the offender is more than forty-eight months older than the victim and in a position of authority over the victim, and uses the position to cause the victim to submit; the offender has a significant relationship to the victim and the victim is under sixteen; the offender has a significant relationship to the victim, the victim is under eighteen, and the abuse involves multiple acts committed over an extended period of time. MINN. STAT. ANN. §§ 609.342 (enacted 1975), 609.343 (enacted 1975). Position of trust includes but is not limited to any person who is a parent. Significant relationship means a situation in which the offender is the victim's parent, stepparent, guardian, brother, sister, stepbrother, stepsister, first cousin, aunt, uncle, nephew, niece, grandparent, great-grandparent, great-uncle, or great-aunt, by blood, marriage, or adoption. MINN. STAT. ANN. § 609.341 (enacted 1975).

MISSISSIPPI: Incest is a felony. Individuals who cohabit, live together as husband and wife, marry, or commit a single act of adultery or fornication within prohibited relationships are guilty of incest. The following relationships are prohibited: son and grandmother, mother, daughter of his father begotten of his stepmother, aunt (his mother or father's sister), or stepmother; brother and sister; father and daughter, legally adopted daughter, or granddaughter; and first cousins with one another. MISS. CODE ANN. §§ 97-29-5 (enacted 1848), 97-29-27 (enacted 1848), 97-29-29 (enacted 1857), 93-1-1 (enacted 1848). It is a felony to engage in sexual penetration with a child under eighteen if the offender is the child's parent, stepparent, aunt, or uncle. MISS. CODE ANN. § 97-3-95 (enacted 1980). It is a felony to handle, touch, or rub with hands or any other part of the offender's body a child under eighteen if the offender is the child's parent, stepparent, aunt, or uncle. MISS. CODE ANN. § 97-29-7 (enacted 1892).

MISSOURI: Incest is a felony. A person commits incest by marrying, purporting to marry, engaging in sexual intercourse or engaging in deviate sexual intercourse with a person he or she knows to be, without regard to legitimacy, an ancestor or descendant by blood or adoption; a stepchild while the marriage creating the relationship exists; a brother or sister of the whole or half blood; or an uncle, aunt, nephew, or niece of the whole blood. MO. ANN. STAT. § 568.020 (enacted 1977).

MONTANA: Incest is a felony. A person commits incest by knowingly marrying, cohabiting with, having sexual intercourse with, or having sexual contact with an ancestor, descendant, brother or sister of the whole or half blood, or stepson or stepdaughter. These relationships include blood relationships without regard to legitimacy and relationships of parent and child by adoption. Consent is a defense to incest upon or with a stepson or stepdaughter, but is ineffective if the victim is under eighteen. MONT. CODE ANN. § 45-5-507 (enacted 1973). It is a misdemeanor for a parent to engage in sexual conduct with a child under eighteen. MONT. CODE ANN. § 45-5-622 (enacted 1973).

NEBRASKA: Incest is a felony. A person commits incest by marrying or engaging in sexual penetration with a parent, child, grandparent, or grandchild of every degree, brother or sister of the whole or half blood, uncle, niece, aunt, nephew, or minor stepchild, in all cases without regard to legitimacy. NEB. REV. STAT. §§ 28-702 (enacted 1943), 28-703 (enacted 1943).

NEVADA: Incest is a felony. A person commits incest by marrying or committing adultery or fornication with a person nearer of kin than second cousins or cousins of the half blood. NEV. REV. STAT. ANN. §§ 122.020 (enacted 1861), 201.180 (enacted 1911).

NEW HAMPSHIRE: Incest is a felony. A person commits incest by marrying, having sexual intercourse with, or living together under the representation of being married to, a person he or she knows to be an ancestor, descendant, brother or sister of the whole or half blood, uncle, aunt, nephew, or niece. No person under eighteen is liable for incest if the other party is at least three years older at the time of the act. The relationships in this section include blood relationships without regard to legitimacy, stepchildren, and relationships of parents and children by adoption. N.H. REV. STAT. ANN. § 639:2 (enacted 1971).

NEW JERSEY: Incest is prohibited as part of the sexual assault provision of the state code, making it a felony. A person is guilty of incest if he or she commits an act of sexual penetration with a victim who is related by blood or affinity to the third degree and who is under eighteen years of age. N.J. STAT. ANN. § 2C:14-2 (enacted 1978).

NEW MEXICO: Incest is a felony. A person commits incest by knowingly marrying or having sexual intercourse with a parent, child, grandparent, or grandchild of every degree, brother or sister of the half or whole blood, uncle, niece, aunt, or nephew. N.M. STAT ANN. § 30-10-3 (enacted 1953).

NEW YORK: Incest is a felony. A person commits incest by marrying or engaging in sexual intercourse or deviate sexual intercourse with a person he or she knows to be related either legitimately or out of wedlock as an ancestor, descendant, brother or sister of the whole or half blood, uncle, aunt, nephew, or niece. N. Y. PENAL LAW § 255.25 (enacted 1965).

NORTH CAROLINA: A person is guilty of incest punishable as a felony when he or she engages in carnal intercourse with a grandparent, grandchild, parent, child, stepchild, legally adopted child, or brother or sister of the whole or half blood. Incest is punishable as a misdemeanor when it consists of carnal intercourse between uncle and niece or aunt and nephew. N.C. GEN. STAT. §§ 14-178 (enacted 1879), 14-179 (enacted 1879). It is a felony for any parent of a child under sixteen to commit or allow the commission of any sexual act on a juvenile. N.C. GEN. STAT. § 14-318.4 (enacted 1979).

NORTH DAKOTA: Incest is a felony. A person who marries, cohabits with, or engages in a sexual act with a person with whom the actor is in any of the following relationships: parent and child including grandparent and grandchild of every degree; brother and sister of the half or whole blood; uncles and nieces of the whole or half blood; aunts and nephews of the whole or half blood; and first cousins of the whole or half blood, commits incest if the actor knows of the relationship. This section applies to illegitimate as well as legitimate children and relatives. N.D. CENT. CODE §§ 12.1-20-11 (enacted 1973), 14-03-03 (enacted 1890). It is a misdemeanor to engage in sexual contact where the victim is a minor at least fifteen and the offender is the victim's parent. N.D. CENT. CODE § 12.1-20-07 (enacted 1973).

OHIO: Incest is a felony prohibited as one form of sexual battery. An actor is guilty of incestuous sexual battery if, being the natural parent, adoptive parent, or stepparent of the victim, the actor engages in sexual conduct with the victim. OHIO REV. CODE ANN. § 2907.03 (enacted 1973).

OKLAHOMA: Incest is a felony. A person commits incest who marries or commits adultery or fornication with a person with whom the actor has any of the following relationships: ancestors and descendants of any degree; stepfather and stepdaughter; stepmother and stepson; uncles and nieces and aunts and nephews except when such relationship is only by marriage; brothers and sisters of the whole or half blood; and first cousins. OKLA. STAT. tit. 21, § 885 (enacted 1910), tit. 43, § 2 (enacted 1910).

OREGON: Incest is a felony. A person is guilty of incest if the person marries or engages in sexual intercourse or deviate sexual intercourse with a person whom the person knows to be related to the person, either legitimately or illegitimately, as an ancestor, descendant, or brother or sister of either whole or half blood. OR. REV. STAT. § 163.525 (enacted 1971).

PENNSYLVANIA: Incest is a felony. A person is guilty of incest if he or she knowingly marries, cohabits, or has sexual intercourse with an ancestor or descendant, a brother or sister of the whole or half blood, or an uncle, aunt, nephew, or niece of the whole blood. The relationships referred to here are without reference to legitimacy, and the relationship of parent and child includes a child by adoption. 18 PA. CONST. STAT. ANN. § 4302 (enacted 1972).

Rhode Island: No statute.

South Carolina: Incest is a felony. A man is guilty of incest who has carnal intercourse with his mother, grandmother, daughter, granddaughter, stepmother, sister, grandfather's wife, son's wife, grandson's wife, wife's mother, wife's grandmother, wife's daughter, wife's granddaughter, brother's daughter, sister's daughter, father's sister, or mother's sister. A woman is guilty of incest who has carnal intercourse with her father, grandfather, son, grandson, stepfather, brother, grandmother's husband, daughter's husband, granddaughter's husband, husband's father, husband's grandfather, husband's son, husband's grandson, brother's son, sister's son, father's brother, or mother's brother. S.C. Code Ann. § 16-15-20 (enacted 1962). It is a felony to engage in sexual penetration with a person who is at least fourteen but under sixteen and the offender is in a familial position to coerce the victim to submit. S.C. Code Ann. § 16-3-655 (enacted 1977).

South Dakota: Incest is a felony. Any person fourteen years of age or older who knowingly engages in sexual contact with another person, other than a spouse, if that other person is under the age of twenty-one, is guilty of incest if the relationship between the two is that of parent and child, ancestor and descendant of every degree, brother and sister of the half and whole blood, uncle and niece, aunt and nephew, cousins of the half or whole blood, stepfather and stepdaughter, or stepmother and stepson. S.D. Codified Laws Ann. §§ 22-22-19.1 (enacted 1982), 25-1-6 (enacted 1877), 25-1-7 (enacted 1877).

Tennessee: Incest is a felony. A person commits incest who engages in sexual penetration with a person he or she knows to be, without regard to legitimacy, the person's natural parent, child, grandparent, grandchild, uncle, aunt, nephew, niece, stepparent, stepchild, adoptive parent, adoptive child, or brother or sister of the whole or half blood or by adoption. Tenn. Code Ann. § 39-15-302 (enacted 1989). It is a felony to engage in sexual penetration or sexual contact with a person under fifteen by the use of parental authority. Tenn. Code Ann. §§ 39-13-501 (enacted 1989), 39-13-503 (enacted 1989), 39-13-505 (enacted 1989).

Texas: Incest is a felony. A person is guilty of incest if he or she engages in sexual intercourse or deviate sexual intercourse with a person he or she knows to be, without regard to legitimacy, an ancestor or descendant by blood or adoption; a stepchild or stepparent while the marriage creating that relationship exists; a parent's brother or sister of the whole or half blood; a brother or sister of the whole or half blood or by adoption; or the children of a brother or sister of the whole or half blood or by adoption. TEX. PENAL CODE ANN. § 25.02 (enacted 1973).

UTAH: Incest is a felony. A person is guilty of incest when he or she has sexual intercourse with a person whom the actor knows to be an ancestor, descendant, brother, sister, uncle, aunt, nephew, niece, or first cousin. These relationships include whole or half blood without regard to legitimacy, the relationship of parent and child by adoption, and the relationship of stepparent and stepchild while the marriage creating the relationship of stepparent and stepchild exists. UTAH CODE ANN. § 76-7-102 (enacted 1953). It is a felony to engage in sexual penetration or sexual contact with a person who is under eighteen where the offender is the victim's parent, stepparent, or adoptive parent. UTAH CODE ANN. § 76-5-406 (enacted 1953).

VERMONT: Incest is a felony. A man is guilty of incest when he commits fornication with his mother, grandmother, daughter, granddaughter, sister, brother's daughter, sister's daughter, father's sister, or mother's sister. A woman is guilty of incest when she commits fornication with her father, grandfather, son, grandson, brother, brother's son, sister's son, father's brother, or mother's brother. If the relationships are based on marriage, the prohibition continues notwithstanding the dissolution of the marriage by death or divorce, unless the divorce is for a cause that shows the marriage to have been originally invalid or void. VT. STAT. ANN. tit. 15, §§ 1 (enacted 1947), 2 (enacted 1947), 3 (enacted 1947), tit. 13, § 205 (enacted 1947). It is a felony to engage in a sexual act where the victim is under eighteen and is entrusted to the care of the offender by authority of law or is the offender's child, grandchild, adopted child, or stepchild. VT. STAT. ANN. tit. 13, § 3252 (enacted 1977).

VIRGINIA: It is a misdemeanor to commit adultery or fornication with an ancestor, descendant, brother or sister, uncle, niece, aunt or nephew, whether by the half or whole blood or adoption, except that it is a felony to commit adultery or fornication with one's daughter or granddaughter, son or grandson, father or mother. VA. CODE ANN. §§ 18.2-366 (enacted 1950), 20-38.1 (enacted 1975). It is a felony for any person eighteen years or older who is a parent, stepparent, grandparent, step-grandparent, or who stands in loco parentis with respect to a child under eighteen, to knowingly and intentionally propose that any such child feel or fondle the sexual or genital parts of such person, or vice versa; propose to such child the performance of an act of sexual intercourse; expose his or her sexual or genital parts to such child; propose that such child expose his or her genital parts to the person; propose to the child that the child engage in sexual intercourse, sodomy, or fondling of sexual or genital parts with another person; or sexually abuse the child. VA. REV. STAT. § 18.2-370.1 (enacted 1950).

WASHINGTON: Incest is a felony. A person is guilty of incest when such person engages in sexual intercourse or sexual contact with a person whom the actor knows to be a relative, either legitimate or illegitimate, as an ancestor, descendant, brother or sister of either the whole or half blood, including stepchildren and adopted children when those children are under eighteen years of age. WASH. REV. CODE ANN. § 9A.64.020 (enacted 1975).

WEST VIRGINIA: Incest is a felony. A person is guilty of incest when such person engages in sexual intercourse, anal intercourse, oral-genital contact, or penetration of the female sex organ or of the anus of any person by an object for the purpose of degrading or humiliating the person or for gratifying the sexual desire of either party with his or her father, mother, brother, sister, daughter, son, grandfather, grandmother, grandson, granddaughter, nephew, niece, uncle, or aunt, including adoptive and step relatives. W. VA. CODE § 61-8-12 (enacted 1882). It is a felony for any parent, guardian, or custodian of a child to engage in or attempt to engage in sexual exploitation of, or sexual intercourse, intrusion, or contact with a child under his or her care, custody, or control, notwithstanding consent or lack of apparent physical, mental, or emotional injury. It is a felony for any parent, guardian, or custodian of a child to procure another person to engage in or attempt to engage in the above actions if the child is under sixteen. It is a misdemeanor if the child is over sixteen. W. VA. CODE ANN. § 61-8D-5 (enacted 1988).

WISCONSIN: Incest is a felony. A person commits incest by having sexual intercourse with a blood relative by the whole or half blood nearer of kin than second cousins, though sexual intercourse between first cousins where the woman has attained the age of fifty-five or where either party can show by a physician's affidavit that one party is sterile are excepted. WIS. STAT. ANN. §§ 944.06 (enacted 1858),

765.03 (enacted 1849). Incest with a child is also a felony consisting of having sexual intercourse or sexual contact with a child one knows is related, either by blood or adoption, and the child is related in a degree of kinship closer than second cousins. One can also be convicted of incest with a child if one is responsible for the child's welfare and has knowledge that another person intends to or did commit incest with the child and one is physically and emotionally capable of taking action to prevent the harm and fails to take action and that failure exposes the child to an unreasonable risk of incest. WIS. STAT. ANN. § 948.06 (enacted 1987).

WYOMING: Incest is a felony. A person commits incest by knowingly engaging in sexual intrusion or sexual contact with an ancestor, descendant, brother or sister of the whole or half blood, including parents and children by adoption, blood relationships without regard to legitimacy, and stepparent and stepchild. WYO. STAT. § 6-4-402 (enacted 1982). It is a felony to engage in sexual penetration or sexual contact where the offender is a parent or relative who, by reason of the position, is able to exercise significant influence over the victim. WYO. STAT. §§ 6-2-301 (enacted 1982), 6-2-303 (enacted 1982), 6-2-305 (enacted 1982).

UNITED STATES: Whoever knowingly transports, or knowingly persuades, induces, entices, or coerces any individual to travel in interstate or foreign commerce, or in any territory or possession of the United States, with intent that such individual engage in any sexual activity for which any person can be charged with a criminal offense, shall be guilty of a felony. 18 U.S.C.A. §§ 2421 (enacted 1948), 2422 (enacted 1948).

11
Bigamy

Technically, bigamy is the state of being married to two people at once. Three makes it trigamy, and so forth, but the statutes generally use "bigamy" to refer to any marriage other than a monogamous one, and the term connotes illegality. Polygamy refers to the practice of having multiple spouses, whether in the form of polygyny—multiple wives—or polyandry—multiple husbands. Most states do not distinguish between the concepts of bigamy and polygamy, punishing all plural marriages as bigamy.

All state codes contain restrictions on who may receive a marriage license: for example, individuals below a specified age, siblings, couples of the same sex, or individuals who are already married to someone else usually may not obtain a license. Individuals who are barred from receiving a legitimate marriage license but attempt to contract a marriage anyway will find the marriage either void or voidable. But bigamy, like incest, is also punishable as a crime. In the vast majority of states, bigamy is a felony carrying a substantial maximum prison sentence.

Bigamy was criminalized by statute in England in 1603, and had been punished by ecclesiastical courts before that time. It has been a criminal offense in this country throughout its history. The historical reasons for criminalizing bigamy were religious ones; Christianity, unlike Islam, for example, condemns plural marriage. Within the United States, the belief by nineteenth-century Mormons that polygamy was a religiously appropriate marriage form led to challenges of the bigamy statutes as infringement of the free exercise of religion. The Supreme Court rejected that contention. *Reynolds v. United States*, 98 U.S. 145 (1878); *Cleveland v. United States*, 329 U.S. 14 (1946). Christian orthodoxy cannot usually stand alone as a justification for criminal laws, and other reasons for criminalizing bigamy have been offered in recent years, while the religious objection has been recharacterized as a concern over offense to the community's moral standards. The primary other reason is the protection of the innocent third party who marries an individual without knowledge of that person's existing marriage. The bigamy prohibition has been used to protect women from confidence men who move into a town and marry without disclosing a prior marriage, only to move on to a new location after relieving each wife of her wealth. Before divorce became easily obtainable, abandoning a spouse without a formal divorce and remarrying in a new location was the easiest way to change spouses. While bigamy prosecutions are far less common today, they do occur sporadically on similar facts.

Concern over injury to the unknowing spouse cannot explain why the Model Penal Code made it a felony to engage in polygamy publicly pursuant to a claim of right, even where all parties agree to the practice, while making it only a misdemeanor to marry a second spouse without a claim of a right to engage in polygamy as a lifestyle. No state has adopted this distinction, with most treating both as the more serious felony.

Most states allow certain defenses; in particular, absence of a spouse for a certain number of years who is presumed dead, or mistaken belief in the validity of a divorce. At common law, bigamy was a strict liability crime, and these mistakes ordinarily provided no relief from prosecution. The exception, where it existed, was for spouses who were abroad for a period of years, usually seven. The statutory time span today is generally five years.

ALABAMA: It is a felony for a person with a living spouse to intentionally contract a marriage. It is a defense to bigamy that the person reasonably believed the previous marriage to be void or dissolved or that the person and the prior spouse had been living apart for five consecutive years during which time the prior spouse was not known to be alive. ALA. CODE § 13A-13-1 (enacted 1977).

ALASKA: It is a misdemeanor for a person to knowingly marry another when either is married to a third person. ALASKA STAT. § 11.51.140 (enacted 1978). A marriage is prohibited and void if either party has a husband or wife living. ALASKA STAT. § 25.05.021 (enacted 1963).

ARIZONA: A person having a spouse living commits a felony by knowingly marrying any other person. It is a defense that the spouse by the former marriage has been absent for five successive years without being known to such person within that time to be living or that a court pronounced the former marriage void, annulled, or dissolved. ARIZ. REV. STAT. ANN. §§ 13-3606, 13-3607 (enacted 1977).

ARKANSAS: It is a misdemeanor for a person, being married, to purport to marry another person. It is an affirmative defense that the person reasonably believed the prior spouse to be dead, the prior spouses lived apart for five consecutive years throughout which time the prior spouse was not known to be alive, the person reasonably believed that a court had ordered a valid termination or annulment of the prior marriage, or the person otherwise reasonably believed he or she was legally eligible to marry. ARK. CODE ANN. § 5-26-201 (enacted 1975).

CALIFORNIA: Every person with a husband or wife living, who marries any other person commits a felony. Every person who knowingly and willfully marries the husband or wife of another commits a felony. CAL. PENAL CODE §§ 281, 283, 284 (enacted 1872). It is a defense to bigamy that the spouse of the former marriage has been absent for five consecutive years without being known to the spouse within that time to be living or that a competent court has pronounced the former marriage void, annulled, or dissolved. CAL. PENAL CODE § 282 (enacted 1872).

COLORADO: It is a felony for any married person to marry or cohabit with someone else. It is an affirmative defense that the accused believed the prior spouse to be dead, the prior spouse had been continually absent for five years during which time the accused did not know the prior spouse to be alive, or the accused reasonably believed he or she was legally eligible to remarry. COLO. REV. STAT. ANN. § 18-6-201 (enacted 1971). It is a misdemeanor for an unmarried person to knowingly marry or cohabit with another under circumstances where the unmarried person knows the other person would be guilty of bigamy. COLO. REV. STAT. ANN. §§ 18-6-202, 18-6-203 (enacted 1971).

CONNECTICUT: It is a felony for a person to marry another if either is lawfully married. It is an affirmative defense that the actor reasonably believed that the prior spouse was dead, a court purported to terminate or annul any prior marriage and the actor did not know that the judgment was invalid, or the single person did not know that the other person was legally married. CONN. GEN. STAT. § 53a-190 (enacted 1969).

DELAWARE: It is a felony for a person to contract a marriage with another person knowing either person has a living spouse. DEL. CODE. ANN. tit. 11, § 1001 (enacted 1953). It is a defense that the accused believed, after diligent inquiry, that the prior spouse was dead, the former spouses lived apart for seven consecutive years throughout which the accused had no reasonable grounds to believe that the prior spouse was alive, a court purported to terminate or annul the prior marriage and the accused did not know that judgment was invalid, or the accused otherwise reasonably believed he or she was legally eligible to remarry. DEL. CODE. ANN. tit. 11, § 1002 (enacted 1953).

DISTRICT OF COLUMBIA: It is a felony for anyone having a husband or wife living to marry another. It is a defense that a person's husband or wife has been continually absent for five successive years without being known to such person to be living within that time, or a court has dissolved the prior marriage or declared the marriage void. D.C. CODE ANN. § 22-601 (enacted 1901).

FLORIDA: It is a felony for anyone having a husband or wife living to marry another person. FLA. STAT. § 826.01 (enacted 1868). It is a defense that the person reasonably believes that the prior spouse is dead; the prior spouse has deserted the person and remained absent for three years continuously, and the moving party does not know the other to be living within that time; the bonds of matrimony have been dissolved, a court has entered an invalid judgment purporting to terminate or annul the prior marriage and the defendant does not know that judgment to be invalid; or the defendant reasonably believes he or she is legally eligible to remarry. FLA. STAT. § 826.02 (enacted 1868). A person who knowingly marries the husband or wife of another person, knowing him or her to be the spouse of another person commits a felony. FLA. STAT. § 826.03 (enacted 1832).

GEORGIA: A person commits a felony by marrying or cohabiting with another person while being married and knowing the prior spouse to be alive. It is an affirmative defense that the prior spouse has been continually absent for seven years, during which time the accused did not know the prior spouse to be alive, or that the accused reasonably believed he or she was eligible to remarry. GA. CODE ANN. § 16-6-20 (enacted 1833).

HAWAII: A person commits a petty misdemeanor by intentionally marrying, knowing that he or she is legally ineligible to do so. HAW. REV. STAT. § 709-900 (enacted 1972).

IDAHO: Every person having a husband or wife living, who marries any other person, commits a felony. IDAHO CODE §§ 18-1101, 18-1103 (enacted 1972). It is a defense that the prior spouse has been absent for five successive years without being known to be living or a competent court pronounced the former marriage void, annulled, or dissolved. IDAHO CODE § 18-1102 (enacted 1972). Every person who knowingly and willfully marries the husband or wife of another commits a felony. IDAHO CODE § 18-1104 (enacted 1972).

ILLINOIS: Any person having a husband or wife who subsequently marries another or cohabits after such marriage commits a felony. It is an affirmative defense that the prior marriage was dissolved or declared invalid, the accused reasonably believed the prior spouse to be dead, the prior spouse had been continually absent for five years during which time the accused did not know the prior spouse to be alive, or the accused reasonably believed he or she was legally eligible to remarry. ILL. REV. STAT. ch. 720, para. 5/11-12 (enacted 1961). It is a misdemeanor for any unmarried person to knowingly marry or cohabit with another knowing circumstances that would render the other guilty of bigamy. ILL. REV. STAT. ch. 720, para. 5/11-13 (enacted 1961).

INDIANA: A person who, being married and knowing that the prior spouse is alive, marries again commits a felony. It is a defense that the accused reasonably believed that he or she was eligible to remarry. IND. CODE § 35-46-1-2 (enacted 1976).

IOWA: It is a serious misdemeanor for any person, having a living husband or wife, to marry another, or for any person to marry another who the person knows has a living husband or wife. It is a defense that the prior marriage was terminated or the person reasonably believes that it was terminated, the person believes that the prior spouse is dead, or the person had no evidence for three years that the prior spouse is alive. IOWA CODE § 726.1 (enacted 1976).

KANSAS: It is a felony for any person who has a living spouse to marry or cohabit or for an unmarried person to marry or cohabit with a person known by the unmarried person to be the spouse of some other person. It is a defense that the accused reasonably believed the prior marriage had been dissolved by death, divorce, or annulment. KAN. STAT. ANN. § 21-3601 (enacted 1969).

KENTUCKY: A person who purports to marry or cohabits with another person knowing he or she has a husband or wife or knowing the other person has a husband or wife commits a felony. It is a defense that the accused believed he or she was legally eligible to remarry. KY. REV. STAT. ANN. § 530.010 (enacted 1974).

LOUISIANA: A person commits a felony in the marriage to or habitual cohabitation with another person who is already married and having a living husband or wife. It is a defense that the former husband or wife has been absent for five successive years without being known to such person to be living, the former marriage has been annulled or dissolved by a competent court, or the person has a reasonable and honest belief that his or her former husband or wife is dead, a valid divorce or annulment has been secured, or that his or her former marriage was invalid. LA. REV. STAT. ANN. § 14:76 (enacted 1942).

MAINE: It is a misdemeanor for a person, having a spouse, to intentionally marry or purport to marry, knowing that he or she is legally ineligible to do so. ME. REV. STAT. ANN. tit. 17-A, § 551 (enacted 1975).

MARYLAND: It is a felony for any individual, while lawfully married to a living individual, to enter into a marriage ceremony with another individual. It is a defense that the prior spouse has been absent for seven continuous years and the person does not know whether or not the spouse is living. MD. ANN. CODE art. 27, § 18 (enacted 1706).

MASSACHUSETTS: Any person, having a former husband or wife living, who marries another person or continues to cohabit with a second husband or wife commits a felony. It is a defense that the prior husband or wife has continually remained beyond sea, or has voluntarily withdrawn from the other and remained absent, for seven consecutive years, during which time the person did not know the other to be living, or there has been a legal divorce. MASS. GEN. L. ch. 272, § 15 (enacted 1694).

MICHIGAN: Any person who has a former husband or wife living, who marries another person, or cohabits with such second husband or wife, commits a felony. It is a defense that the prior spouse remained beyond the sea or voluntarily withdrew himself or herself from the other and remained absent for five years while the party remarrying did not know the other to be living, or that the person has good reason to believe such husband or wife to be dead, or that the person has been legally divorced. MICH. COMP. LAWS § 750.439 (enacted 1931). Any person who knowingly enters into a marriage with another to whom marriage is prohibited by statute commits a felony. MICH. COMP. LAWS § 750.440 (enacted 1931).

MINNESOTA: A person who contracts a marriage in this state knowingly having a prior marriage that is not dissolved or a person who contracts a marriage with another with knowledge that the prior marriage of the other is not dissolved commits a felony. Marriage of another outside the state with knowledge that either of the parties has a prior marriage that has not been dissolved and then living together under the representation or appearance of being married is also a felony. MINN. STAT. § 609.355 (enacted 1963).

MISSISSIPPI: Every person having a husband or wife living, who shall marry again, and every unmarried person who shall knowingly marry the husband or wife of another living person, commits a felony. MISS. CODE ANN. § 97-29-13 (enacted 1848). It is a defense that the prior husband or wife has been absent for seven successive years, without being known by the accused to be living, that the prior husband or wife absented himself or herself from his or her husband or wife and remained outside the United States for seven continuous years, that the former marriage has been dissolved by a competent court, unless the court decree provides that such person is not at liberty to marry again, that the former marriage was pronounced annulled or void by a competent court. MISS. CODE ANN. § 97-29-15 (enacted 1848).

MISSOURI: It is a misdemeanor for a married person to purport to contract another marriage or cohabit in the state after a bigamous marriage in another jurisdiction. It is a defense for a married person that the accused reasonably believes that he or she is legally eligible to remarry. It is a misdemeanor for an unmarried person to purport to contract marriage knowing that the other person is married or to cohabit in this state after a bigamous marriage in another jurisdiction. MO. REV. STAT. § 568.010 (enacted 1977).

MONTANA: A person who knowingly contracts or purports to contract another marriage while married commits a misdemeanor. It is a defense that the offender believes on reasonable grounds that the prior spouse is dead, the offender and the prior spouse have been living apart for five consecutive years throughout which the prior spouse was not known by the offender to be alive, a court purported to terminate or annul any prior disqualifying marriage and the offender does not know that judgment to be invalid, or the offender reasonably believes that he or she is legally eligible to remarry. MONT. CODE ANN. § 45-5-611 (enacted 1973). A person who contracts or purports to contract a marriage with another knowing that the other is committing bigamy commits a misdemeanor. MONT. CODE ANN. § 45-5-612 (enacted 1973).

NEBRASKA: It is a misdemeanor for any married person, having a husband or wife living, to marry any other person or for any unmarried person to knowingly marry a person who is married. It is an affirmative defense that the accused reasonably believes that the prior spouse is dead, the prior spouse had been continually absent for five years during which time the accused did not know the prior spouse to be alive, or the accused reasonably believed that he or she was legally eligible to remarry. NEB. REV. STAT. § 28-701 (enacted 1977).

NEVADA: If any married person marries any other person while the former husband or wife is alive or cohabits in this state after a second marriage has taken place out of state, the person commits a felony. It is a defense that the prior spouse has been continually absent for five years prior to the second marriage, if the offender did not know the prior husband or wife to be living within that time, or that the person is divorced or the former marriage has been declared void by lawful authority. NEV. REV. STAT. § 201.160 (enacted 1911). It is a felony for any unmarried person to knowingly marry the husband or wife of another. NEV. REV. STAT. § 201.170 (enacted 1911).

NEW HAMPSHIRE: It is a felony for a person, having a spouse and knowing that he or she is not legally eligible to marry, to marry another. N.H. REV. STAT. ANN. § 639:1 (enacted 1971).

NEW JERSEY: A married person commits a misdemeanor by contracting or purporting to contract another marriage. The other party to the marriage commits a misdemeanor by contracting or purporting to contract marriage with another knowing that the other is thereby committing bigamy. It is a defense that the actor and the prior spouse had been living apart for five consecutive years throughout which the prior spouse was not known by the actor to be alive, a court purported to terminate or annul any prior disqualifying marriage and the actor does not know that judgment to be invalid, or the actor reasonably believes that he or she is eligible to remarry. N.J. REV. STAT. § 2C:24-1 (enacted 1978).

NEW MEXICO: It is a felony to knowingly enter into a marriage by or with a person who has previously contracted one or more marriages which have not been dissolved by death, divorce, or annulment. N.M. STAT. ANN. § 30-10-1 (enacted 1953).

NEW YORK: A person commits a felony when he or she contracts or purports to contract a marriage with another person when he or she or the other person has a living spouse. N.Y. PENAL LAW § 255.15 (enacted 1965). It is a defense that the defendant acted under reasonable belief that both he or she and the other person to the marriage were unmarried. N.Y. PENAL LAW § 255.20 (enacted 1965).

NORTH CAROLINA: If any person, being married, marries any other person during the life of the former husband or wife, the offender and every person counseling, aiding, or abetting the offender commits a felony. Any married person also commits a felony by marrying any other person outside of the state and thereafter cohabitting with such person in this state. It is a defense that the prior husband or wife has been continually absent from such person for seven years and is not known by such person to be living within that time, that such person is lawfully divorced, or that the former marriage has been declared void by a competent court. N.C. GEN. STAT. § 14-183 (enacted 1790).

NORTH DAKOTA: It is a felony for a person to marry while married to another person. It is a defense that the prior spouse has been absent for five successive years and is believed by the spouse to be dead, the prior spouse voluntarily absented himself or herself and has remained outside the United States continually for five successive years, or the marriage has been pronounced void, annulled, or dissolved by a competent court. N.D. CENT. CODE § 12.1-20-13 (enacted 1973).

OHIO: It is a misdemeanor for a married person to marry another or continue to cohabit with such other person. It is an affirmative defense that the prior spouse was continuously absent for five years immediately preceding the subsequent marriage and was not known by the spouse to be alive. OHIO REV. CODE ANN. § 2919.01 (enacted 1974).

OKLAHOMA: Every person, having been married to another who remains living, who marries any other person commits a felony. OKLA. STAT. tit. 21, §§ 881, 883 (enacted 1910). It is a defense that the prior husband or wife has been absent for five successive years without being known to be living within that time, the prior husband or wife has absented himself or herself from the spouse and has been continually outside the United States for five years together, a competent court has pronounced the former marriage to be void, annulled, or dissolved, or the prior husband or wife has been sentenced to imprisonment for life.

OKLA. STAT. tit. 21, § 882 (enacted 1910). Every person who knowingly marries the husband or wife of another, in any case where such husband or wife would be punishable for bigamy, commits a felony. OKLA. STAT. tit. 21, § 884 (enacted 1910).

OREGON: It is a felony for a person to knowingly marry or purport to marry another person at a time when either is lawfully married. OR. REV. STAT. § 163.515 (enacted 1971).

PENNSYLVANIA: It is a misdemeanor for a married person to contract or purport to contract another marriage. It is a defense that the actor believes the prior spouse is dead, the actor and the prior spouse have been living apart for two consecutive years and the prior spouse was not known by the actor to be alive, or a court purported to terminate or annul any prior disqualifying marriage and the actor does not know that judgment to be invalid. A person also commits a misdemeanor if he or she contracts or purports to contract marriage with another knowing that the other is thereby committing bigamy. 18 PA. CONS. STAT. ANN. § 4301 (enacted 1972).

RHODE ISLAND: Every person, having a former husband or wife living, commits a misdemeanor by marrying another or cohabiting with another as husband and wife. It is a defense that the prior husband or wife was continually out of the state for seven years together and the spouse did not know the other to be living within that time, the person was divorced at the time of the second marriage, or the prior marriage was made when the man was less than fourteen and the woman less than twelve years of age. R.I. GEN. LAWS § 11-6-1 (enacted 1896).

SOUTH CAROLINA: It is a felony for any person who is married to marry another person. It is a defense that the prior spouse has remained beyond the sea or continually absented himself or herself for seven years and the spouse did not know whether he or she was living within that time, the prior marriage took place before the age of consent, the prior spouse is under sentence of imprisonment for life, the former marriage has been annulled, or the prior spouses have been divorced by a competent tribunal. S.C. CODE ANN. § 16-15-10 (enacted 1962).

SOUTH DAKOTA: It is a felony for any person, having been married to another person presently living, to marry any other person. It is a defense that the prior spouse has been absent for five successive years without being known by the spouse to be living, the prior spouse has absented himself or herself from the spouse by being outside the

United States continuously for five years, or the previous marriage has been pronounced void, annulled, or dissolved by a competent court. S.D. CODIFIED LAWS § 22-22-15 (enacted 1877).

TENNESSEE: It is a misdemeanor for a person who is married to purport to marry a person other than his or her spouse and for a person who knows that a person other than his or her spouse is married to purport to marry such person. It is a defense that the person reasonably believed that the marriage had been dissolved by death, divorce, or annulment. TENN. CODE ANN. § 39-15-301 (enacted 1989).

TEXAS: It is a misdemeanor for a legally married person to purport to marry or marry a person other than his or her spouse or live with a person other than his or her spouse under the appearance of being married. It is also a misdemeanor for a person who knows that a person is married to purport to marry that person or live with that person under the appearance of being married. It is a defense that the actor reasonably believed that his or her marriage was void or had been dissolved by death, divorce, or annulment. TEX. CODE ANN. § 25.01 (enacted 1973).

UTAH: A person, knowing he or she has a husband or wife or knowing the other person has a husband or wife, who purports to marry that person or cohabit with that person commits a felony. It is a defense that the accused reasonably believed he or she and the other person were legally eligible to remarry. UTAH CODE ANN. § 76-7-101 (enacted 1953).

VERMONT: It is a felony for a person having a husband or wife living to marry another person or to continue to cohabit with such second husband or wife. It is a defense that the prior spouse has been continually beyond the sea or out of the state for seven consecutive years and the party marrying again does not know the other to be living at that time, or the former marriage has been avoided by divorce or annulled, or was contracted under the age of consent and not afterwards assented to. VT. STAT. ANN. tit. 13, § 206 (enacted 1971).

VIRGINIA: It is a felony for any person, being married, to marry another person during the life of the first husband or wife or to cohabit with such other person. VA. CODE ANN. § 18.2-362 (enacted 1950). It is a defense that the prior husband or wife has been continually absent for seven years and is not known by the spouse to be living within that time, the second marriage was contracted in good faith under a reasonable belief that the former spouse was dead, or the former marriage was ended through divorce or was void. VA. CODE ANN. § 18.2-364 (enacted 1950).

WASHINGTON: It is a felony for a person to intentionally marry or purport to marry another person when either person has a living spouse. It is a defense that the actor reasonably believed that the prior spouse was dead, a court purported to terminate or annul the prior marriage and the actor did not know that the judgment was invalid, or the actor reasonably believed that he or she was legally eligible to marry. WASH. REV. CODE § 9A.64.010 (enacted 1975).

WEST VIRGINIA: Any person, being married, who marries another during the life of the former husband or wife or cohabits with such other person commits a felony. W. VA. CODE § 61-8-1 (enacted 1849).

WISCONSIN: It is a felony for a person to contract a marriage or cohabit with knowledge that his or her prior marriage is not dissolved, or to contract a marriage or cohabit with knowledge that the prior marriage of the person he or she marries or lives with under the representation or appearance of being married is not dissolved. WIS. STAT. § 944.05 (enacted 1849).

WYOMING: It is a felony for a person, being married and knowing that his or her spouse is alive, to marry again. It is a defense that the accused person reasonably believed that he or she was eligible to remarry. WYO. STAT. § 6-4-401 (enacted 1982).

UNITED STATES: Any immigrant who is coming to the United States to practice polygamy is excluded. The alien may be admitted temporarily as a nonimmigrant at the discretion of the Attorney General. 8 U.S.C. § 1182 (enacted 1984).

12

Prostitution

For reasons set forth in the Introduction, operating a house of prostitution or a prostitution enterprise, or permitting property to be used for prostitution, are outside of the scope of this book. We confine ourselves to statutes regulating the activites of prostitutes and their patrons. Most statutes call people prostitutes who engage in prostitution; we have adopted the same convention.

At English common law it was a crime to streetwalk for the purpose of solicitation, but an act of prostitution itself was not a crime. Throughout the twentieth century in the United States, all states have criminalized prostitution in some format, although Nevada delegates the authority to regulate or prohibit prostitution to county governments.

Of the many reasons, both old and new, put forward for prohibiting prostitution, the Model Penal Code emphasizes disease prevention as the primary goal. Other reasons have included suppressing the organized crime surrounding prostitution, protecting the integrity of the family, protecting nonparticipants from unwelcome solicitations, protecting prostitutes from physical abuse, and protecting minors who are coerced into a life of prostitution. The criminalization of prostitution has become controversial in recent years, but the controversy appears not to have led to any changes in state law.

In every state the criminal prohibitions on prostitution extend to a number of crimes surrounding prostitution itself. The norm is to treat pimping (sometimes for female prostitutes only) and pandering more severely than engaging in prostitution. This reflects the Model Penal Code's stated focus on the organizational structures of prostitution as the source of harm rather than individual acts of prostitution.

Some statutes criminalize either the solicitation by a prostitute or the tenancy of the prostitute in a house of prostitution, rather than the act of prostitution itself. This removes from the scope of criminal prohibition any exchanges transacted entirely in private, and incorporates the view of the Model Penal Code drafters that such conduct is of less concern to the public than solicitation. Where the definition of prostitution requires that a person engage in sexual activity as a business, the drafters intended that a single exchange of sex for money would not be adequate to complete the offense; rather, a pattern of prostitution activity would need to be proved.

Many states treat prostitution and patronizing a prostitute with the same severity, but many others do not treat patronizing a prostitute as severely as prostitution. In some states, patronizing a prostitute is a trivial offense that has been criminalized for ease of law enforcement; criminalizing the patron allows police to arrest everyone in a raid on a house of prostitution. Almost all states that criminalize the activities of patrons have done so only in the past forty years.

Prostitution statutes have been challenged in the courts on numerous occasions on the theory that they violate the constitutional right to privacy articulated in *Griswold v. Connecticut*, 381 U.S. 479 (1965); all such challenges have failed.

Prostitution statutes have also been challenged on the ground that they are so vague as to violate due process of law. Those challenges have been unsuccessful in most courts. However, a few prostitution statutes have been struck down as unconstitutionally vague, in particular where the law proscribed "immoral acts" without a definition of the acts, or prohibited "wrongful following."

Statutes prohibiting solicitation have been challenged on First Amendment grounds, with defendants arguing that their right to suggest sexual activity to passersby is protected by the free speech clause. These challenges have been unsuccessful.

ALABAMA: Prostitution is a loitering offense; loitering includes remaining in a public place for the purpose of engaging or soliciting another person to engage in prostitution or deviate sexual intercourse. It is a misdemeanor. ALA. CODE § 13A-11-9 (enacted 1975). Advancing prostitution means acting other than as a prostitute or patron and causing or aiding a person to engage in prostitution. Profiting from prostitution means acting other than as a prostitute and receiving money or other property pursuant to an understanding with any person whereby the offender is to participate in the proceeds of prostitution. ALA. CODE § 13A-12-110 (enacted 1975). It is a misdemeanor to advance or profit from prostitution generally. ALA. CODE § 13A-12-113 (enacted

1975). It is a felony to advance prostitution by compelling a person by force or intimidation to engage in prostitution, to profit from such coercive conduct, or to advance or profit from the prostitution of a person under sixteen. ALA. CODE § 13A-12-111 (enacted 1975).

ALASKA: Prostitution is agreeing to, offering to engage in, or engaging in sexual conduct for a fee. It is a misdemeanor. ALASKA STAT. § 11.66.100 (enacted 1978). It is a misdemeanor to induce or cause a person of at least sixteen years of age to engage in prostitution, or as other than a prostitute to receive or agree to receive money or property pursuant to an understanding that the money or property is derived from prostitution. ALASKA STAT. § 11.66.130 (enacted 1978). It is a felony to induce or cause a person to engage in prostitution through the use of force; acting other than as a prostitute or patron, to induce or cause a person under the age of sixteen to engage in prostitution; or to induce or cause a person in the offender's legal custody to engage in prostitution. ALASKA STAT. § 11.66.110 (enacted 1978).

ARIZONA: It is a misdemeanor to be an employee of a house of prostitution or prostitution enterprise. ARIZ. REV. STAT. ANN. § 13-3208 (enacted 1978). It is a felony to compel, induce, or encourage any person to reside with another person for the purpose of prostitution or to lead a life of prostitution. ARIZ. REV. STAT. ANN. §§ 13-3208 (enacted 1978), 13-3209 (enacted 1978). It is a felony to transport any person for the purpose of prostitution. ARIZ. REV. STAT. ANN. § 13-3210 (enacted 1978). It is a felony to knowingly entice a person or receive a thing of value for procuring a person to enter into a house of prostitution or elsewhere for the purpose of prostitution. ARIZ. REV. STAT. ANN. §§ 13-3201 (enacted 1978), 13-3203 (enacted 1978). It is a felony to receive money or a thing of value from the earnings of a prostitute. ARIZ. REV. STAT. ANN. § 13-3204 (enacted 1978). It is a felony to cause one's spouse by force, fraud, intimidation, or threat to become a prostitute. ARIZ. REV. STAT. ANN. § 13-3205 (enacted 1978). It is a felony for a person to procure another person for illicit carnal relations by fraudulent means, false pretenses, or false representations. ARIZ. REV. STAT. ANN. § 13-3203 (enacted 1978). It is a felony to detain a person in a house of prostitution because of debt. ARIZ. REV. STAT. ANN. § 13-3207 (enacted 1978).

It is a felony to take any minor away from his or her parents for the purpose of prostitution. ARIZ. REV. STAT. ANN. § 13-3206 (enacted 1978). There is a separate statute for child prostitution creating higher felonies for the following crimes: causing any minor to engage in prostitution; using a minor for the purposes of prostitution; permitting a minor under such person's custody to engage in prostitution; receiving any benefit from child prostitution; and transporting or financing the transportation of a minor for the purpose of prostitution. ARIZ. REV. STAT. ANN. § 13-3212 (enacted 1978).

ARKANSAS: It is a misdemeanor to engage in or to offer or agree to engage in sexual activity with another person for a fee. ARK. CODE ANN. § 5-70-102 (enacted 1975). It is a lesser misdemeanor to pay or agree to pay a person to engage in sexual activity or to solicit or request a person to do the same. ARK. CODE ANN. § 5-70-103 (enacted 1975).

A person advances prostitution if acting other than as a prostitute or patron the offender engages in any conduct designed to institute, aid, or facilitate an act or enterprise of prostitution. A person profits from prostitution if, acting other than as a prostitute, the offender accepts or receives anything of value pursuant to an understanding that the offender is participating in the proceeds of prostitution. ARK. CODE ANN. § 5-70-101 (enacted 1975). It is a felony to advance or profit from the prostitution of a person under eighteen; or to advance prostitution by compelling a person by physical force or intimidation to engage in prostitution or to profit from such coercive conduct by others. ARK. CODE ANN. § 5-70-104 (enacted 1975). It is a misdemeanor to advance or profit from prostitution. ARK. CODE ANN. §§ 5-70-105 (enacted 1975), 5-70-106 (enacted 1975).

CALIFORNIA: It is a misdemeanor to solicit, agree to engage in, or engage in any act of prostitution. CAL. PENAL CODE § 647(b) (enacted 1961). It is a felony if upon a previous conviction the defendant tested positive for AIDS. CAL. PENAL CODE § 647f (enacted 1988). It is a misdemeanor to inveigle or entice any unmarried female of previous chaste character under eighteen into any house of ill fame or elsewhere for the purpose of prostitution, or to aid or assist such inveiglement or enticement. CAL. PENAL CODE § 266 (enacted 1872).

Pandering is a felony. A person is guilty of pandering who: procures another person for the purpose of prostitution; by promises, threats, violence or by any other device or scheme, causes, induces, persuades, or encourages another person to become a prostitute; procures for another person a place as inmate in a house of prostitution or any place in which prostitution is encouraged or allowed; by promises, threats, violence or by any device or scheme causes, induces, persuades, or encourages an inmate of any place of prostitution to remain therein as an inmate; by fraud or artifice, or by duress of another person for the purpose of prostitution or for a place of prostitution, procures or attempts to procure another person for the purpose of prostitution. CAL. PENAL CODE § 266I (enacted 1953). It is a felony to take a person under eighteen from the parents, guardian, or other person having legal charge of the minor, without their consent, for the purpose of prostitution. CAL. PENAL CODE § 267 (enacted 1872).

COLORADO: Prostitution is defined as performing, offering, or agreeing to perform any act of sexual intercourse, fellatio, cunnilingus, masturbation, or anal intercourse in exchange for anything of value. It is a misdemeanor. COLO. REV. STAT. § 18-7-201 (enacted 1971). It is a petty offense to patronize a prostitute, meaning to engage in an act of sexual intercourse or deviate sexual conduct with a prostitute, or enter or remain in a place of prostitution with the intent to engage in the same. COLO. REV. STAT. § 18-7-205 (enacted 1971). It is a misdemeanor to solicit another person for prostitution; arrange or offer to arrange a meeting of persons for the purpose of prostitution; arrange or offer to arrange a situation in which a person may practice prostitution; or direct another to a place for prostitution. COLO. REV. STAT. §§ 18-7-202 (enacted 1971), 18-7-203 (enacted 1971). It is a petty offense to endeavor to further the practice of prostitution within public view by word, gesture or action. COLO. REV. STAT. § 18-7-207 (enacted 1971).

It is a felony offense to engage in prostitution or to patronize a prostitute with the knowledge that the offender has HIV. COLO. REV. STAT. §§ 18-7-201.7 (enacted 1990), 18-7-205.7 (enacted 1990). It is a felony to pander by inducing a person by menacing or criminal intimidation to commit prostitution. COLO. REV. STAT. § 18-7-203 (enacted 1971). It is a felony to pimp by deriving support from money or other things of value earned or realized by another person through prostitution. COLO. REV. STAT. § 18-7-206 (enacted 1971). It is a felony to solicit, procure, pimp, or pander for the prostitution of a person under eighteen, or to induce such a person to engage in prostitution, or to patronize such a prostitute. COLO. REV. STAT. §§ 18-7-402 (enacted 1979), 18-7-403 (enacted 1979), 18-7-403.5 (enacted 1983), 18-7-404 (enacted 1979), 18-7-405 (enacted 1979), 18-7-405.5 (enacted 1981), 18-7-406 (enacted 1979).

CONNECTICUT: Prostitution is agreeing to engage in or engaging in sexual conduct in return for a fee. CONN. GEN. STAT. ANN. § 53a-82 (enacted 1969). Patronizing a prostitute means paying or offering to pay or requesting to pay a fee to another person for a person to engage in sexual conduct. CONN. GEN. STAT. ANN. § 53a-83 (enacted 1969). Both are misdemeanors. In both cases, the sex of the parties is immaterial. CONN. GEN. STAT. ANN. § 53a-84 (enacted 1969).

Advancing prostitution means acting other than as a prostitute or patron and causing or aiding a person to engage in prostitution; procuring or soliciting patrons for prostitution; or engaging in any conduct designed to institute, aid, or facilitate prostitution. Profiting from prostitution means acting other than as a prostitute and receiving money or other property pursuant to an understanding with any person whereby the offender is to participate in the proceeds of prostitution. CONN. GEN. STAT. ANN. § 53a-85 (enacted 1969). It is a felony to advance or profit from prostitution. CONN. GEN. STAT. ANN. § 53a-88 (enacted 1969).

DELAWARE: Prostitution is engaging in, agreeing to, or offering to engage in sexual conduct with another person in return for a fee. DEL. CODE ANN. tit. 11, § 1342 (enacted 1953). Patronizing a prostitute means agreeing to pay or paying a fee to a person pursuant to an understanding that in return that person will engage in sexual conduct with the patron; or soliciting or requesting another person to engage in sexual conduct for a fee. DEL. CODE ANN. tit. 11, § 1343 (enacted 1953). If the defendant has a previous conviction for patronizing a prostitute within the previous five years and a vehicle has been used in connection with the subsequent offense, it shall be seized and taken into custody. DEL. CODE ANN. tit. 11, § 1343 (enacted 1953). Both prostitution and patronizing a prostitute are misdemeanors.

It is a felony to knowingly advance or profit from prostitution. DEL. CODE ANN. tit. 11, §§ 1351 (enacted 1953), 1352 (enacted 1953), 1353 (enacted 1953). A person advances prostitution when acting other than as a prostitute or patron, he or she: causes or aids a person to commit or engage in prostitution; procures or solicits patrons for prostitution; provides persons for prostitution; or engages in any other activity designed to institute, aid, or facilitate an act or enterprise of prostitution. DEL. CODE ANN. tit. 11, § 1356 (enacted 1953). A person profits from prostitution when acting other than as a prostitute, he or she accepts or receives money or property pursuant to an agreement to receive proceeds from prostitution. DEL. CODE ANN. tit. 11, § 1356 (enacted 1953).

DISTRICT OF COLUMBIA: It is a misdemeanor to invite, entice, persuade, or address for the purpose of inviting, enticing, or persuading any person or persons for the purpose of prostitution or any other immoral or lewd purposes. Inviting, enticing, or persuading includes, but is not limited to: repeatedly beckoning to, stopping, attempting to stop, or attempting to engage passers-by in conversation for the purpose of prostitution; stopping or attempting to stop motor vehicles for the purpose of prostitution; or repeatedly interfering with the free passage of other persons for the purpose of prostitution. D.C. CODE § 22-2701 (enacted 1935).

"Prostitution" means the engaging, agreeing to engage, or offering to engage in sexual acts or contacts with a person in exchange for a fee. "Arranging for prostitution" means any act to procure or attempt to procure or otherwise arrange for the purpose of prostitution, regardless of whether such procurement or arrangement occurred or a fee was paid. D.C. CODE § 22-2701.1 (enacted 1981). It is a felony to arrange for prostitution, or to accept, receive, levy, or appropriate any money or other valuable thing, without consideration other than the furnishing of a place for prostitution or the servicing of a place for prostitution, from the proceeds or earnings of any female engaged in prostitution. D.C. CODE §§ 22-2707 (enacted 1910), 22-2710 (enacted 1910), 22-2711 (enacted 1910), 22-2712 (enacted 1910).

It is a felony to place or cause, induce, procure, or compel the placing of any female in the charge or custody of any other person, with intent that she shall engage in prostitution. D.C. CODE § 22-2705 (enacted 1910). It is a felony to cause any female, including one's wife, to live a life of prostitution against her will. D.C. CODE §§ 22-2706 (enacted 1910), 22-2708 (enacted 1910), 22-2709 (enacted 1910).

FLORIDA: Prostitution is offering to give or receive or giving or receiving the body for sexual activity for hire; it is a misdemeanor. FLA. STAT. ANN. § 796.07 (enacted 1943). It is a misdemeanor to solicit, induce, entice, or procure another to commit prostitution; to reside in, enter, or remain in a place for the purpose of prostitution; to aid or abet any of these acts; or to purchase the services of anyone engaged in prostitution. FLA. STAT. ANN. § 796.07 (enacted 1943). It is a misdemeanor to offer or agree to secure a person for prostitution; or to direct or transport a person or offer or agree to do the same for the purpose of prostitution. FLA. STAT. ANN. § 796.07 (enacted 1943).

Procuring a person for prostitution who is under the age of sixteen is a felony. FLA. STAT. ANN. § 796.03 (enacted 1993). Forcing, compelling, or coercing another to become a prostitute is a felony. FLA. STAT. ANN. § 796.04 (enacted 1943). It is a felony to derive support from the proceeds of another person's prostitution. FLA. STAT. ANN. § 796.05 (enacted 1993). An offender who has tested positive for HIV on a previous offense commits a separate felony, criminal transmission of HIV. FLA. STAT. ANN. § 775.0877 (enacted 1993). A person who knows he or she has tested positive for a sexually transmissible disease other than HIV and could possibly communicate such disease to another person through sexual activity and who still commits prostitution or procures another for prostitution is guilty of a misdemeanor. If the sexually transmissible disease is HIV, the crime is a felony. The offender can also be convicted and sentenced separately for the underlying crime of prostitution or procurement of prostitution. FLA. STAT. ANN. § 796.08 (enacted 1993).

GEORGIA: Prostitution means performing or offering or agreeing to perform an act of sexual intercourse for money. GA. CODE ANN. § 16-6-9 (enacted 1968). Masturbation for hire means erotically stimulating the genital organs of another by bodily contact or instrumental manipulation for money or the substantial equivalent thereof. GA. CODE ANN. § 16-6-16 (enacted 1975). It is unlawful for a masseur or masseuse to massage any person in a place used for prostitution. GA. CODE ANN. § 16-6-17 (enacted 1975). These are all ordinary misdemeanors. GA. CODE ANN. §§ 16-6-13 (enacted 1968), 16-6-16 (enacted 1975), 16-6-17 (enacted 1975). Solicitation of sodomy means soliciting another to perform or submit to an act of sodomy. It is a misdemeanor except when the person being solicited is under seventeen, in which case it is a felony. GA. CODE ANN. § 16-6-15 (enacted 1968). Pimping means offering or agreeing to procure a prostitute for another; offering or agreeing to arrange a meeting of persons for the purpose of prostitution; directing another to a place for the purpose of prostitution; receiving money or other thing of value from a prostitute without lawful consideration knowing it was earned in part from prostitution; or aiding, abetting, counseling, or commanding a person in the commission of prostitution, or aiding and assisting in prostitution where the proceeds are to be divided on a pro rata basis. GA. CODE ANN. § 16-6-11 (enacted 1968). It is a misdemeanor of a high and aggravated nature. GA. CODE ANN. § 16-6-13 (enacted 1968). Pandering means soliciting a person to perform an act of prostitution or assembling persons at a fixed place for the purpose of being solicited by others to perform acts of prostitution. GA. CODE ANN. § 16-6-12 (enacted 1968). It is also a misdemeanor of a high and aggravated nature. GA. CODE ANN. § 16-6-13 (enacted 1968).

A person convicted of pandering when such offense involves the solicitation of a person under seventeen to perform an act of prostitution or the assembly of two or more persons under seventeen at a fixed place for the purpose of being solicited by others to perform an act of prostitution shall be guilty of a felony. GA. CODE ANN. § 16-6-13 (enacted 1968). Pandering by compulsion is also a felony defined as causing a female to perform an act of prostitution by duress or coercion. GA. CODE ANN. § 16-6-14 (enacted 1968).

A person who offers or consents to perform with another person an act of sexual intercourse for money without disclosing to that other person the presence of the HIV infection prior to such acts, or solicits another person to perform or submit to sodomy for money without disclosing to that person the presence of the HIV infection prior to such acts, after obtaining knowledge of being infected with HIV commits a felony. GA. CODE ANN. § 16-5-60 (enacted 1988).

HAWAII: Prostitution means agreeing or offering to engage in or engaging in sexual conduct with another person for a fee. Prostitution is a petty misdemeanor. HAW. REV. STAT. § 712-1200 (enacted 1972). It is a misdemeanor to knowingly advance or profit from the prostitution of a person over eighteen. HAW. REV. STAT. § 712-1204 (enacted 1972). A person advances prostitution if, acting other than as a prostitute or patron of a prostitute, the offender knowingly causes or aids a person to engage in prostitution; procures or solicits patrons for prostitution; provides persons for prostitution purposes; or engages in any other conduct designed to institute, aid, or facilitate an act or enterprise of prostitution. HAW. REV. STAT. § 712-1201 (enacted 1972). A person profits from prostitution if, acting other than as a prostitute, the offender accepts or receives money or property from prostitution. HAW. REV. STAT. § 712-1201 (enacted 1972). Loitering for the purpose of prostitution occurs when a person remains or wanders about in a public place and repeatedly beckons to or repeatedly stops people, attempts to stop people, attempts to engage passersby in conversation, stops or attempts to stop motor vehicles, or interferes with the free passage of other persons. If the loitering is for the purpose of committing the crime of prostitution, the offender is guilty of a violation; if for the purpose of committing the crime of advancing prostitution, the offender is guilty of a misdemeanor. HAW. REV. STAT. § 712-1206 (enacted 1991).

It is a felony to advance or profit from the prostitution of a person under eighteen; or to advance prostitution by compelling a person by criminal coercion to engage in prostitution, or to profit from such coercive conduct by another. HAW. REV. STAT. §§ 712-1202 (enacted 1972), 712-1203 (enacted 1972).

IDAHO: Prostitution means engaging in or offering or agreeing to engage in sexual intercourse or deviate sexual intercourse with another person for a fee; any touching of the sexual organs or other intimate parts of a person not married to the actor for the purpose of arousing or gratifying the sexual desire of either party for a fee; being an inmate of a house of prostitution; or loitering in or within view of any public place for the purpose of being hired to engage in sexual contact. Prostitution is a misdemeanor for the first two offenses and a felony for the third or subsequent offense. IDAHO CODE ANN. § 18-5613 (enacted 1977). Patronizing a prostitute means entering or remaining in a house of prostitution or paying, offering, or agreeing to pay another person a fee for the purposes of engaging in an act of sexual intercourse, deviate sexual intercourse, or any touching of the sexual organs. Patronizing a prostitute is a misdemeanor for the first two offenses and a felony for the third or subsequent offense. IDAHO CODE ANN. § 18-5614 (enacted 1977).

It is a felony to import or export or induce, entice, or procure a person to enter or leave the state for the purpose of prostitution. IDAHO CODE ANN. § 18-5601 (enacted 1972). It is a felony to induce, compel, entice, or procure another person to engage in acts as a prostitute or to provide or receive money or any object of value to procure a prostitute. IDAHO CODE ANN. §§ 18-5602 (enacted 1972), 18-5603 (enacted 1972), 18-5604 (enacted 1972). Detention for prostitution is a felony meaning to hold, detain, or restrain, or attempt to hold, detain, or restrain for the purpose of compelling a person to engage in prostitution. IDAHO CODE ANN. § 18-5605 (enacted 1972). It is a felony to knowingly accept or appropriate any money or item of value from the earnings of any person engaged in prostitution as part of a joint venture. IDAHO CODE ANN. § 18-5606 (enacted 1972). It is a felony to induce or attempt to induce a person under eighteen to engage in prostitution or to patronize a prostitute. IDAHO CODE ANN. § 18-5609 (enacted 1972), 18-5611 (enacted 1972).

ILLINOIS: Prostitution means offering or agreeing to perform or performing any act of sexual penetration or touching of genitals for money or anything of value. ILL. ANN. STAT. ch. 720, para. 5/11-14 (enacted 1961). A person patronizes a prostitute by engaging in sexual penetration with a prostitute who is not that person's spouse or entering or remaining in a place of prostitution with the intent to engage in an act of sexual penetration. The patronizing statute does not mention compensation. ILL. ANN. STAT. ch. 720, para. 5/11-18 (enacted 1961). Soliciting for a prostitute means arranging or offering to arrange a meeting of persons for the purpose of prostitution or directing another for the purpose of prostitution. ILL. ANN. STAT. ch. 720, para. 5/11-15 (enacted 1961). Pimping means receiving money or other property from a prostitute without lawful consideration knowing it was earned in part from prostitution. ILL. ANN. STAT. ch. 720, para. 5/11-19 (enacted 1961). All of these offenses begin as misdemeanors for the first two convictions and become felonies on the third conviction.

Pandering means either compelling a person to become a prostitute or arranging or offering to arrange a situation in which a person may practice prostitution. Pandering is a felony. ILL. ANN. STAT. ch. 720, para. 5/11-16 (enacted 1961). It is a felony to solicit or pimp for a person under sixteen or for an institutionalized severely profoundly mentally retarded person. ILL. ANN. STAT. ch. 720, paras. 5/11-15.1 (enacted 1961), 5/11-19.1 (enacted 1961). Patronizing a prostitute under seventeen is a felony. ILL. ANN. STAT. ch. 720, para. 5/11-18.1 (enacted 1961). Pimping for a prostitute who is under sixteen or who is an institutionalized severely or profoundly mentally retarded person is a felony. ILL. ANN. STAT. ch. 720, para. 5/11-19.1 (enacted 1961). Exploitation of a child includes confining a person under sixteen or an institutionalized severely profoundly mentally retarded person by the infliction or threat of imminent infliction of great bodily harm or by administering any alcohol or drug and compelling the person to become a prostitute; arranging a situation in which the person may practice prostitution; or receiving money or property from the person knowing it was obtained in whole or in part from prostitution. Exploitation of a child is a felony. ILL. ANN. STAT. ch. 720, para. 5/11-19.2 (enacted 1961).

INDIANA: Prostitution is performing or offering or agreeing to perform sexual intercourse, deviate sexual conduct, or fondling the genitals of another person for money or other property. Patronizing a prostitute means paying or offering or agreeing to pay money or other property for the acts constituting prostitution. Both are misdemeanors for the first two offenses and become felonies on the third conviction. IND. CODE ANN. §§ 35-45-4-2 (enacted 1971), 35-45-4-3 (enacted 1976).

Promoting prostitution is a felony. Promoting prostitution means enticing or compelling another person to become a prostitute; procuring or offering or agreeing to procure a person for another person for the purpose of prostitution; receiving money or property from a prostitute without lawful consideration knowing it was earned in whole or in part from prostitution; or conducting or directing a person to a place for the purpose of prostitution. IND. CODE ANN. § 35-45-4-4 (enacted 1976).

IOWA: A person who sells or offers to sell the person's services as a partner in a sex act, or one who purchases or offers to purchase such services is guilty of prostitution, an aggravated misdemeanor. IOWA CODE ANN. § 725.1 (enacted 1976).

A person who solicits a patron for a prostitute or who shares in the earnings of a prostitute commits a felony called pimping. IOWA CODE ANN. § 725.2 (enacted 1976).

Pandering is a felony consisting of persuading, arranging, coercing, or otherwise causing a person to become a prostitute or to return to the practice of prostitution after having abandoned it. IOWA CODE ANN. § 725.3 (enacted 1976). Detention in a brothel is a felony meaning the use of force, intimidation, or false pretense to entice another who is not a prostitute to enter a brothel with the intent that the person become an inmate thereof or to detain another person against his or her will with the intent that the detainee engage in prostitution. IOWA CODE ANN. § 709.7 (enacted 1976).

KANSAS: Prostitution is performing or offering or agreeing to perform for hire sexual intercourse, sodomy, or manual or other bodily contact stimulation of the genitals with the intent to arouse. It is a misdemeanor. KAN. CRIM. CODE ANN. § 21-3512 (enacted 1969). It is a misdemeanor to enter into intercourse, sodomy, or any other unlawful act with a prostitute, or to hire a prostitute to engage in any of these acts. KAN. CRIM. CODE ANN. § 21-3515 (enacted 1969). Promoting prostitution includes procuring a prostitute for a house of prostitution; inducing another to become a prostitute; soliciting a patron for a prostitute or a house of prostitution; procuring a prostitute for a patron; procuring transportation for, paying for the transportation of, or transporting a person within the state for assisting or promoting that person's prostitution; or being employed to do any of the foregoing. Promoting prostitution is a misdemeanor if the prostitute is at least sixteen and it is the offender's first conviction for promoting prostitution. If the prostitute is under sixteen, or it is not the first conviction for promoting prostitution, the crime is a felony. KAN. CRIM. CODE ANN. §21-3513 (enacted 1969).

KENTUCKY: Prostitution means engaging in or offering or agreeing to engage in sexual conduct with another person for a fee. KY. REV. STAT. ANN. § 529.020 (enacted 1974). Loitering for prostitution purposes means remaining in a public place for the purpose of engaging or agreeing or offering to engage in prostitution. KY. REV. STAT. ANN. § 529.080 (enacted 1984). These offenses are misdemeanors, and it is not an offense to patronize a prostitute.

It is a felony to advance prostitution by compelling a person by force or intimidation to engage in prostitution or to facilitate or profit from the prostitution of a person under eighteen. KY. REV. STAT. ANN. §§ 529.030 (enacted 1986), 529.040 (enacted 1986). It is a misdemeanor to facilitate or profit from the prostitution of a person eighteen or over. KY. REV. STAT. ANN. § 529.050 (enacted 1974). It is a felony to commit, offer, or agree to commit, or procure another to commit prostitution by engaging in sexual activity in a manner likely to transmit HIV if the offender knew, prior to the commission of the crime, that he or she had tested positive for HIV and that the sexual activity could transmit HIV. A person who commits prostitution and who, prior to the commission of the crime, knew that he or she had tested positive for a sexually transmitted disease and knew that the sexual activity might transmit the disease to another person is guilty of a misdemeanor. Note that a person may be convicted and sentenced separately for this crime and for the underlying crime of prostitution. KY. REV. STAT. ANN. § 529.090 (enacted 1992).

LOUISIANA: Prostitution is the practice or solicitation of indiscriminate sexual intercourse with others for compensation. It is a misdemeanor with a mandatory jail term when it is the third such offense or if the offense occurred as a result of solicitation while the offender was on a public road, highway, sidewalk, or walkway. LA. REV. STAT. ANN. § 82 (enacted 1977). It is a misdemeanor to solicit, invite, induce, direct, or transport a person to any place with the intention of promoting prostitution. LA. REV. STAT. ANN. § 83 (enacted 1980). It is a misdemeanor to aid, abet, or assist in an enterprise for profit in which customers are charged a fee for services which include prostitution, the offender knows or reasonably should know that his or her conduct is for prostitution, and when the proceeds or profits are to be in any way divided by the prostitute and the offender. LA. REV. STAT. ANN. § 83.1 (enacted 1984). Prostitution by massage is a misdemeanor consisting of the erotic stimulation of the genital organs by any person by instrumental manipulation, touching with the hands, or other bodily contact exclusive of sexual intercourse or unnatural carnal copulation, when done for money. LA. REV. STAT. ANN. §83.3 (enacted 1984). It is also a misdemeanor for any masseur, masseuse, or any other person in a massage parlor to expose, touch, caress, or fondle the genitals, anus, or pubic hairs of any person or the nipples of the female breast or to perform any acts of sadomasochistic abuse, flagellation, or torture in the context of sexual conduct. LA. REV. STAT. ANN. § 83.4 (enacted 1984). Prostitutes and persons who live in a house of ill fame or who habitually associate with prostitutes are guilty of vagrancy. LA. REV. STAT. ANN. §107 (enacted 1952).

It is a felony for a person over seventeen to engage in sexual intercourse with a person under seventeen who is practicing prostitution where there is an age difference of greater than two years, or for any parent or tutor of any person under the age of seventeen to consent to the person's entrance or detention in the practice of prostitution. LA. REV. STAT. ANN. § 82.1 (enacted 1985). Pandering is a felony consisting of any of the following: enticing, placing, persuading, encouraging, or causing a person to enter the practice of prostitution by force, threats, promises, or any device or scheme; detaining a person in a place of prostitution by force, threats, promises, or by any other device or scheme; receiving as a substantial part of support or maintenance anything of value which is known to be from the earnings of a prostitute; consenting as a parent or tutor to a person's entrance or detention into the practice of prostitution; or transporting a person for the purpose of promoting prostitution. LA. REV. STAT. ANN. §§ 84 (enacted 1978), 86 (enacted 1978).

MAINE: It is a misdemeanor to engage in prostitution or to engage a prostitute, meaning to provide or agree to provide pecuniary benefit in return for a sexual act. It is a misdemeanor to promote prostitution, meaning to cause or aid another to become a prostitute; to publicly solicit patrons for prostitution; to provide persons for the purpose of prostitution; to transport a person for prostitution purposes; or to accept or receive, or agree to accept or receive, a pecuniary benefit pursuant to an understanding with any person other than with a patron, whereby the offender is to participate in the proceeds of prostitution.

ME. REV. STAT. ANN. tit. 17-A, §§ 851 (enacted 1975), 853 (enacted 1975), 853-A (enacted 1975), 853-B (enacted 1981).

It is a felony to promote prostitution by compelling a person to enter or remain in prostitution or to promote the prostitution of a person under eighteen. Compelling includes but is not limited to the use of a drug or intoxicating substance to render a person incapable of controlling his or her conduct or appreciating its nature or withholding or threatening to withhold a narcotic drug or alcoholic liquor from a physically or psychically drug- or alcohol-dependent person. ME. REV. STAT. ANN. tit. 17-A, § 852 (enacted 1975).

MARYLAND: Prostitution means offering or receiving the body for sexual intercourse for hire. MD. CRIM. LAW CODE ANN. § 16 (enacted 1951). It is a misdemeanor. MD. CRIM. LAW CODE ANN. §§ 15 (enacted 1951), 17 (enacted 1951). It is a misdemeanor to direct, transport, or offer to transport a person for the purpose of prostitution; to procure or solicit or offer to procure or solicit for the purpose of prostitution; or to reside or remain in a place of prostitution. MD. CRIM. LAW CODE ANN. § 15 (enacted 1951). A person is guilty of pandering who harbors, inveighs, entices, persuades, encourages, either by threat or promise, or by any device or scheme takes or places, or causes to be taken or placed, any other person to any place against his or her will, for the purpose of prostitution or illegal sexual intercourse, or being a parent or guardian of another person consents to the taking of that charge by another for the purpose of prostitution or illegal sexual intercourse. The crime of pandering also includes placing a person in a house of prostitution with the intent that that person shall live a life of prostitution or compelling a person to live with someone for the purpose of prostitution or compelling a person to live a life of prostitution. MD. CRIM. LAW CODE ANN. §§ 426 (enacted 1951), 427 (enacted 1951). Pandering carries similar penalties to the prostitution felonies below, but it is not named a felony.

It is a felony to, by force, fraud, intimidation, or threats, place or leave one's spouse in a house of prostitution, or procure another to cause one's spouse to lead a life of prostitution. MD. CRIM. LAW CODE ANN. § 429 (enacted 1951). It is a felony to receive money or any valuable thing without lawful consideration from the earnings of a person engaged in prostitution. MD. CRIM. LAW CODE ANN. § 430 (enacted 1951). It is a felony to detain a person in a house of prostitution because of any debt that person has contracted while living in the house.

MD. CRIM. LAW CODE ANN. § 431 (enacted 1951). It is a felony to transport, aid, or assist in obtaining transportation for any person for the purpose of prostitution or with the intent to induce or compel the person to become a prostitute. MD. CRIM. LAW CODE ANN. § 432 (enacted 1951).

MASSACHUSETTS: It is a misdemeanor to engage in, or to offer or agree to engage in sexual conduct with another person in return for a fee, or to pay, or agree to an offer to pay another person to engage in sexual conduct. MASS. GEN. LAWS ch. 272, § 53A (enacted 1983). It is a misdemeanor to fraudulently and deceitfully entice or take away a person for the purpose of prostitution or to aid or assist in the same. MASS. GEN. LAWS ch. 272, § 2 (enacted 1845). It is a misdemeanor to solicit or receive compensation for soliciting for a prostitute. MASS. GEN. LAWS ch. 272, § 8 (enacted 1910).

It is a felony to induce a minor to become a prostitute or aid and assist such inducement, or to live or derive support or maintenance in whole or in part from the earnings or proceeds of prostitution committed by a minor. MASS. GEN. LAWS ch. 272, §§ 4A (enacted 1979), 4B (enacted 1979). It is a felony to live on or derive support or maintenance in whole or part from the earnings or proceeds of prostitution. MASS. GEN. LAWS ch. 272, § 7 (enacted 1910). It is a felony to knowingly procure, entice, or send a person to practice prostitution or to enter as an inmate or a servant a house of prostitution or other place resorted to for prostitution, or to aid or abet in these acts. MASS. GEN. LAWS ch. 272, § 12 (enacted 1910). It is a felony for any length of time to detain or attempt to detain or provide or administer any drug or liquor for the purpose of detaining a person in a house of ill fame or other place resorted to for prostitution, or to aid or abet in these acts. MASS. GEN. LAWS ch. 272, § 13 (enacted 1888).

MICHIGAN: It is a misdemeanor to do any of the following: to accost, solicit, or invite another in any public place or in or from a vehicle or building, by word, gesture, or any other means to commit prostitution; to offer to or to receive or admit any person into any place for the purpose of prostitution or to allow such person to remain for that purpose; for any male to engage or offer to engage the services of a female not his wife for the purposes of prostitution; or to aid or abet in any of the above. MICH. COMP. LAWS ANN. §§ 750.448 (enacted 1931), 750.449 (enacted 1931), 750.449a (enacted 1931), 750.450 (enacted 1931). Third convictions for these crimes are felonies. MICH. COMP.

LAWS ANN. § 750.451 (enacted 1931). It is a misdemeanor to take or convey or suffer to remain in any house of prostitution or place of resort for prostitution any female under eighteen for any purpose other than prostitution. MICH. COMP. LAWS ANN. § 750.462 (enacted 1931).

It is a felony to do any of the following: to procure a female inmate for a house of prostitution; to induce, persuade, or encourage a female person to become a prostitute; by promise, threat, or other scheme to cause or encourage a female to become an inmate of a house of prostitution or any place where prostitution is encouraged or allowed, or to remain therein; to inveigle or encourage a female to come into this state or leave the state for the purpose of prostitution; to receive or give or agree to receive or give any money or thing of value for procuring or attempting to procure any female person to become a prostitute or to come into this state or leave this state for the purpose of prostitution; to knowingly accept, receive, or appropriate any thing of value without consideration from the proceeds of the earnings of any woman engaged in prostitution; to live or derive support or maintenance in whole or in part from the earnings or proceeds of the prostitution of a female; to detain a female in a house of prostitution because of debts she is said to have contracted while living in the house; to take or detain a female for the purpose of sexual intercourse upon the pretense of marriage; to force one's wife to lead a life of prostitution; or to transport any person for the purpose of prostitution. MICH. COMP. LAWS ANN. §§ 750.452 (enacted 1931), 750.455 (enacted 1931), 750.456 (enacted 1931), 750.457 (enacted 1931), 750.458 (enacted 1931), 750.459 (enacted 1931).

MINNESOTA: Prostitution means engaging or offering or agreeing to engage in sexual penetration or sexual contact for hire. Patronizing a prostitute means hiring or offering or agreeing to hire a person to engage in sexual penetration or sexual contact. The offenses are misdemeanors where the other party is eighteen or over and felonies where the other party is under eighteen. MINN. STAT. ANN. §§ 609.321 (enacted 1979), 609.324 (enacted 1979).

Promoting the prostitution of a person occurs where the offender solicits or procures patrons for a prostitute, or transports an individual to induce a person to practice prostitution. It is a felony to solicit or induce a person to practice prostitution or to promote prostitution. MINN. STAT. ANN. §§ 609.321 (enacted 1979), 609.322 (enacted 1979).

It is a misdemeanor for a person acting other than as a prostitute or patron to intentionally receive profit, knowing or having reason to know that it is derived from the prostitution or the promotion of the prostitution of an individual eighteen or older. MINN. STAT. ANN. § 609.323 (enacted 1979). However, it is a felony to profit from prostitution as described above under any of the following circumstances: where the prostitute is under eighteen; where the prostitute has been induced or solicited to practice prostitution by means of force; where a position of authority has been used to induce or solicit the person to practice prostitution; where the person has been induced or solicited to practice prostitution by means of trick, fraud, or deceit; or where an individual in a position of authority has consented to the prostitute being taken or detained for the purpose of prostitution. The offender must know of the circumstances making the offense a felony. These provisions do not apply to the sale of goods or services to a prostitute in the ordinary course of a lawful business. MINN. STAT. ANN. §§ 609.321 (enacted 1979), 609.322 (enacted 1979), 609.323 (enacted 1979).

MISSISSIPPI: It is a misdemeanor to do any of the following: to engage in prostitution or aid or abet prostitution or procure or solicit for the purpose of prostitution; enter or remain in any place for the purpose of prostitution; to become an inmate in a house of prostitution; to receive any person for the purpose of prostitution into any vehicle or place; to offer or agree to transport or direct a person for the purpose of prostitution; to cause a female to become a prostitute, an inmate of a house of prostitution, or to cross state lines for the purpose of prostitution; or to receive any thing of value without consideration from a prostitute or from the proceeds of prostitution. MISS. CODE ANN. §§ 97-29-49 (enacted 1942), 97-29-51 (enacted 1942).

MISSOURI: Prostitution, meaning offering or agreeing to engage in or engaging in sexual conduct with another person in exchange for something of value, is a misdemeanor. MO. ANN. STAT. §§ 567.010 (enacted 1977), 567.020 (enacted 1977). Patronizing a prostitute is also a misdemeanor. It means giving or agreeing to give something of value in exchange for a person engaging in sexual conduct or having engaged in sexual conduct when the payment is pursuant to a prior understanding, or requesting or soliciting another person to engage in sexual conduct in return for something of value. MO. ANN. STAT. §§ 567.010 (enacted 1977), 567.030 (enacted 1977). In either case, the gender of the parties is irrelevant. MO. ANN. STAT. §§ 567.040 (enacted 1977).

It is a felony to promote prostitution, a crime to which people acting as prostitutes and patrons are not themselves subject. It is the mildest degree of felony to cause or aid a person to commit or engage in prostitution; procure or solicit patrons for prostitution; accept or receive or agree to accept or receive something of value pursuant to an understanding that the offender is participating in the proceeds of prostitution activity; or engage in any conduct designed to institute, aid, or facilitate an act or enterprise of prostitution. MO. ANN. STAT. §§ 567.010 (enacted 1977), 567.070 (enacted 1977). It is a more serious degree of a felony to promote prostitution by compelling a person to enter into, engage in, or remain in prostitution through forcible compulsion, the use of drugs or intoxicating substances to render a person incapable of controlling her conduct or appreciating its nature, or withholding or threatening to withhold dangerous drugs or a narcotic from a drug-dependent person. It is also a more serious degree of offense to promote the prostitution of a person under sixteen. MO. ANN. STAT. §§ 567.050 (enacted 1977).

MONTANA: Prostitution means engaging in or agreeing to or offering to engage in sexual intercourse with another person for compensation. It is a misdemeanor. MONT. CODE ANN. § 45-5-601 (enacted 1973). Promoting prostitution means encouraging or causing a person to become a prostitute; soliciting a person to patronize a prostitute; procuring a prostitute for a patron; transporting or arranging to transport a person to promote prostitution; or living in part upon the earnings of a person engaged in prostitution. Promoting prostitution is a misdemeanor. MONT. CODE ANN. § 45-5-602 (enacted 1973).

Aggravated promotion of prostitution means compelling another to engage in or promote prostitution; promoting prostitution of a person under eighteen; or promoting the prostitution of one's spouse, child, or ward. Aggravated promotion is a felony. MONT. CODE ANN. § 45-5-603 (enacted 1973).

NEBRASKA: It is a misdemeanor to perform, offer, or agree to perform any act of sexual penetration in exchange for money or a thing of value. NEB. REV. STAT. § 28-801 (enacted 1977).

It is a felony to entice another to become a prostitute; to inveigle, entice, persuade, encourage, or procure any person to come into or leave the state for the purpose of prostitution or debauchery; or to receive or give or agree to receive or give any money or thing of value for procuring or attempting to procure any person to become a prostitute or commit an act of prostitution. NEB. REV. STAT. § 28-802 (enacted 1977).

NEVADA: Prostitution means engaging in sexual conduct for a fee. NEV. REV. STAT. § 201.295 (enacted 1979). It is a prohibited misdemeanor except in a licensed house of prostitution. NEV. REV. STAT. § 201.354 (enacted 1987). Any person who works as a prostitute after testing positive for HIV and receiving notice of that fact is guilty of a felony. NEV. REV. STAT. § 201.358 (enacted 1987).

Pandering is prohibited and is expansively defined. The crime of pandering includes: inducing, persuading, inveigling, enticing, or compelling a person to become a prostitute or to continue to engage in prostitution; causing, inducing, persuading, encouraging, taking, placing, harboring, inveigling, or enticing a person by threats, violence, or by any device or scheme to become an inmate of a place of prostitution; by threats, violence, any device or scheme, fraud, artifice, duress of person or goods, abuse of any position of confidence or authority, or having legal charge, taking, placing, harboring, inveigling, enticing, persuading, encouraging, or procuring a person to enter any place within this state where prostitution is practiced for the purpose of prostitution or in the same manner causing a person of previous chaste character to enter any place within this state where prostitution is practiced for the purpose of sexual intercourse; agreeing to receive or give or receiving or giving any money or thing of value for procuring or attempting to procure any person to become a prostitute or cross state lines for the purpose of prostitution; attempting to detain any person in a house of prostitution because of any debt the other has contracted while living in the house; transporting or aiding in obtaining transportation for any person with the intent to induce, persuade, encourage, inveigle, entice, or compel that person to become or remain a prostitute; compelling another person to reside in a house of prostitution or with the offender or a third person for the purpose of prostitution; placing a person in the custody of a third person with intent that the other person engage in prostitution; asking or receiving any compensation or promise thereof for placing a person somewhere for the purpose of cohabiting with someone who is not the person's spouse; giving, offering, or promising any compensation to procure a person to engage in prostitution against that person's will; as a spouse, parent, or guardian of a person under eighteen permitting, conniving at, or consenting to the minor's being or remaining in a house of prostitution; living with or accepting any earnings of a common prostitute, or enticing or soliciting any person to go to a house of prostitution to engage in sexual conduct with a common prostitute; decoying, enticing, procuring, or in any manner inducing any person to become a prostitute or to become an inmate of a house of prostitution for purposes of prostitution or for purposes of employment or for any purpose whatsoever when that person does not know that it is a house of prostitution; decoying, enticing, procuring, or in any manner inducing a person under twenty-one, to go into or visit, upon any pretext or for any reason whatever, any house of ill fame or prostitution, or any room or place inhabited or frequented by any prostitute, or used for purposes of prostitution; or by force, fraud, intimidation, or threats placing, or procuring another person to place, one's spouse in a house of prostitution or compelling one's spouse to lead a life of prostitution. Pandering does not apply to customers of a prostitute. Pandering carries a one year minimum jail term if physical force or the immediate threat of such force is used upon the person. NEV. REV. STAT. §§ 201.300 (enacted 1913), 201.310 (enacted 1913), 201.330 (enacted 1913), 201.340 (enacted 1913), 201.360 (enacted 1913). Accepting, receiving, levying, or appropriating any money or other valuable thing without consideration from the proceeds of any prostitute is prohibited; any such acceptance, receipt, levy, or appropriation in a proceeding for violation of this section is presumptive evidence of lack of consideration. NEV. REV. STAT. §§ 201.320 (enacted 1919).

NEW HAMPSHIRE: It is a misdemeanor to solicit, agree to perform, or engage in; or to induce or otherwise purposely cause another to engage in; or to transport another into or within the state with the purpose of promoting or facilitating a person in engaging in; or to be supported in whole or in part by the proceeds of a person engaging in sexual penetration or sexual contact in return for consideration. It is a felony to do any of the above by compelling another person by force or intimidation. N.H. REV. STAT. ANN. §§ 645:2 (enacted 1971), 632-A:1 (enacted 1975).

NEW JERSEY: Prostitution is sexual activity with another person in exchange for something of economic value. It is the mildest level of offense, called a "disorderly persons" offense. It is a felony to solicit a person to patronize a prostitute, procure a prostitute for a patron, or procure transportation or transport a person for prostitution. More serious felonies are encouraging, inducing, or otherwise causing a person to become or remain a prostitute; compelling another to engage in prostitution; promoting the prostitution of one's spouse; or engaging in prostitution or solicitation with a person under eighteen. The most serious felonies are promoting the prostitution of a person under eighteen or promoting the prostitution of one's child or ward. Mistake concerning the age of the prostitute is not a defense to the age-based offenses. N.J. STAT. ANN. § 2C:34-1 (enacted 1978).

NEW MEXICO: Prostitution means engaging in or offering to engage in a sexual act for hire. N.M. STAT ANN. § 30-9-2 (enacted 1953). Patronizing a prostitute means entering or remaining in a place where prostitution is practiced with the intent of engaging in a sexual act with a prostitute, or hiring, or offering to hire a person to engage in sexual conduct. N.M. STAT ANN. § 30-9-3 (enacted 1953). Both prostitution and patronizing a prostitute are petty misdemeanors for a first offense and misdemeanors for subsequent offenses. Attempting to persuade or entice or persuading or enticing a child under sixteen to enter any secluded place with the intent to commit an act of prostitution is a misdemeanor called "enticing a child." N.M. STAT. ANN. § 30-9-1 (enacted 1953).

It is a felony to promote prostitution. Promoting prostitution includes any of the following when the offender is not acting as a prostitute or patron: encouraging or allowing prostitution; inducing another to become a prostitute; soliciting a patron for a prostitute or place of prostitution; procuring a prostitute for a patron and receiving compensation for it; procuring transportation or transporting a person for prostitution; or under the pretense of marriage, detaining a person or causing a person to travel across state lines for prostitution. N.M. STAT. ANN. § 30-9-4 (enacted 1953). It is a felony to accept the earnings of a prostitute by receiving or appropriating money or anything of value without consideration from the proceeds of prostitution. N.M. STAT. ANN. § 30-9-4.1 (enacted 1981).

NEW YORK: Prostitution means offering, agreeing to, or engaging in sexual conduct in return for a fee. N.Y. PENAL LAW § 230.00 (enacted 1965). Patronizing a prostitute means paying a fee pursuant to a prior understanding as compensation for another person engaging in sexual conduct or soliciting a person or agreeing in advance to pay a person for engaging in sexual conduct. N.Y. PENAL LAW § 230.02 (enacted

1965). Prostitution is a misdemeanor. Patronizing a prostitute is a misdemeanor of the same degree as prostitution, unless the prostitute is under seventeen years of age and the patron is at least twenty-one, in which case patronizing a prostitute is a misdemeanor of a more serious degree. N.Y. PENAL LAW §§ 230.03 (enacted 1978), 230.04 (enacted 1978). Patronizing a prostitute under fourteen when the patron is over eighteen is a felony, and patronizing a prostitute under eleven is a felony of a more serious degree. N.Y. PENAL LAW §§ 230.05 (enacted 1978), 230.06 (enacted 1978). It is a misdemeanor to remain or wander about a public place and repeatedly beckon, stop, or attempt to stop passersby or cars; engage passersby in conversation; or interfere with the free passage of other people for the purpose of prostitution or patronizing a prostitute. N.Y. PENAL LAW § 240.37 (enacted 1976).

Advancing prostitution means causing or aiding a person in engaging in prostitution, procuring or soliciting patrons for prostitution, or providing persons for prostitution, while not acting as a prostitute or patron. Profiting from prostitution means receiving money or property pursuant to an understanding with anyone to participate in the proceeds of prostitution. N.Y. PENAL LAW § 230.15 (enacted 1965). It is a misdemeanor to knowingly advance or profit from prostitution. N.Y. PENAL LAW § 230.20 (enacted 1965). It is a felony to advance or profit from prostitution by a person under nineteen. N.Y. PENAL LAW § 230.25 (enacted 1965).

It is a felony to advance prostitution by compelling a person to engage in prostitution with force or intimidation or to profit from such coercive conduct of others. It is also a felony to advance or profit from the prostitution of a person under sixteen. N.Y. PENAL LAW § 230.30 (enacted 1965). In a prosecution for advancing or profiting from prostitution, the prostitute under seventeen cannot be deemed an accomplice. N.Y. PENAL LAW § 230.35 (enacted 1978).

NORTH CAROLINA: Prostitution is either offering or receiving the body for sexual intercourse for hire or for indiscriminate sexual intercourse without hire. N.C. GEN. STAT. § 14-203 (enacted 1919). All prostitution crimes are misdemeanors unless they involve minors. N.C. GEN. STAT. §§ 14-207 (enacted 1919), 14-208 (enacted 1919). It is a misdemeanor to engage in prostitution or to aid or abet prostitution; to remain or wander about a public place and repeatedly beckon, stop, or attempt to stop passersby or cars or engage passersby in conversation or interfere with the free passage of other people for the purpose of prostitution; to direct or transport or agree to transport a person to a place for prostitution; to procure or solicit or offer to do so for prostitution; or to reside in, enter, or remain in any place for prostitution. N.C. GEN. STAT. §§ 14-204 (enacted 1919), 14-204.1 (enacted 1979).

It is a felony to patronize a minor prostitute if the patron is not also a minor. Patronizing a minor prostitute means soliciting or requesting a minor to participate in prostitution or paying or agreeing to pay a minor for prostitution past or future. N.C. GEN. STAT. § 14-190.19 (enacted 1985). Promoting the prostitution of a minor is also a felony consisting of enticing, forcing, encouraging, or facilitating a minor to participate in prostitution, or supervising, supporting, advising, or protecting the prostitution of a minor. N.C. GEN. STAT. § 14-190.18 (enacted 1985).

NORTH DAKOTA: Prostitution is a misdemeanor consisting of being an inmate of a house of prostitution or otherwise engaging in sexual activity as a business, or of soliciting another person with the purpose of being hired to engage in sexual activity. N.D. CENT. CODE § 12.1-29-03 (enacted 1973). It is a misdemeanor to facilitate prostitution by soliciting a person to patronize a prostitute; procuring a prostitute for a patron; or inducing or causing a person to remain a prostitute. A person who is supported in substantial part by the proceeds of prostitution is presumed to be inducing a person to remain a prostitute. N.D. CENT. CODE § 12.1-29-02 (enacted 1973). Facilitating prostitution becomes a felony if the offender causes a person to remain a prostitute by force or threat, or the prostitute is the offender's spouse, child, or ward, or is less than sixteen. N.D. CENT. CODE § 12.1-29-02 (enacted 1973).

It is a felony to promote prostitution by inducing or causing a person to become engaged in sexual activity as a business. N.D. CENT. CODE § 12.1-29-01 (enacted 1973).

OHIO: It is a misdemeanor to engage in sexual activity for hire. OHIO REV. CODE ANN. § 2907.25 (enacted 1972). It is also a misdemeanor to solicit another person to engage in sexual activity for hire. OHIO REV. CODE ANN. § 2907.24 (enacted 1972). It is the misdemeanor of procuring to entice or solicit a person to patronize a prostitute or brothel; to procure a prostitute for another to patronize; or to direct or take another person somewhere for the purpose of patronizing a prostitute. OHIO REV. CODE ANN. § 2907.23 (enacted 1972).

It is a felony to transport or arrange the transportation of a person across state or county lines to facilitate prostitution. OHIO REV. CODE ANN. § 2907.22 (enacted 1972). It is a felony of a more serious degree to compel a person to engage in sexual activity for hire; to induce, solicit, or request a minor to engage in sexual activity for hire; or to pay or agree to pay a minor either directly or through an agent for the minor having engaged in sexual activity. Ignorance of age is not a defense to this offense. OHIO REV. CODE ANN. § 2907.21 (enacted 1988).

OKLAHOMA: Prostitution means the giving or receiving of the body for sexual intercourse, fellatio, cunnilingus, masturbation, anal intercourse, or lewdness in exchange for anything of value; or the making of any appointment or engagement for these sexual activities for anything of value. OKLA. STAT. ANN. tit. 21, § 1030 (enacted 1943). To engage in prostitution, to attempt to patronize a prostitute, to patronize a prostitute, to enter or remain in a house of prostitution for the purpose of engaging in prostitution, or to aid or abet in any of the foregoing are all misdemeanors. OKLA. STAT. ANN. tit. 21, § 1029 (enacted 1943). If the offense involves a child under sixteen, it is a felony. OKLA. STAT. ANN. tit. 21, § 1030 (enacted 1943), 1031 (enacted 1943). Offering to procure or procuring a person for prostitution is a misdemeanor, as is receiving, offering or agreeing to receive a person, or allowing a person to remain in any place to engage in prostitution. It is also a misdemeanor to direct or transport or arrange transportation for the purpose of prostitution. OKLA. STAT. ANN. tit. 21, § 1028 (enacted 1943). It is a misdemeanor to receive any thing of value without consideration from a prostitute or from the proceeds of a woman engaged in prostitution. OKLA. STAT. ANN. tit. 21, § 1028 (enacted 1943).

A person who engages in prostitution knowing of personal HIV infection is guilty of a felony. OKLA. STAT. ANN. tit. 21, § 1031 (enacted 1991).

OREGON: It is a misdemeanor to engage in or offer or agree to engage in sexual conduct or contact for a fee; or to pay or offer or agree to pay a fee to engage in sexual conduct or contact. OR. REV. STAT. § 167.007 (enacted 1971).

It is a felony to promote prostitution, by inducing a person to engage in prostitution or remain in a place of prostitution or engaging in any conduct that institutes or facilitates an act or enterprise of prostitution. Promoting prostitution also includes receiving or agreeing to receive money or property pursuant to an understanding that the money or property is derived from prostitution services, but this definition does not include prostitutes receiving compensation for personally rendered prostitution services. OR. REV. STAT. § 167.012 (enacted 1971). It is a felony of a more serious degree to compel prostitution by using force or intimidation to induce a person to engage in prostitution or by inducing or causing either a person under eighteen or a person's spouse, child, or stepchild to engage in prostitution. OR. REV. STAT. § 167.017 (enacted 1971).

PENNSYLVANIA: Prostitution is a misdemeanor consisting of being an inmate in a house of prostitution, engaging in sexual activity as a business, or loitering within view of a public place for the purpose of being hired to engage in sexual activity. Patronizing a prostitute means hiring a person to engage in sexual activity or entering or remaining in a house of prostitution to engage in sexual activity. If the prostitute is under sixteen, the offense is a misdemeanor equivalent to the offense of prostitution. If the prostitute is sixteen or older, patronizing a prostitute is called a "summary offense." It is also a misdemeanor to solicit a person to patronize a prostitute or procure a prostitute for a patron, or to transport or arrange the transportation of a person for the purpose of prostitution.

It is a misdemeanor to encourage, induce, or intentionally cause a person to become or remain a prostitute; however, this offense is a felony where the offender compels another person to promote or engage in prostitution or where the offender promotes the prostitution of a person under sixteen or who is the offender's spouse, child, or dependent. 18 PA. CONS. STAT. ANN. § 5902 (enacted 1972).

RHODE ISLAND: It is a misdemeanor to loiter on a street or ride in or drive a car and attempt to engage passersby in conversation or detain cars for the purpose of prostitution, or to patronize or otherwise induce a person to commit such an act. R.I. GEN. LAWS §§ 11-34-8 (enacted 1980), 11-34-8.1 (enacted 1984).

Pandering is a felony. To pander is to do any of the following: facilitate or encourage a person to become a prostitute or an inmate of a house of prostitution, or receive or give or agree to receive or give anything of value for doing the foregoing. It is a felony to detain a person in a place where prostitution takes place for the purpose of prostitution or the payment of debts. R.I. GEN. LAWS § 11-34-1 (enacted 1896). Pandering may be prosecuted in Rhode Island even if all of the relevant acts take place outside of Rhode Island. R.I. GEN. LAWS § 11-34-2 (enacted 1909). Anyone involved for pecuniary gain in the transportation or direction of another for the purpose of prostitution, or in receiving or allowing a person to remain in a place for the purpose of prostitution commits a felony. R.I. Gen. Laws § 11-34-5 (enacted 1909). It is a felony to derive any support or maintenance from earnings or proceeds of prostitution. R.I. Gen. Laws § 11-34-5.1 (enacted 1978). All of the felonies related to prostitution carry a mandatory minimum jail term.

South Carolina: All crimes involving adults and prostitution carry equal punishment and are misdemeanors. S.C. Code Ann. § 16-15-110 (enacted 1952). Prohibited crimes include: prostitution; aiding or abetting prostitution; procuring or soliciting prostitution; entering or remaining in a place of prostitution; directing, transporting, or assisting in transporting a person for prostitution; causing or persuading a female to become or remain a prostitute by any means; inducing or encouraging a female to come into or leave the state to become a prostitute or an inmate of a house of prostitution; receiving or giving or agreeing to receive or give anything of value for attempting to procure or procuring a female to become a prostitute or an inmate of a house of prostitution; knowingly accepting or receiving any thing of value without consideration from a prostitute; or aiding, abetting, or participating in any of the foregoing acts. S.C. Code Ann. §§ 16-15-90 (enacted 1952), 16-15-100 (enacted 1952).

It is a felony carrying a mandatory minimum sentence to patronize a minor prostitute when the offender is not also a minor, or to entice, force, offer to pay, pay (enacted directly or through an agent), encourage, promote, supervise, support, advise, request, or otherwise facilitate a minor to participate in prostitution. Mistake of age is not a defense. S.C. Code Ann. §§ 16-15-415 (enacted 1987), 16-15-425 (enacted 1987).

It is a felony for a person who knows that he or she is infected with HIV to knowingly commit an act of prostitution with another person. S.C. Code Ann. § 44-29-145 (enacted 1988).

South Dakota: It is a misdemeanor to be an inmate of a house of prostitution or to loiter within view of any public place to be hired for sexual activity or to otherwise engage in sexual activity for a fee. S.D. Codified Laws Ann. § 22-23-1 (enacted 1903). It is also a misdemeanor to hire a person for a fee to engage in sexual activity or to enter or remain in a house of prostitution to engage in sexual activity. S.D. Codified Laws Ann. § 22-23-9 (enacted 1976).

Procuring or promoting prostitution and pimping are felonies. Procuring or promoting means encouraging, inducing, or causing a person to become or remain a prostitute or promoting the prostitution of a minor, one's child, ward, or spouse. S.D. CODIFIED LAWS ANN. § 22-23-2 (enacted 1877). Pimping means soliciting another person to patronize a prostitute; procuring a prostitute for a patron; transporting or arranging transportation for a person to promote that person's prostitution; or soliciting, receiving, or agreeing to receive any benefit for doing or agreeing to pimp. S.D. CODIFIED LAWS ANN. § 22-23-8 (enacted 1976).

TENNESSEE: Prostitution means engaging in sexual activity as a business or being an inmate of a house of prostitution or loitering in a public place to be hired to engage in sexual activity. Patronizing a prostitute means soliciting or hiring another person for prostitution or entering or remaining in a house of prostitution to engage in sexual activity. Both are misdemeanors. TENN. CODE ANN. §§ 39-13-512 (enacted 1989), 39-13-513 (enacted 1989), 39-13-514 (enacted 1989).

Promoting prostitution is a felony. It means encouraging or causing a person to become a prostitute; soliciting a person to patronize a prostitute; procuring a prostitute for a patron; or soliciting, receiving, or agreeing to receive any benefit for engaging in any of these activities. TENN. CODE ANN. §§ 39-13-512 (enacted 1989), 39-13-515 (enacted 1989).

It is a felony called aggravated prostitution for a person to engage in sexual activity as a business or to be an inmate of a house of prostitution or to loiter in a public place for the purpose of being hired to engage in sexual activity if that person knows that he or she is infected with HIV or any other identified causative agent of AIDS. It is not necessary for an HIV infection to have occurred for the person to be found guilty of aggravated prostitution. TENN. CODE ANN. § 39-13-516 (enacted 1989).

TEXAS: Prostitution means agreeing to engage or engaging in sexual conduct for a fee, or soliciting another in a public place to do so. The offense is prostitution whether a person is to receive the fee or to pay the fee. The offense is a misdemeanor with an increase in the degree upon a second conviction. TEX. PENAL CODE ANN. § 43.02 (enacted 1973). Sexual conduct includes any touching of breast, anus, or genitals of another with the intent to arouse. TEX. PENAL CODE ANN. § 43.01 (enacted 1973). Promoting prostitution is also a misdemeanor, and it includes receiving money or other property from the proceeds of prostitution pursuant to an agreement or soliciting a person to engage in sexual conduct with another person for compensation. TEX. PENAL CODE ANN. § 43.03 (enacted 1973).

It is a felony to cause another person by force, threat, or fraud to commit prostitution or to cause a person under seventeen to commit prostitution. TEX. PENAL CODE ANN. § 43.05 (enacted 1973).

UTAH: The offense of prostitution is committed by being an inmate of a house of prostitution, loitering within view of a public place for the purpose of being hired to engage in sexual activity, or engaging in sexual activity with another person for a fee. Sexual activity includes masturbation, intercourse, oral sex, or anal sex, regardless of the gender of the parties. Patronizing a prostitute means paying or agreeing to pay for sexual activity or entering or remaining in a house of prostitution for the purpose of engaging in sexual activity. Both prostitution and patronizing a prostitute are misdemeanors of the same degree; however, second offenses are a more serious class of misdemeanor for prostitutes only. UTAH CODE ANN. §§ 76-10-1301 (enacted 1953), 76-10-1302 (enacted 1953), 76-10-1303 (enacted 1953). Aiding a prostitute is a misdemeanor and consists of soliciting, attempting to procure, or procuring a prostitute for a patron, or agreeing to receive any benefit for doing these things. UTAH CODE ANN. § 76-10-1304 (enacted 1953).

Exploiting a prostitute is a felony. A person exploits a prostitute by encouraging or aiding a person in becoming or remaining a prostitute, transporting or procuring transportation for a person to promote that person's prostitution, or sharing in the proceeds of prostitution pursuant to an understanding with a prostitute. UTAH CODE ANN. § 76-10-1305 (enacted 1953). Aggravated exploitation of a prostitute is a felony, and it means exploiting a prostitute using force, threat, or fear against any person or exploiting one's wife or a person under eighteen. UTAH CODE ANN. § 76-10-1306 (enacted 1953).

An HIV-positive individual with actual knowledge of his or her infection suffers enhanced penalties for other sexual crimes. UTAH CODE ANN. § 76-10-1309 (enacted 1993).

VERMONT: Prostitution is the offering or receiving of the body for sexual intercourse for hire and also includes offering or receiving the body for indiscriminate sexual intercourse without hire. VT. STAT. ANN. tit. 13, § 2631 (enacted 1947). The following acts are misdemeanors: directing or taking a person to a place with reasonable cause to know that the purpose of going to the place is prostitution; remaining in a place for the purpose of prostitution; engaging in prostitution; aiding or abetting prostitution by any means. VT. STAT. ANN. tit. 13, § 2632 (enacted 1947).

"White slave traffic" is a felony. It consists of inducing or procuring a female person to come into the state or leave the state for prostitution, to enter or live in a house of prostitution, or to live a life of prostitution. It also includes aiding in a female's placement in a house of prostitution or aiding in her transportation into the state for prostitution. VT. STAT. ANN. tit. 13, § 2635 (enacted 1971). Receiving money or other valuable things for placing a female in a house of prostitution is also a felony. VT. STAT. ANN. tit. 13, § 2636 (enacted 1947). Detaining a female person in a house of prostitution to compel her to perform service or labor to liquidate her debt to the house is a felony, as is receiving money or other valuable things from the earnings of a prostitute. VT. STAT. ANN. tit. 13, § 2637 (enacted 1947).

VIRGINIA: Prostitution is a misdemeanor defined as adultery, fornication, anal or oral sex, or an offer of any of these accompanied by a substantial act in furtherance of the offer in exchange for money or its equivalent. Patronizing a prostitute means offering money or its equivalent for any of the acts above and thereafter doing a substantial act in furtherance of the offer. It is also a misdemeanor. VA. CODE ANN. § 18.2-346 (enacted 1950).

It is unlawful to reside in or visit for immoral purposes a "bawdy" place, meaning a place used for lewdness or prostitution. VA. CODE ANN. § 18.2-347 (enacted 1950). It is unlawful to take or transport a person or to offer to take or transport a person to a place where prostitution occurs if the offender has good reason to know of the immoral purpose of the visit, or to assist a person by giving any information or direction with intent to enable that person to commit an act of prostitution. VA. CODE ANN. § 18.2-348 (enacted 1950). An owner or chauffeur of a vehicle is barred from using or allowing the vehicle to be used for prostitution or used to aid or promote prostitution. VA. CODE ANN. § 18.2-349 (enacted 1950).

Taking a person into or persuading a person to enter a bawdy place for the purpose of prostitution or consenting to the same as the guardian or parent of a minor child is pandering which is a felony. VA. CODE ANN. § 18.2-355 (enacted 1950). Receiving money or another valuable thing for procuring or placing a prostitute for another is a felony. VA. CODE ANN. § 18.2-356 (enacted 1950). Receiving money from the earnings of a prostitute unless it is in exchange for lawful consideration is a felony. VA. CODE ANN. § 18.2-357 (enacted 1950). It is a felony to detain a person who wishes to leave a bawdy place. VA. CODE ANN. § 18.2-358 (enacted 1950). It is a felony to place or leave one's wife by force, fraud, intimidation, or threats in a bawdy place for the purpose of prostitution. VA. CODE ANN. § 18.2-368 (enacted 1950).

WASHINGTON: Prostitution is engaging or agreeing to or offering to engage in sexual intercourse or contact for a fee, and it is a misdemeanor. WASH. REV. CODE ANN. § 9A.88.030 (enacted 1975). The gender of any party is immaterial. WASH. REV. CODE ANN. § 9A.88.050 (enacted 1975). Patronizing a prostitute is requesting or offering to pay or paying a fee for sexual contact, and it is also a misdemeanor. WASH. REV. CODE ANN. § 9A.88.110 (enacted 1988). Patronizing a minor prostitute is a felony. WASH. REV. CODE ANN. § 9.68A.100 (enacted 1984).

A person advances prostitution by causing or aiding a person to engage in prostitution, procuring or soliciting customers for prostitution, providing persons for prostitution, or engaging in any other conduct designed to institute or facilitate prostitution. Advancing prostitution or profiting from prostitution is a felony. WASH. REV. CODE ANN. §§ 9A.88.070 (enacted 1975), 9A.88.080 (enacted 1975).

WEST VIRGINIA: Prostitution itself is not defined. Offering, or offering to secure, another for the purpose of prostitution; or directing or transporting or offering or agreeing to direct or transport a person for the purpose of prostitution; or aiding or abetting such acts is a misdemeanor with a mandatory minimum jail term and increased penalties for a second offense. W. VA. CODE § 61-8-5(a) (enacted 1860). Engaging in prostitution, being in a place for the purpose of prostitution, soliciting, inducing, or enticing another to commit an act of prostitution, or aiding or abetting or participating in any of these acts is a misdemeanor carrying a mandatory minimum jail term. For a pimp, panderer, solicitor, or operator a second offense will lead to an increased sentence. W. VA. CODE § 61-8-5(b) (enacted 1860).

Detaining a person in a place of prostitution for the purpose of compelling that person to pay a debt is a misdemeanor with a mandatory minimum jail term and increased penalties for a second offense. If the person detained is a minor, the offense becomes a felony. W. VA. CODE

§ 61-8-6 (enacted 1911). Pandering is procuring or inducing a person to become a prostitute and is a misdemeanor with a mandatory minimum sentence and increased penalties for a second offense. W. VA. CODE § 61-8-7 (enacted 1911). Any person who knows another person to be a prostitute and derives support from the earnings of the prostitute is guilty of pimping which is a misdemeanor with a mandatory minimum jail term and increased penalties for a second offense. If the prostitute is a minor, pimping is a felony. W. VA. CODE § 61-8-8 (enacted 1911).

Past notorious prostitution provides grounds for the annulment of a marriage. W. VA. CODE § 48-2-2 (enacted 1849).

WISCONSIN: Prostitution is committing, offering to commit, or requesting to commit, in exchange for anything of value, any of the following: nonmarital sexual intercourse, oral sex, anal sex, masturbation, or sexual contact. Prostitution also includes being an inmate of a place of prostitution. WIS. STAT. ANN. § 944.30 (enacted 1993). Patronizing a prostitute means entering or remaining in any place of prostitution with intent to perform any of the acts constituting prostitution with a prostitute. WIS. STAT. ANN. § 944.31 (enacted 1993). Both offenses are misdemeanors.

Soliciting or causing a person to practice prostitution is a felony. WIS. STAT. ANN. §§ 944.32 (enacted 1987), 948.08 (enacted 1987). Pandering, which means soliciting a person to have intercourse, anal sex, oral sex, to masturbate, or have sexual contact with a prostitute, or transporting a prostitute or a patron to one another, is a misdemeanor. However, if a person receives compensation for pandering from the prostitute's earnings the crime is a felony. WIS. STAT. ANN. § 944.33 (enacted 1983). A prostitute who loiters on the streets or where alcohol is served is guilty of vagrancy, which is a misdemeanor. WIS. STAT. ANN. § 947.02 (enacted 1993).

WYOMING: Prostitution includes performing or agreeing to perform or permit acts involving sexual intrusion for money or other property. Patronizing a prostitute means paying or offering or agreeing to pay the prostitute or any other person money or other property for sexual intrusion. Prostitution and patronizing a prostitute are both misdemeanors. WYO. STAT. §§ 6-4-101 (enacted 1982), 6-4-102 (enacted 1982). Sexual intrusion means sexual intercourse, cunnilingus, fellatio, analingus, anal intercourse, or any intrusion by any object or any part of a person's body into the genital or anal opening of a person's body for the purposes of sexual arousal, gratification, or abuse. WYO. STAT. § 6-2-301 (enacted 1982).

Promoting prostitution includes enticing or compelling another person to become a prostitute; procuring or offering or agreeing to procure a person for another person for the purpose of prostitution; or receiving money or property from a prostitute without lawful consideration knowing that the money was earned at least in part from prostitution. Promoting prostitution is a felony. WYO. STAT. § 6-4-103 (enacted 1982).

No person may induce a child to enter or remain in a place where prostitution occurs. WYO. STAT. § 6-4-403 (enacted 1982). Towns are given general powers to control and punish prostitution. WYO. STAT. § 15-1-103 (enacted 1965).

UNITED STATES: It is a misdemeanor to engage in, aid, abet, procure, or solicit for purposes of prostitution within a reasonable distance of any military or naval camp, station, fort, post, yard, base, cantonment, training or mobilization place. "Reasonable distance" shall be determined by the Secretary of the Army, the Secretary of the Navy, the Secretary of the Air Force, or any two of them, or all of them together. 18 U.S.C.A. § 1384 (enacted 1948).

It is a felony to, directly or indirectly, import or attempt to import an alien into the United States for the purpose of prostitution, or to hold or attempt to hold any alien for such purpose. 8 U.S.C.A. § 1328 (enacted 1952). It is a felony to transport any individual in interstate or foreign commerce, or in any territory or possession of the United States, with intent that such individual engage in prostitution. 18 U.S.C.A. §§ 2421 (enacted 1948), 2423 (enacted 1948). It is a felony to knowingly persuade, induce, entice, or coerce any individual to travel in interstate or foreign commerce, or in any territory or possession of the United States, to engage in prostitution. 18 U.S.C.A. § 2422 (enacted 1948).

13

Possession of Obscene Materials

This chapter covers personal consumption of obscene materials. It includes crimes for which an individual who is not a producer or distributor of obscene materials may be convicted. It is focused on possession or receipt of obscene materials by individuals who do not intend to disseminate those materials. Retail display, dissemination, and production of such materials are excluded from our coverage. Many states prohibit possession of obscenity depicting children. Most states do not prohibit the possession of obscenity that depicts adults. Obscenity was first criminalized in the eighteenth century in England; before that time it had been regulated in ecclesiastical courts.

Obscenity has a particular meaning in constitutional law. It does not receive protection as speech under the First Amendment, and may be regulated or prohibited without running afoul of the Constitution. *Roth v. United States*, 354 U.S. 476 (1957). The task becomes defining what are "obscene" materials that a state can freely regulate, and distinguishing obscene materials from materials that receive free speech protection. If the material has a dominant theme that appeals to the prurient interest in sex, is patently offensive in affronting community standards regarding the description of sexual matters, and the material, taken as a whole, lacks serious literary, artistic, political, or scientific value, the material is designated as "obscene." *Miller v. California*, 413 U.S. 15 (1973). No expert testimony on what exactly the community standards are is required. *Hamling v. United States*, 418 U.S. 87, 125-27 (1974). Juries decide most cases, subject to limited judicial review. *Jenkins v. Georgia*, 418 U.S. 153 (1974). In deciding whether material that is otherwise obscene can be protected because it possesses serious literary, artistic, political, or scientific value, the work is viewed as a whole so that the prohibition against obscenity will not be evaded by incorporating a single reference to a serious idea in an otherwise obscene work. *Miller v. California*, 413 U.S. 15, 25 n. 7 (1973)

("A quotation from Voltaire in the flyleaf of a book will not constitutionally redeem an otherwise obscene publication").

At one time, it appeared as though the Supreme Court would decide that regulation of the private possession of obscene materials was not constitutionally permissible on the basis of both privacy and First Amendment interests; possession would thus be a protected activity. *Stanley v. Georgia*, 394 U.S. 557 (1969). However, the Court soon limited the *Stanley* decision. It would only protect possession of obscene materials within the home, while distribution or production would remain unprotected by the Constitution, and thus be eligible for criminal sanctions. *United States v. Reidel*, 402 U.S. 351 (1971). The privacy right to possess obscene materials within the home articulated in *Stanley* does not extend to carrying obscene materials across state lines: *United States v. Orito*, 413 U.S. 139 (1973) (the Court decided that the home is the limit of the *Stanley* protection); nor does the *Stanley* right extend to viewing obscene materials at a movie theatre. *Paris Adult Theatre I v. Slaton*, 413 U.S. 49 (1973).

The current First Amendment jurisprudence, then, only protects from criminalization the possession of obscene materials within a person's home. The protection, moreover, does not extend to the possession of child pornography. *Osborne v. Ohio*, 495 U.S. 103 (1990). The Court in *Osborne* held that the state had a legitimate interest in protecting minors from the psychological and physical effects of the pornography production experience and from potential victimization by pedophiles. Many of the statutes reach as far as constitutionally permissible, regulating the possession of child obscenity but not of adult obscenity in the home.

ALABAMA: It is a felony to knowingly possesses any obscene matter containing a visual reproduction of a person under seventeen engaged in any act of sadomasochistic abuse, sexual intercourse, sexual excitement, masturbation, genital nudity, or any touching of the genitals, pubic areas, or buttocks of the human male or female, or the breasts of the female, whether alone or with others, or between humans and animals in an act of apparent sexual stimulation or gratification. ALA. CODE § 13A-12-192 (enacted 1978). The above material is obscene if it lacks serious literary, artistic, political, or scientific value, unless it is used to describe matter that contains a visual reproduction of breast nudity without any of the other elements above, in which case it is obscene if applying contemporary community standards, on the whole, it appeals to the prurient interest; and it is patently offensive; and on the whole it lacks serious literary, artistic, political, or scientific value. ALA. CODE § 13A-12-190 (enacted 1978).

ALASKA: No statute.

ARIZONA: It is a felony to purchase or possess any visual or print medium in which minors are engaged in sexual conduct. ARIZ. REV. STAT. ANN. § 13-3553 (enacted 1978). It is a misdemeanor to purchase any visual or print medium whose text, title, or visual representation depicts a participant in sexual conduct as a minor even though the participant is an adult. ARIZ. REV. STAT. ANN. § 13-3554 (enacted 1978). Sexual conduct means actual or simulated: sexual intercourse, including genital-genital, oral-genital, anal-genital, or oral-anal contact between any two persons; penetration of the vagina or rectum by any object except when done as part of a recognized medical procedure; sexual bestiality; masturbation, for the purpose of sexual stimulation of the viewer; sadomasochistic abuse for the purpose of sexual stimulation of the viewer; lewd exhibition of the genitals, pubic, or rectal areas of any person; or defecation or urination for the purpose of sexual stimulation of the viewer. ARIZ. REV. STAT. ANN. § 13-3551 (enacted 1978).

ARKANSAS: It is a misdemeanor for any person to have in possession any literature or matter the shipment or transportation of which has been refused by and rejected from the United States mails, or which literature or literature of like character the United States will not permit to be sold, shipped, or handled. ARK. CODE ANN. § 5-68-202 (enacted 1931). It is a misdemeanor to possess obscene film of any type. ARK. CODE ANN. § 5-68-203 (enacted 1967). It is a misdemeanor to possess, with knowledge of its content, any obscene materials that do not have second-class mailing privileges, or that do have mailing privileges where the offender knows the material has been judicially found to be obscene. ARK. CODE ANN. §§ 5-68-403 (enacted 1961), 5-68-405 (enacted 1961). Material is obscene if to the average person, applying contemporary community standards, the dominant theme of the material taken as a whole appeals to prurient interest. ARK. CODE ANN. § 5-68-403 (enacted 1961).

It is a felony for any person with knowledge of the character of the material to knowingly receive, purchase, possess, or view any visual or print medium depicting a child engaging in actual or simulated: sexual intercourse, including genital-genital, oral-genital, anal-genital, or oral-anal contact; bestiality; masturbation; sadomasochistic abuse for the purpose of sexual stimulation; or lewd exhibition of the genitals or pubic area of any person. ARK. CODE ANN. §§ 5-27-304 (enacted 1981), 5-27-302 (enacted 1981).

CALIFORNIA: It is a misdemeanor for the first offense and a felony for subsequent offenses to knowingly possess or control any matter the production of which involves the use of a person under eighteen, knowing that the matter depicts a person under eighteen personally engaging in or simulating sexual conduct. CAL. PENAL CODE § 311.11 (enacted 1989). Sexual conduct means actual or simulated: sexual intercourse; oral copulation; anal intercourse; anal-oral copulation; masturbation; bestiality; sexual sadism; sexual masochism; penetration of the vagina or rectum by any object in a lewd or lascivious manner; exhibition of the genitals, pubic, or rectal area for the purposes of sexual stimulation of the viewer; or excretory functions performed in a lewd or lascivious manner: whether or not any of the above conduct is performed alone or between members of the same or opposite sex or between humans and animals. CAL. PENAL CODE § 311.4 (enacted 1961).

COLORADO: It is a misdemeanor for a first offense and a felony for subsequent offenses to possess or control any sexually exploitative material for any purpose, but this does not apply to peace officers or court personnel in the performance of their official duties, or to physicians, psychologists, therapists, or social workers, so long as such persons are licensed in Colorado and they possess the materials in the course of a bona fide treatment or evaluation program at the treatment or evaluation site. Sexually exploitative material means any photograph, motion picture, videotape, print, negative, slide, or other mechanically, electronically, or chemically reproduced visual material which depicts a person under eighteen engaged in, participating in, observing, or being used for sexual intercourse, erotic fondling, erotic nudity, masturbation, sadomasochism, or sexual excitement. COLO. REV. STAT. ANN. § 18-6-403 (enacted 1979).

CONNECTICUT: No statute.

DELAWARE: It is a misdemeanor to knowingly possess any visual matter depicting a child engaging in a prohibited sexual act or the simulation of such an act. DEL. CODE ANN. tit. 11, § 1111 (enacted 1990). Prohibited sexual acts include: sexual intercourse; anal intercourse; masturbation; bestiality; sadism; masochism; fellatio; cunnilingus; nudity, if such nudity is to be depicted for the purpose of the sexual stimulation or the sexual gratification of any individual who may view such depiction; or sexual contact. DEL. CODE ANN. tit. 11, § 1103 (enacted 1953).

DISTRICT OF COLUMBIA: No statute.

FLORIDA: It is a misdemeanor for a person to knowingly have in his or her possession, custody, or control: any obscene book, magazine, periodical, pamphlet, newspaper, comic book, story paper, written or printed story or article, writing, paper, card, picture, drawing, photograph, motion-picture film, film; any sticker, decal, emblem or other device attached to a motor vehicle containing obscene descriptions, photographs, or depictions; any obscene figure, image, phonograph record, or wire or tape or other recording, or any written, printed, or recorded matter of any such character which may or may not require mechanical or other means to be transmuted into auditory, visual, or sensory representations of such character; or any article or instrument for obscene use, or purporting to be for obscene use or purpose, without intent to sell, lend, give away, distribute, transmit, show, transmute, or advertise the same. FLA. STAT. ANN. § 847.011 (enacted 1961). Obscene means the status of material which: the average person, applying contemporary community standards, would find, taken as a whole, appeals to the prurient interest; depicts or describes, in a patently offensive way, sexual conduct as specifically defined herein; and taken as a whole lacks serious literary, artistic, political, or scientific value. Sexual conduct means actual or simulated sexual intercourse, deviate sexual intercourse, sexual bestiality, masturbation, or sadomasochistic abuse; actual lewd exhibition of the genitals; actual physical contact with a person's clothed or unclothed genitals, pubic area, buttocks, or, if such person is a female, breast, with the intent to arouse or gratify the sexual desire of either party; or any act or conduct which constitutes sexual battery or simulates that sexual battery. A mother's breast-feeding of her baby does not under any circumstance constitute sexual conduct. FLA. STAT. ANN. § 847.001 (enacted 1986).

It is a felony for any person to knowingly possess a photograph, motion picture, exhibition, show, representation, or other presentation which, in whole or in part, includes any sexual conduct by a person under eighteen. FLA. STAT. ANN. § 827.071 (enacted 1983).

It is a misdemeanor for any minor to falsely represent that such minor is seventeen or older, with the intent to procure admission to premises exhibiting, or videotape showing, a motion picture, exhibition, show, representation, or other presentation which, in whole or in part, depicts nudity, sexual conduct, sexual excitement, sexual battery, bestiality, or sadomasochistic abuse, and is harmful to minors. FLA. STAT. ANN. § 847.013 (enacted 1969).

It is a misdemeanor to knowingly compile, reproduce, buy, or receive by means of a computer any visual depiction of a minor engaged in sexual conduct. FLA. STAT. ANN. § 847.0135 (enacted 1986).

GEORGIA: It is a misdemeanor for any person to knowingly possess or control any material which depicts a minor engaged in any sexually explicit conduct. It is a felony for any person to knowingly purchase any medium which provides information as to where any visual medium which depicts a minor engaged in any sexually explicit conduct may be found or purchased, unless the person is a law enforcement or prosecution agent acting in the investigation and prosecution of criminal offenses, or the conduct pertains to legitimate medical, scientific, or educational activities. Sexually explicit conduct means actual or simulated: sexual intercourse, including genital-genital, oral-genital, anal-genital, or oral-anal contact; bestiality; masturbation; lewd exhibition of the genitals or pubic area of any person; flagellation or torture by or upon a person who is nude; condition of being fettered, bound, or otherwise physically restrained on the part of a person who is nude; physical contact in an act of apparent sexual stimulation or gratification with any person's unclothed genitals, pubic area, or buttocks, or with a female's nude breasts; defecation or urination for the purpose of sexual stimulation of the viewer; or penetration of the vagina or rectum by any object except when done as part of a recognized medical procedure. GA. CODE ANN. § 16-12-100 (enacted 1978).

HAWAII: No statute.

IDAHO: It is a felony to knowingly and willfully possess any sexually exploitative material. IDAHO CODE § 18-1507A (enacted 1987). Sexually exploitative material means any photograph, motion picture, videotape, print, negative, slide, or other mechanically, electronically, or chemically reproduced visual material which depicts a child engaged in, participating in, observing, or being used for explicit sexual conduct. Explicit sexual conduct means sexual intercourse, erotic fondling, erotic nudity, masturbation, sadomasochism, sexual excitement, or bestiality. IDAHO CODE § 18-1507 (enacted 1983).

ILLINOIS: A person commits the felony offense of child pornography who, with knowledge of the nature or content thereof, possesses any film, videotape, photograph, or other similar visual reproduction of any child or institutionalized severely or profoundly mentally retarded person whom the offender knows or reasonably should know to be under the age of eighteen or to be an institutionalized severely or profoundly mentally retarded person, engaged in any actual or simulated: act of sexual intercourse with any person or animal, or any act of sexual contact involving the sex organs of the child or mentally retarded person and the mouth, anus, or sex organs of another person or animal; or which involves the mouth, anus, or sex organs of the child or mentally retarded person and the sex organs of another person or an animal; or any act of masturbation, or portrayal of an object of, or otherwise engaged in any act of lewd fondling, touching, or caressing, involving another person or animal; or any act of excretion or urination within a sexual context; or portrayal or depiction as bound, fettered, or subject to sadistic or masochistic abuse in any sexual context; or depiction or portrayal in any pose, posture, or setting involving a lewd exhibition of the unclothed genitals, pubic area, buttocks, or, if such person is a female, a fully or partially developed breast of the child or other person. ILL. ANN. STAT. ch. 720, para. 5/11-20.1 (enacted 1961).

INDIANA: It is a misdemeanor to knowingly or intentionally possess a picture, drawing, photograph, negative image, undeveloped film, motion picture, videotape, or any pictorial representation that depicts or describes sexual conduct by a child who is, or appears to be, under sixteen and that lacks serious literary, artistic, political, or scientific value. Sexual conduct means sexual intercourse, deviate sexual conduct, exhibition of the uncovered genitals intended to satisfy or arouse the sexual desires of any person, sadomasochistic abuse, sexual intercourse or deviate sexual conduct with an animal, or any fondling or touching of a child by another person or of another person by a child intended to arouse or satisfy the sexual desires of either the child or the other person. IND. CODE ANN. § 35-42-4-4 (enacted 1978).

IOWA: It is a serious misdemeanor to knowingly purchase or possess a negative, slide, book, magazine, or other print or visual medium depicting a person under eighteen engaging in a prohibited sexual act or the simulation of a prohibited sexual act. This section does not apply to law enforcement officers, court personnel, licensed physicians, licensed psychologists, or attorneys in the performance of their official duties. IOWA CODE ANN. § 728.12 (enacted 1978). Prohibited sexual act means: any sexual contact between two or more persons by penetration of the penis into the vagina or anus, by contact between the mouth and genitalia or by contact between the genitalia of one person and the genitalia or anus of another person or by use of artificial sexual organs or substitutes thereof in contact with the genitalia or anus; bestiality; fondling or touching the pubes or genitals; sadomasochistic abuse of a child, or of another person by a child, for the purpose of arousing or satisfying the sexual desires of a person who may view a depiction of the abuse; or nudity of a child for the purpose of arousing or satisfying the sexual desires of a person who may view a depiction of the nude child. IOWA CODE ANN. § 728.1 (enacted 1976).

KANSAS: It is a felony to possess any film, photograph, negative, slide, book, magazine, or other printed or visual medium, or any audio tape recording in which a child under sixteen years of age is shown or heard engaging in sexually explicit conduct with intent to arouse or satisfy the sexual desires or appeal to the prurient interest of the offender, the child, or another. Sexually explicit conduct means actual or simulated: exhibition in the nude, sexual intercourse or sodomy, including genital-genital, oral-genital, anal-genital, or oral-anal contact; masturbation; sadomasochistic abuse for the purpose of sexual stimulation; or lewd exhibition of the genital or pubic area of any person. KAN. STAT. ANN. § 21-3516 (enacted 1978).

KENTUCKY: It is a misdemeanor for a first offense and a felony for subsequent offenses to knowingly possess or control any matter which visually depicts an actual sexual performance by a minor person. KY. REV. STAT. ANN. § 531.335 (enacted 1992). Sexual performance means any performance or part thereof which includes: acts of masturbation, homosexuality, lesbianism, bestiality, sexual intercourse or deviant sexual intercourse, actual or simulated; physical contact with, or willful or intentional exhibition of the genitals; flagellation or excretion for the purpose of sexual stimulation or gratification; or the exposure, in an obscene manner, of the unclothed or apparently unclothed human male or female genitals, pubic area or buttocks, or the female breast, whether or not subsequently obscured by a mark placed thereon, or otherwise altered, in any resulting motion picture, photograph, or other visual representation, exclusive of exposure portrayed in matter of a private, family nature not intended for distribution outside of the family. KY. REV. STAT. ANN. § 531.300 (enacted 1986).

LOUISIANA: It is a felony to intentionally possess any photograph, films, videotape, or other visual reproduction of any performance or part thereof involving a child under seventeen that includes actual or simulated sexual intercourse, deviate sexual intercourse, sexual bestiality, masturbation, sadomasochistic abuse, or lewd exhibition of the genitals. Lack of knowledge of the child's age shall not be a defense. LA. REV. STAT. ANN. § 14:81.1 (enacted 1981).

MAINE: No statute.

MARYLAND: It is a misdemeanor to knowingly possess any film, videotape, photograph, or other visual representation depicting an individual under sixteen engaged as a subject of sadomasochistic abuse or in sexual conduct, or in a state of sexual excitement. MD. ANN. CODE, art. 27, § 419B (enacted 1957). Sadomasochistic abuse means flagellation or torture by or upon a human who is nude, or clad in undergarments, or in a revealing or bizarre costume, or the condition of one who is nude or so clothed and is being fettered, bound, or otherwise physically restrained. Sexual conduct means human masturbation; sexual intercourse; or any touching or contact with genitals; pubic areas or buttocks of the human male or female, or the breasts of the female, whether alone or with others, or between humans and animals. Sexual excitement means the condition of human male or female genitals, or the breasts of the female, when in a state of sexual stimulation, or the sensual experiences of humans engaging in or witnessing sexual conduct or nudity. MD. ANN. CODE, art. 27, § 416A (enacted 1971).

MASSACHUSETTS: No statute.

MICHIGAN: No statute.

MINNESOTA: It is a gross misdemeanor to possess a photographic representation of sexual conduct which involves a minor, knowing or with reason to know its content and character and where an actual minor is an actor or photographic subject in it. This section does not apply to the performance of official duties by peace officers, court personnel, or attorneys, nor to licensed physicians, psychologists, or social workers in the course of a bona fide treatment or professional education program. Sexual conduct means any of the following if the act involves a minor: an act of sexual intercourse, normal or perverted, actual or simulated, including genital-genital, anal-genital, or oral-genital intercourse, whether between human beings or a human being and an animal; sadomasochistic abuse, meaning flagellation, torture, or similar demeaning acts inflicted by or upon a person who is nude or clad in undergarments or in a revealing costume, or the condition of being fettered, bound, or otherwise physically restrained on the part of one so clothed; masturbation or lewd exhibitions of the genitals; or physical contact or simulated physical contact with the clothed or unclothed pubic areas or buttocks of a human male or female, or the breasts of the female, whether alone or between members of the same or opposite sex or between humans and animals in an act of apparent sexual stimulation or gratification. MINN. STAT. ANN. §§ 617.246 (enacted 1977), 617.247 (enacted 1982).

MISSISSIPPI: It is a felony to knowingly and for the purpose of sexual gratification of the sender or the recipient to transport, ship, or mail any photograph, drawing, sketch, film, or video depicting a child under eighteen engaging in all forms of sexual intercourse, actual or simulated, masturbation, bestiality, sadomasochistic abuse, sodomy, or other sexual activity or nudity when such nudity is depicted for the purpose of sexual stimulation or gratification of any individual who may view such nude depiction. MISS. CODE ANN. §§ 97-5-33 (enacted 1979), 97-5-31 (enacted 1979).

MISSOURI: It is a misdemeanor for a first offense and a felony for subsequent offenses to possess or control any obscene material that has a minor as one of its participants or portrays a minor as an observer of sexual conduct, sexual contact, or a sexual performance; or to possess or control any material that shows a minor participating or engaging in sexual conduct. MO. ANN. STAT. § 573.037 (enacted 1987). Material is obscene if, applying contemporary community standards, its predominant appeal is to prurient interest in sex, and taken as a whole by the average person, applying contemporary community standards, it depicts or describes sexual conduct in a patently offensive way, and taken as a whole, it lacks serious literary, artistic, political, or scientific value. MO. ANN. STAT. § 573.010 (enacted 1977). Sexual conduct means actual or simulated, normal or perverted acts of: human masturbation; deviate sexual intercourse; sexual intercourse; or physical contact with a person's clothed or unclothed genitals, pubic area, buttocks, or the breast of a female in an act of apparent sexual stimulation or gratification; or any sadomasochistic abuse or acts including animals or any latent objects in an act of apparent sexual stimulation or gratification. MO. ANN. STAT. § 573.010 (enacted 1977).

MONTANA: It is a misdemeanor to possess any visual or print medium in which children are engaged in actual or simulated sexual conduct. MONT. CODE ANN. § 45-5-625. Sexual conduct means actual or simulated: sexual intercourse, whether between persons of the same or opposite sex; penetration of the vagina or rectum by any object, except when done as part of a recognized medical procedure; bestiality; masturbation; sadomasochistic abuse; lewd exhibition of the genitals, breasts, pubic, or rectal area, or other intimate parts of any person; or defecation or urination for the purpose of the sexual stimulation of the viewer. MONT. CODE ANN. § 45-5-620 (enacted 1993).

NEBRASKA: It is a misdemeanor for any person to knowingly possess any visual depiction of sexually explicit conduct which has a minor as one of its participants or portrayed observers. NEB. REV. STAT. § 28-1463.02 (enacted 1986). Sexually explicit conduct means: real or simulated intercourse, whether genital-genital, oral-genital, anal-genital, or oral-anal between persons of the same or opposite sex or between a human and an animal or with an artificial genital; real or simulated masturbation; real or simulated sadomasochistic abuse; erotic fondling; erotic nudity; or real or simulated defecation or urination for the purpose of sexual gratification or sexual stimulation of one or more persons involved. NEB. REV. STAT. § 28-813.01 (enacted 1988).

NEVADA: It is a gross misdemeanor for the first offense and a felony for subsequent offenses to knowingly and willfully possess any film, photograph, or other visual presentation depicting a person under sixteen engaging in or simulating, or assisting others to engage in or simulate, sexual conduct. NEV. REV. STAT. § 200.730 (enacted 1983). Sexual conduct means sexual intercourse, lewd exhibition of genitals, fellatio, cunnilingus, bestiality, anal intercourse, excretion, sadomasochistic abuse, masturbation, or the penetration of any part of a person's body, or any object manipulated or inserted by a person into the genital or anal opening of the body of another. NEV. REV. STAT. § 200.700 (enacted 1983).

NEW HAMPSHIRE: It is a midemeanor to buy, procure, possess, control, bring into the state, or cause to be brought into the state, any visual representation of a child engaging in sexual activity. N.H. REV. STAT. ANN. § 649-A:3 (enacted 1983). Sexual activity means human masturbation, the touching of the actor's or other person's sexual organs in the context of a sexual relationship, actual or simulated sexual intercourse, normal or perverted, whether alone or between members of the same or opposite sex or between humans and animals; any lewd exhibition of the genitals, flagellation, or torture. N.H. REV. STAT. ANN. § 649-A:2 (enacted 1983).

NEW JERSEY: It is a felony for any person to knowingly possess, procure, or view any photograph, film, videotape, or any other reproduction or reconstruction which depicts a person under sixteen engaging in a prohibited sexual act. Prohibited sexual acts are sexual intercourse, anal intercourse, masturbation, bestiality, sadism, masochism, fellatio, cunnilingus, and nudity, if depicted for the purpose of sexual stimulation or gratification of any person who may view such depiction. N.J. STAT. ANN. § 2C:24-4 (enacted 1978).

NEW MEXICO: No statute.

NEW YORK: No statute.

NORTH CAROLINA: It is a felony to possess material that contains a visual representation of a minor engaging in sexual activity if the offender knows the character or content of the material. Mistake of age is not a defense. N.C. GEN. STAT. § 14-190.17A (enacted 1989). Sexual activity means: masturbation, alone or with another person or an animal; vaginal, anal, or oral intercourse with another person or an animal; touching, in an act of apparent sexual stimulation or sexual abuse, of the clothed or unclothed genitals, pubic area, or buttocks of another person or breasts of a human female; an act or condition that depicts torture, physical restraint by being fettered or bound, or flagellation of or by a person clad in undergarments or in revealing or bizarre costume; excretory functions; or the insertion of any part of a person's body, other than the male sexual organ, or of any object into another person's anus or vagina, except when done as a part of a recognized medical procedure. N.C. GEN. STAT. § 14-190.13 (enacted 1985).

NORTH DAKOTA: It is a misdemeanor for a first offense and a felony for subsequent offenses for a person, knowing of its character and content, to knowingly possess any motion picture, photograph, or other visual representation that includes sexual conduct by a minor. N.D. CENT. CODE § 12.1-27.2-04.1 (enacted 1989). Sexual conduct means actual or simulated: sexual intercourse; sodomy; sexual bestiality;

masturbation; sadomasochistic abuse; excretion; or lewd exhibition of the male or female genitals. N.D. CENT. CODE § 12.1-27.1-01 (enacted 1975).

OHIO: It is a felony to buy, procure, possess, or control any obscene material that has a minor as one of its participants. OHIO REV. CODE ANN. § 2907.321 (enacted 1988). Any material is considered "obscene" if, when considered as a whole, and judged with reference to ordinary adults, or if designed for another specially susceptible group, judged with reference to that group: its dominant appeal is to prurient interest and its dominant tendency is to arouse lust by displaying or depicting sexual activity, masturbation, sexual excitement, or nudity in a way that tends to represent human beings as mere objects or sexual appetite; bestiality or extreme or bizarre violence, cruelty or brutality; human bodily functions of elimination in a way that inspires disgust or revulsion in persons with ordinary sensibilties, without serving any genuine scientific, educational, sociological, moral, or artistic purpose. OHIO REV. CODE ANN. § 2907.01 (enacted 1990).

It is a misdemeanor to receive, possess, or control any material that shows a minor participating or engaging in sexual activity, masturbation, or bestiality. OHIO REV. CODE ANN. § 2907.322 (enacted 1988). Sexual activity means vaginal intercourse between a male and female, and anal intercourse, fellatio, and cunnilingus between persons regardless of sex, any touching of an errogenous zone of another, including without limitation the thigh, genitals, buttock, pubic region, or if the person is a female, a breast, for the purpose of sexually arousing or gratifying either person. OHIO REV. CODE ANN. § 2907.01 (enacted 1990).

It is a misdemeanor to possess or view any material or performance that shows a minor who is not the person's child or ward in a state of nudity, unless one of the following applies: the material or performance is possessed or controlled for a bona fide artistic, medical, scientific, educational, religious, governmental, judicial, or other proper purpose, by or to a physician, psychologist, sociologist, scientist, teacher, person pursuing bona fide studies or research, librarian, clergyman, prosecutor, judge, or other person having a proper interest in the material or performance; or the person knows that the parents, guardian or custodian has consented in writing to the photographing or use of the minor in a state of nudity and to the manner in which the material or performance is used or transferred. OHIO REV. CODE ANN. § 2907.322 (enacted 1988).

Oklahoma: It is a felony to knowingly possess any of the following materials involving the participation of any person under eighteen: any film, motion picture, videotape, photograph, negative, slide, drawing, painting, play, or performance where the minor is engaged in or portrayed, depicted, or represented as engaging in any act of sexual intercourse, in any act of fellatio or cunnilingus, in any act of excretion in the context of sexual activity, or in any lewd exhibition of the uncovered genitals having the purpose of sexual stimulation of the viewer. Okla. Stat. Ann. tit. 21, § 1021.2 (enacted 1978). It is a felony to buy, procure, or possess obscene material. Okla. Stat. Ann. tit. 21, § 1024.2 (enacted 1981). Obscene material means any photographic product depicting actual human models or actors, whether in the form of still photographs, undeveloped photographs, motion pictures, undeveloped film, videotape, or a purely photographic product or reproduction of such product, where the obscene material has as one of its participants or portrayed observers a child under eighteen or who appears as prepubescent; or contains depictions or descriptions of sexual conduct which are patently offensive; taken as a whole has as the dominant theme an appeal to prurient interest, as found by the average person applying contemporary community standards; and taken as a whole lacks serious literary, artistic, educational, political, or scientific purposes or value. Sexual conduct means sexual intercourse including any intercourse which is normal or perverted, actual or simulated; deviate sexual conduct including oral and anal sodomy; masturbation; sadomasochistic abuse; excretion in a sexual context, or exhibition of the human genitals or pubic areas. Okla. Stat. Ann. tit. 21, § 1024.1 (enacted 1981).

It is a felony to knowingly buy any picture, moving picture, drawing, electronic video game, diagram, or photograph of any person or animal or caricature thereof in an act of sexual intercourse or unnatural copulation. Okla. Stat. Ann. tit. 21, § 1040.51 (enacted 1968).

Oregon: It is a felony to knowingly possess or control any photograph, motion picture, videotape, or other visual recording of sexually explicit conduct involving a child. Or. Rev. Stat. § 163.672 (enacted 1991). Sexually explicit conduct means actual or simulated: sexual intercourse or deviant sexual intercourse; genital-genital, oral-genital, anal-genital, or oral-anal contact, whether between persons of the same or opposite sex or between humans and animals; object penetration of the vagina or rectum, other than as part of a medical diagnosis or treatment or as part of a personal hygiene practice; masturbation, sadistic or masochistic abuse; or lewd exhibition of the genitals or pubic area. OR. REV. STAT. § 163.665 (enacted 1985).

PENNSYLVANIA: It is a felony to knowingly possess or control any book, magazine, pamphlet, slide, photograph, film, videotape, computer depiction, or other material depicting a child under eighteen engaging in or simulating any of the following acts: sexual intercourse, including intercourse per os or per anus, masturbation, bestiality, sadism, masochism, fellatio, cunnilingus, lewd exhibition of the genitals, or nudity if such nudity is depicted for the purpose of sexual stimulation or gratification of any person who might view the depiction. 18 PA. CONS. STAT. ANN. § 6312 (enacted 1977).

RHODE ISLAND: No statute.

SOUTH CAROLINA: It is a felony to receive, purchase, exchange, solicit, or possess materials that contain a visual representation of a minor engaging in sexual activity. S.C. CODE ANN. §§ 16-15-405 (enacted 1987), 16-15-410 (enacted 1991). Sexual activity includes any of the following acts or simulations thereof: masturbation, alone or with another person or animal; vaginal, oral, or anal intercourse with another human or an animal; touching, in an act of apparent sexual stimulation or sexual abuse, of the clothed or unclothed genitals, pubic area, or buttocks of another person, or the clothed or unclothed breasts of a human female; an act or condition that depicts bestiality, sadomasochistic abuse, meaning flagellation or torture by or upon a person who is nude or clad in undergarments or in a costume which reveals the pubic hair, anus, vulva, genitals, or female breast nipples, or the condition of being fettered, bound, or otherwise physically restrained on the part of the one so clothed; excretory functions; or the insertion of any part of a person's body, other than the male sexual organ, or of any object into another person's anus or vagina, except when done as a part of a recognized medical procedure. S.C. CODE ANN. § 16-15-375 (enacted 1987).

SOUTH DAKOTA: It is a misdemeanor to knowingly possess any book, magazine, pamphlet, slide, photograph, or film depicting a person under eighteen engaging in a prohibited sexual act or in the simulation of such act. S.D. CODIFIED LAWS ANN. § 22-22-23.1 (enacted 1987). Prohibited sexual act means: sexual intercourse, anal intercourse, masturbation, bestiality, sadism, masochism, fellatio, cunnilingus, incest, or any other sexual activity including nudity if such sexual activity is depicted for the purpose of sexual stimulation or gratification of any person who might view such depiction. S.D. CODIFIED LAWS ANN. § 22-22-22 (enacted 1978).

TENNESSEE: It is a felony to knowingly possess material that includes a minor engaged in sexual activity or engaged in simulated sexual activity that is patently offensive, meaning that it goes substantially beyond customary limits of candor in describing or representing such matters. TENN. CODE ANN. §§ 39-17-1002 (enacted 1990), 39-17-1003 (enacted 1990). Sexual activity means any of the following acts: vaginal, anal, or oral intercourse with another person or an animal; masturbation, whether done alone or with another person or an animal; patently offensive, as determined by contemporary community standards, physical contact with or touching of a person's clothed or unclothed genitals, pubic area, buttocks, or breasts in an act of apparent sexual stimulation or sexual abuse; sadomasochistic abuse including flagellation, torture, physical restraint, domination, or subordination by or upon a person for the purpose of sexual gratification of any person; the insertion of any part of a person's body or of any object into another person's anus or vagina, except when done as part of a recognized medical procedure by a licensed professional; patently offensive, as determined by contemporary community standards, conduct, representations, depictions, or descriptions of excretory functions; or lascivious exhibition of the genitals or pubic area of any person. TENN. CODE ANN. § 39-17-1002 (enacted 1990).

TEXAS: It is a felony to knowingly or intentionally possess material containing a film image that visually depicts a child under seventeen at the time the film image of the child was made, who is engaging in sexual conduct. TEX. PENAL CODE ANN. § 43.26 (enacted 1985). Sexual conduct means actual or simulated sexual intercourse, deviate sexual intercourse, sexual bestiality, masturbation, sadomasochistic abuse, or lewd exhibition of the genitals. TEX. PENAL CODE ANN. § 43.25 (enacted 1977).

UTAH: It is a felony to possess material depicting a nude or partially nude minor for the purpose of sexual arousal of any person or any person's engagement in sexual conduct with the minor. UTAH CODE ANN. § 76-5a-3 (enacted 1983). Sexual conduct means and includes the following acts, whether actual or simulated, regardless of the gender or state of dress of the participants: sexual intercourse or deviate sexual intercourse; masturbation; sodomy or bestiality; sadomasochistic activities; the fondling or touching of the genitals, pubic region, buttocks, or female breast; or the explicit representations of the defecation or urination functions. UTAH CODE ANN. § 76-5a-2 (enacted 1983).

VERMONT: No statute.

VIRGINIA: It is a misdemeanor for a first offense, and a felony for subsequent offenses, to knowingly possess any sexually explicit visual material utilizing or having as a subject a person under eighteen, unless the prohibited material comes into the offender's possession from a law-enforcement officer or law-enforcement agency, or where the material is possessed for a bona fide artistic, medical, scientific, educational, religious, governmental, judicial, or other proper purpose by a physician, psychologist, sociologist, scientist, teacher, person pursuing bona fide studies or research, librarian, clergyman, prosecutor, judge, or other person having a proper interest in the material. VA. CODE ANN. § 18.2-374.1:1 (enacted 1992). Sexually explicit visual material means a picture, photograph, drawing, sculpture, motion-picture film, or similar visual representation which depicts sexual bestiality, a lewd exhibition of nudity, or sexual excitement, sexual conduct, or sadomasochistic abuse, or a book, magazine, or pamphlet which contains such a visual representation. An undeveloped photograph or similar visual material may be sexually explicit material notwithstanding that processing or other acts may be required to make its sexually explicit content apparent. VA. CODE ANN. § 18.2-374.1 (enacted 1979).

WASHINGTON: It is a felony to knowingly possess visual or printed matter depicting a minor engaged in sexually explicit conduct. WASH. REV. CODE ANN. § 9.68A.070 (enacted 1969). Sexually explicit conduct means actual or simulated sexual intercourse, including genital-genital, oral-genital, anal-genital, or oral-anal contact, whether between persons or with an animal; penetration of the vagina or rectum by any object; masturbation; sadomasochistic abuse for the purpose of sexual stimulation of the viewer; exhibition of the genitals or unclothed pubic or rectal areas of any minor or the unclothed breast of a female minor for the purpose of sexual stimulation of the viewer; defecation or urination for the purpose of sexual stimulation of the viewer; and touching of a person's clothed or unclothed genitals, pubic area, buttocks, or breast area for the purpose of sexual stimulation of the viewer. WASH. REV. CODE ANN. § 9.68A.011 (enacted 1984).

It is a misdemeanor for any minor to misrepresent his true age or his true status as the child, stepchild, or ward of a person accompanying him for the purpose of purchasing or obtaining access to any erotic material. WASH. REV. CODE ANN. § 9.68.080 (enacted 1969). Erotic material means printed material, photographs, pictures, motion pictures, sound recordings, and other material the dominant theme of which taken as a whole appeals to the prurient interest of minors in sex; which is patently offensive because it affronts contemporary community standards relating to the description or representation of sexual matters or sadomasochistic abuse; and which is utterly without redeeming social value. WASH. REV. CODE ANN. § 9.68.050 (enacted 1969).

WEST VIRGINIA: It is a felony to knowingly possess any visual material portraying a child under eighteen engaged in any sexually explicit conduct. W. VA. CODE § 61-8C-3 (enacted 1979). Sexually explicit conduct includes actually performed or simulated genital to genital intercourse, fellatio, cunnilingus, anal intercourse, oral to anal intercourse, bestiality, masturbation, sadomasochistic abuse, excretory functions in a sexual context, or exhibition of the genitals, pubic, or rectal areas of any person in a sexual context. W. VA. CODE § 61-8C-1 (enacted 1979).

WISCONSIN: It is a felony to knowingly possess any undeveloped film, photographic negative, photograph, motion picture, videotape, or other pictorial reproduction of a person under eighteen engaged in sexually explicit conduct. WIS. STAT. ANN. § 948.12 (enacted 1989). Sexually explicit conduct means actual or simulated sexual intercourse, meaning vulvar penetration as well as cunnilingus, fellatio, or anal intercourse between persons, or any other intrusion, however slight, of any part of a person's body or of any object into the genital or anal opening; bestiality; masturbation; sexual sadism or sexual masochism; or lewd exhibition of genitals or pubic area. WIS. STAT. ANN. § 948.01 (enacted 1989).

WYOMING: No statute.

UNITED STATES: It is a felony to bring into the United States, or any place subject to the jurisdiction thereof, or to knowingly use any express company or other common carrier, for carriage in interstate or foreign commerce any obscene, lewd, lascivious, or filthy book, pamphlet, picture, motion-picture film, paper, letter, writing, print, or other matter of indecent character; or any obscene, lewd, lascivious, or filthy phonograph recording, electrical transcription, or other article, or thing capable of producing sound. It is also a felony to take from such express company or other common carrier any matter or thing the carriage of which is herein made unlawful. 18 U.S.C.A. § 1462 (enacted 1948).

It is a felony for any person to knowingly transport or ship in interstate or foreign commerce by any means including by computer or mails any visual depiction, if the producing of such visual depiction involves the use of a minor engaging in sexually explicit conduct; and such visual depiction is of such conduct. It is a felony for any person to knowingly receive or distribute any visual depiction that has been mailed, or has been shipped and transported in interstate or foreign commerce, or which contains materials which have been mailed or so shipped or transported, by any means including by computer, if the producing of such visual depiction involves the use of a minor engaging in sexually explicit conduct, and such visual depiction is of this conduct. It is a felony for any person either, in the special maritime and territorial jurisdiction of the United States, or on any land or building owned by, leased to, or otherwise used by or under the control of the government of the United States, or in the Indian country as defined by federal law, to knowingly possess three or more books, magazines, periodicals, films, videotapes, or other matter which contain any visual depiction that has been mailed, or has been shipped or transported in interstate or foreign commerce, or which was produced using materials which have been mailed or so shipped or transported by any means including by computer, if the producing of such visual depiction involves the use of a minor engaging in sexually explicit conduct; and such visual depiction is of such conduct. 18 U.S.C.A. § 2252 (enacted 1978).

14
Bestiality

This chapter covers sex acts between a person and an animal, but excludes crimes involving animals that are prohibited for an unrelated reason—for example, that the act is committed in public or forced on a child.

At common law, bestiality was a form of sodomy, as were nonprocreative sex acts between consenting adults, including married couples. Many early American sodomy statutes prohibited sodomy by making it a crime to commit "the abominable crime against nature with man or beast." There is some evidence that bestiality was particularly reviled because of fear that it would produce monsters. Some of the early statutes remain in place today, and typically carry heavier penalties than sodomy statutes that have been modernized and focus on human conduct.

At early common law, there was no offense of cruelty to animals. However, such statutes have been in place in the United States for quite some time. The focus of such statutes is different from that of the traditional sodomy statute; anticruelty statutes are concerned both with the treatment of the animal and with the offense to community standards, while antibestiality provisions embodied in the sodomy statutes are aimed only at offenses to community standards.

Modern cases enforcing bestiality provisions exist. *State v. Bonynge*, 450 N.W.2d 331 (Minn. App. 1990) (defendant convicted on one count of bestiality for an act he performed with a dog, and four counts of aiding and abetting bestiality for acts he encouraged adult women to perform with a dog). The general language in sodomy statutes has been interpreted to encompass all sexual contact between a human and an animal, rather than particular acts. *People v. Carrier*, 254 N.W.2d 35 (Mich. App. 1977) (bestiality prohibition encompasses a broader range of acts than sodomy prohibition between two humans).

ALABAMA: No statute.

ALASKA: No statute.

ARIZONA: A person commits public sexual indecency by intentionally or knowingly engaging contact between the offender's mouth, vulva, or genitals and the anus or genitals of an animal if another person is present and the offender is reckless about whether the witness, being a reasonable person, would be offended or alarmed by the act. Public sexual indecency is a misdemeanor. If the offender knowingly or intentionally engages in any of the listed acts and such person is reckless as to whether a minor under the age of fifteen is present, the offender has committed a felony. ARIZ. REV. STAT. ANN. § 13-1403 (enacted 1977).

ARKANSAS: It is a misdemeanor for a person to perform any act of sexual gratification involving: the penetration of the anus, vagina, or mouth of an animal by the penis or any body member of a person; or the penetration of the anus, vagina, or mouth of a person by the penis or any body member of an animal. ARK. CODE ANN. § 5-14-122 (enacted 1977).

CALIFORNIA: Any person who sexually assaults an animal for the purpose of arousing or gratifying the sexual desire of the offender is guilty of a misdemeanor. CAL. PENAL CODE § 286.5 (enacted 1975).

COLORADO: No statute.

CONNECTICUT: It is a misdemeanor to engage in sexual contact with an animal. CONN. GEN. STAT. ANN. § 53a-73a (enacted 1975).

DELAWARE: It is a felony to intentionally engage in any sexual contact, penetration, or intercourse with the genitalia of an animal, or intentionally cause another person to engage in any such sexual act with an animal for purposes of sexual gratification. DEL. CODE ANN. tit. 11, § 777 (enacted 1993). A person is guilty of a felony if he or she permits or advances an exhibition, display, or performance of a child engaging in bestiality or the simulation of such an act. DEL. CODE ANN. tit. 11, §§ 1103 (enacted 1953), 1108 (enacted 1961).

DISTRICT OF COLUMBIA: It is a felony for a person to take into that person's mouth or anus the sexual organ of an animal or to place that person's sexual organ in the mouth or anus of an animal. It is a violation to commit a lewd or indecent act. D.C. CODE ANN. §§ 22-3502 (enacted 1948), 22-1112 (enacted 1948).

Florida: No statute.

Georgia: It is a felony to perform or submit to any sexual act with an animal involving the sex organs of one and the mouth, anus, penis, or vagina of the other. Ga. Code Ann. § 16-6-6 (enacted 1968). It is unlawful to perform bestiality on premises licensed for alcholic beverages. Ga. Stat. Ann. § 3-3-41 (enacted 1988).

Hawaii: No statute.

Idaho: It is a felony to engage in the infamous crime against nature involving any penetration with any animal. Idaho Code §§ 18-6605 (enacted 1972), 18-6606 (enacted 1972). It is a misdemeanor for a person to knowingly exhibit or display, or permit to be displayed, an actual or simulated sex act or sexual contact between humans and animals. Idaho Code § 18-4105 (enacted 1973).

Illinois: No statute.

Indiana: No statute.

Iowa: No statute.

Kansas: Oral or anal copulation or sexual intercourse between a person and an animal is a misdemeanor. Kan. Crim. Code Ann. §§ 21-3501 (enacted 1969), 21-3505 (enacted 1969).

Kentucky: No statute.

Louisiana: The unnatural carnal copulation by a human being with an animal is a crime against nature and a felony. La. Rev. Stat. Ann. § 14:89 (enacted 1975).

Maine: No statute.

Maryland: It is a felony for an offender to take the sexual organs of an animal into the offender's mouth; to place the offender's sexual organs into the mouth of an animal; or to commit any other unnatural or perverted sexual practice with any other person or with an animal. Md. Ann. Code, art. 27, § 554 (enacted 1951).

Massachusetts: It is a felony to commit the abominable and detestable crime against nature with a beast. Mass. Gen. Laws ch. 272, § 34 (enacted 1902).

Michigan: It is a felony to commit the abominable and detestable crime against nature with any animal. Mich. Comp. Laws § 750.158 (enacted 1970).

MINNESOTA: Whoever carnally knows an animal or bird is guilty of a misdemeanor. If knowingly done in the presence of another, the misdemeanor carries a maximum penalty of imprisonment of not more than one year or a fine of not more than $3,000 or both. MINN. STAT. § 609.294 (enacted 1967).

MISSISSIPPI: It is a felony to engage in the detestable and abominable crime against nature committed with a beast. MISS. CODE ANN. § 97-29-59 (enacted 1848).

MISSOURI: No statute.

MONTANA: It is a felony to engage in any form of sexual penetration with an animal. MONT. CODE ANN. §§ 45-2-101 (enacted 1973), 45-5-505 (enacted 1973).

NEBRASKA: It is a misdemeanor to subject an animal to sexual penetration. Sexual penetration shall mean sexual intercourse in its ordinary meaning, cunnilingus, fellatio, anal intercourse, or any intrusion, however slight, of any part of the actor's or victim's body, or any object manipulated by the actor into the genital or anal openings of the victim's body which can be reasonably construed as being for nonmedical or nonhealth purposes. Sexual penetration shall not require emission of semen. NEB. REV. STAT. §§ 28-1010 (enacted 1977), 28-318 (enacted 1977).

NEVADA: No statute.

NEW HAMPSHIRE: No statute.

NEW JERSEY: No statute.

NEW MEXICO: No statute.

NEW YORK: It is a misdemeanor to engage in sexual conduct with an animal. N.Y. PENAL LAW § 130.20 (enacted 1965).

NORTH CAROLINA: It is a felony to commit the crime against nature with a beast. N.C. GEN. STAT. § 14-177 (enacted 1979).

NORTH DAKOTA: It is a misdemeanor to engage in any form of sexual contact with an animal or bird with the intent to arouse or gratify the offender's sexual desire. N.D. CENT. CODE §§ 12.1-20-12 (enacted 1973), 12.1-20-02 (enacted 1973).

OHIO: No statute.

Oklahoma: It is a felony to commit the detestable and abominable crime against nature with a beast. Any penetration, however slight, is sufficient to complete the crime against nature. Okla. Stat. tit. 21, §§ 886 (enacted 1910), 887 (enacted 1910).

Oregon: It is a felony to intentionally cause a person under eighteen to touch or contact the mouth, anus, or sex organs of an animal for the purpose of arousing or gratifying the sexual desire of a person. Or. Rev. Stat. § 163.427 (enacted 1991).

Pennsylvania: It is a misdemeanor to engage in any form of sexual intercourse with an animal. 18 Pa. Cons. Stat. §§ 3101 (enacted 1972), 3124 (enacted 1972).

Rhode Island: It is a felony to commit the abominable and detestable crime against nature with an animal. If convicted, the defendant shall be imprisoned not less than seven years. R.I. Gen. Laws § 11-10-1 (enacted 1956).

South Carolina: It is a felony to commit the abominable crime of buggery with a beast. S.C. Code Ann. § 16-15-120 (enacted 1962).

South Dakota: No statute.

Tennessee: No statute.

Texas: A person commits a misdemeanor if that person knowingly engages in an act involving contact between the offender's mouth or genitals and the anus or genitals of an animal or fowl in a public place or in a private place where the offender is reckless about whether another person is present who will be offended or alarmed by the act. Tex. Penal Code Ann. § 21.07 (enacted 1973).

Utah: It is a misdemeanor to engage in sexual contact between a person and an animal involving the genitals of one and the mouth or anus of the other, or involving the offender's use of an object in contact with the genitals or anus of the animal with the intent of sexually gratifying the offender. Animal means any live, nonhuman, vertebrate creature, including fowl. Utah Code Ann. § 76-9-301.8 (enacted 1953).

Vermont: No statute.

Virginia: It is a felony to carnally know in any manner any brute animal, or to voluntarily submit to such carnal knowledge. Va. Code Ann. § 18.2-361 (enacted 1950).

WASHINGTON: No statute.

WEST VIRGINIA: No statute.

WISCONSIN: It is a misdemeanor to do any of the following: to commit an act of sexual gratification involving the offender's sex organ and the sex organ, mouth, or anus of an animal; or to commit an act of sexual gratification involving the offender's sex organ, mouth, or anus and the sex organ of an animal. WIS. STAT. § 944.17 (enacted 1983). Sexual intercourse and sexual gratification, defined as oral or anal sex or bestiality, where a person might be viewed or in the presence of a third party, is a misdemeanor. WIS. STAT. ANN. §§ 944.15 (enacted 1983), 944.17 (enacted 1983).

WYOMING: No statute.

UNITED STATES: No statute.

15

Necrophilia

We have included prohibitions on sexual conduct with human remains where the statute is explicit on the subject. We have omitted statutes that prohibit offensive treatment of human remains in general where no sexual conduct is suggested.

Indecent treatment of a corpse was a crime at common law, and most states have had a statute regarding the treatment of corpses for quite some time. The Model Penal Code language makes it a misdemeanor to treat a corpse in a way that "would outrage ordinary family sensibilities." The purpose of this provision is to prevent emotional harm to the friends and family of the deceased individual, rather than to deter sexual conduct in general. The more modern treatment does not distinguish between sexual offenses to a corpse and other disrespectful treatment, such as opening a grave or illegal disposal of body parts, so there is no specific statutory provision focusing on sex acts. The trend is for states to treat this offense in a separate section of the state code from sexual offenses, but as is apparent below, a number of states still do treat it as an explicitly sexual crime.

ALABAMA: It is a misdemeanor to knowingly treat a human corpse in a way that would outrage ordinary family sensibilities. ALA. CODE § 13A-11-13 (enacted 1977). Any person who willfuly or maliciously desecrates, injures, defaces, removes, or destroys any tomb, monument, structure, or container of human remains, and invades or mutilates the human corpse or remains, shall be guilty of a felony. ALA. CODE § 13A-7-23.1 (enacted 1980).

ALASKA: It is a misdemeanor to engage in sexual penetration of a corpse. ALASKA STAT. § 11.61.130 (enacted 1978).

ARIZONA: No statute.

ARKANSAS: No statute.

CALIFORNIA: No statute.

COLORADO: No statute.

CONNECTICUT: It is a misdemeanor to engage in sexual contact with a dead body. CONN. GEN. STAT. ANN. § 53a-73a (enacted 1975).

DELAWARE: No statute.

DISTRICT OF COLUMBIA: No statute.

FLORIDA: No statute.

GEORGIA: It is a felony to perform any sexual act with a dead human body involving the sex organs of one and the mouth, anus, penis, or vagina of the other. GA. CODE ANN. § 16-6-7 (enacted 1977).

HAWAII: No statute.

IDAHO: No statute.

ILLINOIS: No statute.

INDIANA: A person who knowingly or intentionally has sexual intercourse or deviate sexual conduct with a corpse commits a felony. IND. CODE § 35-45-11.2 (enacted 1993).

IOWA: No statute.

KANSAS: No statute.

KENTUCKY: No statute.

LOUISIANA: No statute.

MAINE: No statute.

MARYLAND: No statute.

MASSACHUSETTS: No statute.

MICHIGAN: No statute.

MINNESOTA: Whoever carnally knows a dead body is guilty of a misdemeanor. If knowingly done in the presence of another, the person commits a felony. MINN. STAT. ANN. § 609.294 (enacted 1967).

MISSISSIPPI: No statute.

MISSOURI: No statute.

MONTANA: No statute.

Nebraska: No statute.

Nevada: It is a felony to engage in cunnilingus, fellatio, or any intrusion of any part of a person's body, or any object manipulated or inserted by a person into the genital or anal openings of the body of another where the offender performs these acts on the dead body of a human being. Nev. Rev. Stat. Ann. § 201.450 (enacted 1983).

New Hampshire: No statute.

New Jersey: No statute.

New Mexico: Any person who unlawfully uses an unclaimed body is guilty of a felony. N.M. Stat Ann. § 24-12-3 (enacted 1973).

New York: It is a misdemeanor to engage in sexual conduct with a dead human body. N.Y. Penal Law § 130.20 (enacted 1965).

North Carolina: No statute.

North Dakota: It is a misdemeanor to engage in any form of sexual contact with a dead person with the intent to arouse or gratify the offender's sexual desire. N.D. Cent. Code §§ 12.1-20-12 (enacted 1973), 12.1-20-02 (enacted 1973).

Ohio: Any person, except as authorized by law, who treats a corpse in a way that he knows would outrage reasonable family sensibilities is guilty of a misdemeanor. Any person, except as authorized by law, who treats a corpse in a way that he knows would outrage reasonable community sensibilities is guilty of a felony. Ohio Rev. Code Ann. § 2927.01 (enacted 1978).

Oklahoma: No statute.

Oregon: It is a felony to engage in sexual activity with a corpse or involving a corpse. Or. Rev. Stat. § 166.087 (enacted 1993).

Pennsylvania: Any person, except as authorized by law, who treats a corpse in a way that he knows would outrage reasonable family sensibilities is guilty of a misdemeanor. 18 Pa. Cons. Stat. Ann. § 5510 (enacted 1972).

Rhode Island: No statute.

South Carolina: No statute.

South Dakota: No statute.

TENNESSEE: A person commits a felony if he physically mistreats a corpse in a manner offensive to the sensibilities of an ordinary person. TENN. CODE ANN. § 39-17-312 (enacted 1989).

TEXAS: No statute.

UTAH: It is a felony to commit or attempt to commit sexual penetration, sexual intercourse, object rape, sodomy, or object sodomy upon any dead body. UTAH CODE ANN. § 76-9-704 (enacted 1973).

VERMONT: No statute.

VIRGINIA: No statute.

WASHINGTON: No statute.

WEST VIRGINIA: No statute.

WISCONSIN: All sexual assault crimes apply whether a victim is dead or alive at the time of the sexual contact or sexual intercourse. WIS. STAT. ANN. § 940.225 (enacted 1987).

WYOMING: No statute.

UNITED STATES: No statute.

16

Obscene Communications

These statutes are aimed at communications that either seek to harass or have the effect of harassing or offending, primarily through use of the telephone. The offense of placing a harassing phone call is usually a misdemeanor, with many states raising the level of the offense to a felony if the defendant has multiple convictions for it.

Almost all states and the federal government have statutes prohibiting this conduct, and many of those statutes have been challenged in state and federal courts as unconstitutional. The challenges have proceeded on two theories: first, that these statutes infringe the right of free speech, and second, that they are unconstitutionally vague.

A number of courts have found statutes aimed at obscene phone calls unconstitutional, while a number of courts have held the opposite. The Supreme Court has not addressed the question yet, explicitly declining to decide the issue in *Gormley v. Director, Connecticut State Dept. of Probation*, 632 F.2d 938 (2d Cir. 1980), cert. denied, 449 U.S. 1023 (1980); and *Thorne v. Bailey*, 846 F.2d 241 (4th Cir. 1988), cert. denied, 488 U.S. 984 (1988).

Obscenity is not protected by the First Amendment, so the portions of the harassment statutes directed at obscene communications are generally constitutionally sound. The same is probably true for profanity. *Chaplinsky v. New Hampshire*, 315 U.S. 568 (1942). The more difficult issues arise over language that is "offensive," "annoying," or "indecent." The courts that uphold statutes which contain such language generally do so when the offender must have a specific intent to offend or annoy the victim. See, for example, *Gormley v. Director*, cited above; *State v. Hagen*, 558 P.2d 750 (Ariz. App. 1976). Courts tend to find statutes unconstitutional where they criminalize offensive communications not intended to harass or give offense. See, e.g., *Walker v. Dillard*, 523 F.2d 3 (4th Cir. 1975).

Vague statutes are constitutional when a history of judicial interpretation gives them reasonable specificity. Some courts have held that a specific intent requirement saves a phone harassment statute because it provides clarity as to the state of mind of the defendant, while removing the focus from the question of which words precisely will complete the crime, a question that the statutes tend not to answer.

Courts have placed other requirements on phone harassment statutes in order to pass constitutional muster. In *State v. Elder*, 382 So. 2d 687 (Fla. 1980), the court said that a call must be unwanted, nonconsensual, or unsolicited for it to be a constitutionally valid crime. In *City of Everett v. Moore*, 683 P.2d 617 (Wash. App. 1984), the court decided that a harassment statute was unconstitutionally vague, but probably could be rescued if the legislature added language requiring that the victim receive the call in a place where the victim can reasonably expect privacy. *Jones v. Municipality of Anchorage*, 754 P.2d 275 (Alaska App. 1988), the court held that there is no First Amendment problem when a call is anonymous, because anonymous calls are "essentially noncommunicative." This decision may be weakened by a recent Supreme Court decision protecting anonymous leafleting from regulation on First Amendment grounds. *McIntyre v. Ohio Elections Commission*, 115 S. Ct. 1511 (1995).

ALABAMA: A person commits the crime of harassing communications if, with intent to harass or alarm another person, he telephones another person and addresses to or about such other person any lewd or obscene words or language. Harassing communications is a misdemeanor. ALA. CODE § 13A-11-8(b) (enacted 1977).

ALASKA: A person commits the crime of harassment if, with intent to harass or annoy another person, that person makes an anonymous or obscene telephone call or a telephone call that threatens personal injury. Harassment is a misdemeanor. ALASKA STAT. § 11.61.120(a)(2) (enacted 1978).

ARIZONA: It shall be unlawful for any person with intent to terrify, intimidate, threaten, harass, annoy, or offend, to use a telephone and use any obscene, lewd, or profane language, or suggest any lewd or lascivious act, or threaten to inflict injury or physical harm on the person or property of any person. The use of obscene, lewd, or profane language or the making of a threat or statement as set forth in this section shall be prima facie evidence of intent to terrify, intimidate, threaten, harass, annoy, or offend. Any offense committed by use of a telephone as set forth in this section shall be deemed to have been committed at either the place where the telephone call or calls originated or at the place where the telephone call or calls were received. Any person who violates the provisions of this section is guilty of a misdemeanor. ARIZ. REV. STAT. ANN. § 13-2916 (enacted 1977).

It is a felony for any person to knowingly make by means of a telephone, directly or by a recording device, any obscene or indecent communication for commercial purposes to any person under eighteen. The communication is unlawful regardless of whether the maker of the communication placed the call. ARIZ. REV. STAT. ANN. § 13-3512 (enacted 1988).

ARKANSAS: No statute.

CALIFORNIA: Every person who, with intent to annoy, telephones another and addresses to or about the other person any obscene language or addresses to the other person any threat to inflict injury to the person or property of the person addressed or any member of his or her family is guilty of a misdemeanor. Any offense committed by use of a telephone as provided in this section may be deemed to have been committed at either the place at which the telephone call or calls were made or at the place where the telephone call or calls were received. This section is violated when the person acting with intent to annoy makes a telephone call requesting a return call and performs the acts prohibited upon receiving the return call. CAL. PENAL CODE § 653m(a),(d),(e) (enacted 1963).

COLORADO: A person commits harassment if, with intent to harass, annoy, or alarm another person, he or she initiates communication with a person, anonymously or otherwise, by telephone, in a manner intended to harass or threaten bodily injury or property damage, or makes any comment, request, suggestion, or proposal by telephone, which is obscene. As used in this section, unless the context otherwise requires, obscene means a patently offensive description of ultimate sexual acts or solicitation to commit ultimate sexual acts, whether or not said ultimate sexual acts are normal or perverted, actual or simulated, including masturbation, cunnilingus, fellatio, analingus, or excretory functions. Harassment pursuant to this section is a misdemeanor. COLO. REV. STAT. § 18-9-111 (enacted 1971).

CONNECTICUT: A person is guilty of harassment in the second degree when: (1) by telephone, he addresses another in or uses indecent or obscene language; or (2) with intent to harass, annoy, or alarm another person, he communicates with a person by telegraph or mail, by electronically transmitting a facsimile through connection with a telephone network, or by any other form of written communication, in a manner likely to cause annoyance or alarm; or (3) with intent to harass, annoy, or alarm another person, he makes a telephone call, whether or not a conversation ensues, in a manner likely to cause annoyance or alarm. For purposes of this section such offense may be deemed to have been committed either at the place where the telephone call was made, or at the place where it was received. The court may order any person convicted under this section to be examined by one or more psychiatrists. Harassment is a misdemeanor. CONN. STAT. § 53a-183 (enacted 1969).

DELAWARE: A person is guilty of aggravated harassment when, in the course of a telephone call, he uses obscene, profane, or vulgar language, or language suggesting that the recipient of the call engage with him or another person in sexual relations of any sort, knowing that he is thereby likely to cause annoyance or alarm to the recipient of the call; or knowingly permits any telephone under his control to be used for a purpose prohibited by this section. Aggravated harassment is a misdemeanor. DEL. CODE ANN. tit. 11, § 1312 (enacted 1953).

DISTRICT OF COLUMBIA: No statute.

FLORIDA: Whoever makes a telephone call to a location at which the person receiving the call has a reasonable expectation of privacy; during such call makes any comment, request, suggestion, or proposal which is obscene, lewd, lascivious, filthy, vulgar, or indecent; and by such call or such language intends to offend, annoy, abuse, threaten, or harass any person at the called number, is guilty of a misdemeanor. Whoever knowingly permits any telephone under his control to be used for any purpose prohibited by this section is guilty of a misdemeanor. FLA. STAT. ANN. § 365.16 (enacted 1969).

A subscriber of a telephone service who makes any obscene or indecent communication by means of a telephone, in person or through an electronic recording device, in exchange for remuneration is guilty of a misdemeanor, regardless of whether he placed, initiated, or received the telephone call. A subscriber of telephone service who knowingly permits the use of a telephone or telephone facility under his control to make any obscene or indecent communication prohibited by this section is guilty of a misdemeanor, if the telephone or telephone facility is connected to a local exchange telephone. For purposes of this subsection, each day of the violation constitutes a separate offense. For purposes of this section, the term obscene means that status of a communication which: (1) the average person applying contemporary community standards would find, taken as a whole, appeals to the prurient interests; (2) describes, in a patently offensive way, deviate sexual intercourse, sadomasochistic abuse, sexual battery, bestiality, sexual conduct, or sexual excitement; and (3) taken as a whole, lacks serious literary, artistic, political, or scientific value. Deviate sexual intercourse means sexual conduct between persons consisting of contact between the penis and the anus, the mouth and the penis, or the mouth and the vulva. Sadomasochistic abuse means flagellation or torture by or upon a person, or the condition of being fettered, bound, or otherwise physically restrained, for the purpose of deriving sexual satisfaction from inflicting harm on another or receiving such harm oneself. Sexual battery means oral, anal, or vaginal penetration by, or union with, the sexual organ of another or the anal or vaginal penetration of another by any other object. Bestiality means any sexual act between a person and an animal involving the sexual organ of the one, and the mouth, anus, or vagina of the other. Sexual conduct means actual or simulated sexual intercourse, deviate sexual intercourse, sexual bestiality, masturbation, or sadomasochistic abuse; or any act or conduct which constitutes sexual battery. Sexual excitement means the condition of the human male or female genitals when in a state of sexual stimulation or arousal. FLA. STAT. ANN. § 365.161 (enacted 1995).

It is a misdemeanor for any telephone subscriber to sell, offer for sale, or transmit, over telephone lines, any obscene material or messages described and promoted as "adult" and of a nature which is commonly understood to be for the purposes of sexually oriented entertainment. FLA. STAT. ANN. § 847.0147 (enacted 1991).

GEORGIA: A person commits a misdemeanor, who, without provocation, uses obscene and vulgar or profane language by telephone to a person under the age of fourteen years which threatens an immediate breach of the peace. GA. CODE ANN. § 16-11-39 (enacted 1968).

It shall be a misdemeanor for any person, by means of telephone communication in this state, to make any comment, request, suggestion, or proposal which is obscene, lewd, lascivious, filthy, or indecent. Any person who knowingly permits any telephone under his control to be used for any purpose prohibited by this code section shall be guilty of a misdemeanor. GA. CODE ANN. § 46-5-21 (enacted 1968).

It is a misdemeanor for any person, by means of a telephone communication for commercial purposes, to make directly or by means of an electronic recording device, any comment, request, suggestion, or proposal which is obscene, lewd, lascivious, filthy, or indecent. Any person who makes any such comment, request, suggestion, or proposal may be subject to prosecution under this code section regardless of whether such person placed or initiated the telephone call. It is a misdemeanor for any person to permit knowingly any telephone or telephone facility connected to a local exchange telephone under such person's control to be used for any purpose prohibited by this code section. For purposes of this section, each day of a violation shall constitute a separate offense. GA. CODE ANN. § 46-5-22 (enacted 1981).

HAWAII: No statute.

IDAHO: Every person who, with intent to annoy, terrify, threaten, intimidate, harass, or offend, telephones another and addresses to or about such person any obscene, lewd, or profane language, or makes any request, suggestion, or proposal which is obscene, lewd, lascivious, or indecent, shall be guilty of a misdemeanor. Upon a second or subsequent offense, the defendant shall be guilty of a felony. The use of obscene, lewd, or profane language or the making of a threat or obscene proposal may be prima facie evidence of intent to annoy, terrify, threaten, intimidate, harass, or offend. For the purposes of this section, the term telephone shall mean any device which provides transmission of messages, signals, facsimiles, video images, or other communication between persons who are physically separated from each other, by means of telephone, telegraph, cable, wire, or the projection of energy without physical connection. IDAHO CODE § 18-6710 (enacted 1980).

ILLINOIS: Any person in this state who sends messages or uses language or terms which are obscene, lewd, or immoral with the intent to offend by means of or while using a telephone or telegraph facilities, equipment, or wires of any person, firm, or corporation engaged in the transmission of news or messages between states or within the state of Illinois is guilty of a misdemeanor. The use of language or terms which are obscene, lewd, or immoral is prima facie evidence of the intent to offend. ILL. ANN. STAT. ch. 720, para. 135/1 (enacted 1957). Harassment by telephone is use of telephone communication for the purpose of making any comment, request, suggestion, or proposal which is obscene, lewd, lascivious, filthy, or indecent with an intent to offend; or knowingly permitting any telephone under one's control to be used for the purpose mentioned above. ILL. ANN. STAT. ch. 720, para. 135/1-1 (enacted 1957). Any person who violates any of the provisions of the above sections is, upon conviction, guilty of a misdemeanor. ILL. ANN. STAT. ch. 720, para. 135/2 (enacted 1957).

INDIANA: No statute.

IOWA: A person shall not knowingly disseminate obscene material by the use of telephones or telephone facilities to a minor. A person who violates this subsection upon conviction is guilty of an aggravated misdemeanor. However, second and subsequent offenses of this subsection by a person who has been previously convicted of violating this subsection are felonies. As used in this subsection, a "person" excludes any information-access service provider that merely provides transmission capacity without control over the content of the transmission. It shall be a defense in any prosecution for a violation of this section by a person who knowingly disseminates obscene material by the use of telephones or telephone facilities to a minor that the defendant has taken either of the following measures to restrict access to the obscene material: (1) required the person receiving the obscene material to use an authorized access or identification code, as provided by the information provider, before transmission of the obscene material begins, where the defendant has previously issued the code by mailing it to the applicant after taking reasonable measures to ascertain that the applicant was eighteen years of age or older and has established a procedure to immediately cancel the code of any person after receiving notice, in writing or by telephone, that the code has been lost, stolen, or used by persons under the age of eighteen years or that the code is no longer desired; or (2) required payment by credit card before transmission of the obscene material. IOWA CODE ANN. § 728.15 (enacted 1989).

KANSAS: Harassment by telephone is use of telephone communication for any of the following purposes: making or transmitting any comment, request, suggestion, or proposal which is obscene, lewd, lascivious, filthy, or indecent; knowingly permitting use of any telephone or telefacsimile communication machine under one's control for any of the purposes mentioned herein. As used in this section, telephone communication shall include telefacsimile communication which is the use of electronic equipment to send or transmit a copy of a document via telephone lines. Harassment by telephone is a misdemeanor. KAN. STAT. ANN. § 21-4113 (enacted 1969).

KENTUCKY: No statute.

LOUISIANA: No person shall engage in or institute a telephone call, telephone conversation, or telephone conference, with another person, anonymously or otherwise, and therein use obscene, profane, vulgar, lewd, lascivious, or indecent language, or make any suggestion or proposal of an obscene nature or threaten any illegal or immoral act with the intent to coerce, intimidate, or harass another person; engage in a telephone call, conference, or recorded communication by using obscene language, when by making a graphic description of a sexual act, and the offender knows or reasonably should know that such obscene or graphic language is directed to, or will be heard by, a minor; or knowingly permit any telephone under his control to be used for any purpose prohibited by this section. Where age is relevant to the crime, lack of knowledge of age is not a defense. Any offense committed by use of a telephone as set forth in this section shall be deemed to have been committed at either the place where the telephone call or calls originated or at the place where the telephone call or calls were received. A first violation of this section is a misdemeanor. Second or subsequent offenses of this section are felonies. LA. REV. STAT. ANN. § 14:285 (enacted 1954).

MAINE: A person is guilty of harassment by telephone if he makes any comment, request, suggestion, or proposal which is, in fact, offensively coarse or obscene, without the consent of the person called, or he knowingly permits any telephone under his control to be used for any purpose prohibited by this section. The crime defined in this section may be prosecuted and punished in the county in which the defendant was located when he used the telephone, or in the county in which the telephone called or made to ring by the defendant was located. Harassment by telephone is a Class E crime. ME. REV. STAT. ANN. tit. 17-A, § 506 (enacted 1975).

MARYLAND: It is unlawful for any person to make use of telephone facilities or equipment for any comment, request, suggestion, or proposal which is obscene, lewd, lascivious, filthy, or indecent. Any person violating any one of the provisions of this section is guilty of a misdemeanor. MD. CRIM. LAW CODE ANN. § 555A (enacted 1961).

Massachusetts: Whoever telephones another person, or causes any person to be telephoned, repeatedly, for the sole purpose of harassing, annoying, or molesting such person or his family, whether or not conversation ensues, or whoever telephones a person repeatedly, and uses indecent or obscene language to such person, shall be guilty of a misdemeanor. Mass. Gen. Laws ch. 269, § 14A (enacted 1964). Persons who with offensive or disorderly acts accost or annoy persons of the opposite sex; lewd, wanton, and lascivious persons in speech or behavior; commit a misdemeanor. Mass. Gen. Laws ch. 272, § 53 (enacted 1943).

Michigan: Any person is guilty of a misdemeanor who maliciously uses any service provided by a communications common carrier with intent to terrorize, frighten, intimidate, threaten, harass, molest, or annoy any other person by using any vulgar, indecent, obscene, or offensive language, or suggesting any lewd or lascivious act in the course of a telephone conversation. Any person violating this section commits a misdemeanor. An offense is committed under this section if the communication either originates or terminates or both originates and terminates in this state, and may be prosecuted at the point of origination or termination. Mich. Comp. Laws Ann. § 750.540e (enacted 1969).

Minnesota: Whoever, by means of a telephone, makes any comment, request, suggestion, or proposal which is obscene, lewd, or lascivious, or, having control of a telephone, knowingly permits it to be used for such purpose, shall be guilty of a misdemeanor. The offense may be prosecuted either at the place where the call is made or where it is received. Minn. Stat. Ann. § 609.79 (enacted 1963).

Mississippi: It shall be unlawful for any person or persons to make any comment, request, suggestion, or proposal over a telephone which is obscene, lewd, or lascivious with intent to abuse, threaten, or harass any party to a telephone conversation; or to knowingly permit any telephone under his or her control to be used for any purpose prohibited by this section. Any person who shall be convicted of a violation of this section shall be guilty of a misdemeanor. Any person violating this section may be prosecuted in the county where the telephone call, conversation, or language originates in the state of Mississippi. In case the call, conversation, or language originates outside the state of Mississippi, then such person shall be prosecuted in the county to which it is transmitted. Miss. Code Ann. § 97-29-45 (enacted 1982).

Missouri: Obscenity shall be judged with reference to its impact on ordinary adults. It is unlawful for any person, by means of a telephone communication for commercial purposes, to make directly or by means of an electronic recording device, any comment, request, suggestion, or proposal which is obscene or indecent. Any person who makes any such comment, request, suggestion, or proposal shall be in violation of the provisions of this section regardless of whether such person placed or initiated the telephone call. It is unlawful for any person to permit knowingly any telephone or telephone facility connected to a local exchange telephone under such person's control to be used for any purpose prohibited by this section. Any person who violates any provision of this section is guilty of a misdemeanor unless such person has pleaded guilty to or has been found guilty of the same offense committed at a different time, in which case the violation is a felony. For purposes of this section, each violation constitutes a separate offense. These prohibitions are not applicable to a telecommunications company, over whose facilities prohibited communications may be transmitted. As used in this section, indecent means language or material that depicts or describes, in terms patently offensive as measured by contemporary community standards, sexual or excretory activities or organs; obscene means any comment, request, suggestion, or proposal is obscene if (1) applying contemporary community standards, its predominant appeal is to prurient interest in sex; (2) taken as a whole with respect to the average person, applying contemporary community standards, it depicts or describes sexual conduct in a patently offensive way; and (3) taken as a whole, it lacks serious literary, artistic, political, or scientific value. MO. ANN. STAT. § 573.100 (enacted 1989).

MONTANA: A person commits the offense of violating privacy in communications if he knowingly or purposely, with the purpose to terrify, intimidate, threaten, harass, annoy, or offend, communicates with any person by telephone and uses any obscene, lewd, or profane language, or suggests any lewd or lascivious act. The use of obscene, lewd, or profane language or the making of lewd or lascivious suggestions is prima facie evidence of an intent to terrify, intimidate, threaten, harass, annoy, or offend. A person convicted of the offense of violating privacy in telephone communications is guilty of a misdemeanor on the first offense, and a felony on subsequent offenses. MONT. CODE ANN. § 45-8-213 (enacted 1973).

NEBRASKA: A person commits the offense of intimidation by phone call if with intent to terrify, intimidate, threaten, harass, annoy, or offend, he telephones another and uses indecent, lewd, lascivious, or obscene language or suggests any indecent, lewd, or lascivious act. The use of indecent, lewd, or obscene language or the making of a threat or lewd suggestion shall be prima facie evidence of intent to terrify, intimidate, threaten, harass, annoy, or offend. The offense shall be deemed to have been committed either at the place where the call was made or where it was received. Intimidation by phone call is a misdemeanor. NEB. REV. STAT. § 28-1310 (enacted 1977).

NEVADA: Any person who willfully makes a telephone call and addresses any obscene language, representation, or suggestion to or about any person receiving such call, or addresses to such other person any threat to inflict injury to the person or property of the person addressed or any member of his family, is guilty of a misdemeanor. Any violation is committed at the place at which the telephone call or calls were made and at the place where the telephone call or calls were received, and may be prosecuted at either place. NEV. REV. STAT. § 201.255 (enacted 1967).

NEW HAMPSHIRE: A person is guilty of a misdemeanor, and subject to prosecution in the jurisdiction where the telephone call originated or was received, if, with a purpose to annoy or alarm another, he makes repeated communications at extremely inconvenient hours or in offensively coarse language. N.H. REV. STAT. ANN. § 644:4 (enacted 1971).

NEW JERSEY: No statute.

NEW MEXICO: It shall be unlawful for any person, with intent to terrify, intimidate, threaten, harass, annoy, or offend, to telephone another person and use any obscene, lewd, or profane language, or suggest any lewd, criminal, or lascivious act, or threaten to inflict injury or physical harm on the person or property of any person. The use of obscene, lewd, or profane language or the making of a threat or statement as set forth in the previous sentence shall be prima facie evidence of intent to terrify, intimidate, threaten, harass, annoy, or offend. Any offense committed by use of a telephone as set forth in this section shall be deemed to have been committed at either the place where the telephone call or calls originated or at the place where the telephone call or calls were received. Whoever violates this section is guilty of a misdemeanor, unless such person has previously been convicted of such offense or of an offense under the laws of another state or of the United States which would have been an offense under this section if committed in this state, in which case such person is guilty of a felony. N.M. STAT ANN. § 30-20-12 (enacted 1967).

NEW YORK: No statute.

NORTH CAROLINA: It shall be unlawful for any person to use in telephonic communications any words or language of a profane, vulgar, lewd, lascivious, or indecent character, nature, or connotation; to telephone another and knowingly make any false statement concerning death, injury, illness, disfigurement, indecent conduct, or criminal conduct of the person telephoned or of any member of his or her family or household, with the intent to abuse, annoy, threaten, terrify, harass, or embarrass; or to knowingly permit any telephone under his or her control to be used for any purpose prohibited by this section. Any of the above offenses may be deemed to have been committed at either the place at which the telephone call or calls were made or at the place where the telephone call or calls were received. For purposes of this section, the term "telephonic communications" shall include communications made or received by way of a telephone answering machine or recorder, telefacsimile machine, or computer modem. Anyone violating the provisions of this section shall be guilty of a misdemeanor. N.C. STAT. § 14-196 (enacted 1967).

NORTH DAKOTA: No statute.

OHIO: No person shall knowingly make or cause to be made a telephone call, or knowingly permit a telephone call to be made from a telephone under his or her control, to another, if the caller describes, suggests, requests, or proposes that the caller, recipient of the telephone call, or other person engage in any sexual activity, and the recipient of the telephone call, or another person at the premises to which the telephone call is made, has requested, in a previous telephone call or in the immediate telephone call, that the caller not make a telephone call to the recipient of the telephone call or to the premises to which the telephone call is made; or during the telephone call, cause another to believe that the offender will cause serious physical harm to the person or property of the victim or members of the victim's immediate family. No person shall make or cause to be made a telephone call, or permit a telephone call to be made from a telephone under his or her control, with purpose to abuse, threaten, annoy, or harass another person. Whoever violates this section is guilty of telephone harassment, a misdemeanor. If the offender has previously been convicted of a violation of this section, then telephone harassment is a felony. OHIO REV. CODE ANN. §§ 2903.21 (enacted 1972), 2917.21 (enacted 1974).

OKLAHOMA: Every person who willfully speaks any words by means of a telephone to any person which are offensive to decency or are calculated to excite vicious or lewd thoughts or acts, or who speaks any other communicable words which are offensive to decency or are adapted to excite vicious or lewd thoughts or acts, shall be guilty, upon conviction, of a felony. Every person who willfully solicits or aids a minor child to perform, or shows, exhibits, loans, or distributes to a minor child any obscene or indecent writing, paper, book, picture, motion picture, figure, or form of any description for the purpose of inducing said minor to participate in any act specified above, shall be guilty of a more serious felony. OKL. STAT. ANN. tit. 21, § 1021 (enacted 1910). It shall be unlawful for a person, by means of a telephone, to willfully either make any comment, request, suggestion, or proposal which is obscene, lewd, lascivious, filthy, or indecent, or knowingly permit any telephone under his or her control to be used for such purpose. Use of a telephone facility under this section shall include all use made of such a facility between points of origin and reception. Any offense under this act is a continuing offense and shall be deemed to have been committed at either the place of origin or the place of reception. A first offense is a misdemeanor, subsequent offenses are felonies. OKL. STAT. ANN. tit. 21, § 1021 (enacted 1969).

OREGON: No statute.

PENNSYLVANIA: A person commits a misdemeanor if, with intent to harass another, he or she makes a telephone call without intent of legitimate communication or addresses to or about such person any lewd, lascivious, or indecent words or language; or makes repeated communications in offensively coarse language. Any offense committed under this section may be deemed to have been committed at either the place at which the telephone call or calls were received or at the place where the telephone call or calls were made. 18 PA. CONS. STAT. ANN. § 5504 (enacted 1972).

RHODE ISLAND: Whoever shall originate a transmission by facsimile machine, or other telecommunication device, or shall telephone any person for the purpose of using any vulgar, indecent, obscene, or immoral language over the telephone, shall be guilty of a misdemeanor. This section shall not be construed to impose any liability upon providers of telecommunications services. R.I. GEN. LAWS § 11-35-17 (enacted 1956).

SOUTH CAROLINA: It is unlawful for a person to use in a telephone communication any words or language of a profane, vulgar, lewd, lascivious, or an indecent nature, or to communicate or convey by telephone an obscene, vulgar, indecent, profane, suggestive, or immoral message to another person; or knowingly permit a telephone under his control to be used for any purpose prohibited by this section. A person who violates this section is guilty of a felony, unless he or she only knowingly permitted a telephone under his or her control to be used to violate this section, in which case he or she is guilty of a misdemeanor. S.C. CODE ANN. § 16-17-430 (enacted 1962).

SOUTH DAKOTA: It is a misdemeanor for a person to use a telephone to call another person with intent to terrorize, intimidate, threaten, harass, or annoy such person using obscene or lewd language or by suggesting a lewd or lascivious act. It is also a misdemeanor for a person to knowingly permit a telephone under his or her control to be used for a purpose prohibited by this section. S.D. CODIFIED LAWS ANN. 49-31-31 (enacted 1967).

TENNESSEE: No statute.

TEXAS: A person commits an offense if, with intent to harass, annoy, alarm, abuse, torment, or embarass another, he or she initiates communication by telephone or in writing and in the course of the communication makes a comment, request, suggestion, or proposal that is obscene; or knowingly permits a telephone under his or her control to be used by a person to commit an offense under this section. For purposes of this section, obscene means containing a patently offensive description of or a solicitation to commit an ultimate sex act, including sexual intercourse, masturbation, cunnilingus, fellatio, or analingus, or a description of an excretory function. An offense under this section is a misdemeanor. TEX. PENAL CODE ANN. § 42.07 (enacted 1973).

UTAH: A person is guilty of telephone harassment and subject to prosecution in the jurisdiction where the telephone call originated or was received if, with intent to annoy, alarm another, intimidate, offend, abuse, threaten, harass, or frighten any person at the called number or recklessly creating a risk thereof, the person makes a telephone call and uses any lewd or profane language or suggests any lewd or lascivious act. Telephone harassment is a misdemeanor. UTAH CODE ANN. § 76-9-201 (enacted 1973).

VERMONT: A person with the intent to terrify, intimidate, threaten, harass, or annoy, telephones another and makes any request, suggestion, or proposal which is obscene, lewd, lascivious, or indecent, is guilty of a misdemeanor. Intent to terrify, threaten, harass, or annoy may be inferred by the trier of fact from the use of obscene, lewd, lascivious, or indecent language, and any trial court may in its discretion include a statement to this effect in its jury charge. An offense committed by use of a telephone as set forth in this section shall be considered to have been committed at either the place where the telephone call or calls originated or at the place where the telephone call or calls were received. VT. STAT. ANN. tit. 13, § 1027 (enacted 1967).

VIRGINIA: If any person shall use obscene, vulgar, profane, lewd, lascivious, or indecent language, or make any suggestion or proposal of an indecent nature, or threaten any illegal or immoral act with the intent to coerce, intimidate, or harass any person, over any telephone or citizens band radio, that person shall be guilty of a misdemeanor. VA. CODE ANN. § 18.2-427 (enacted 1950).

WASHINGTON: Every person who, with intent to harass, intimidate, torment, or embarass any other person, shall make a telephone call to such other person using any lewd, lascivious, profane, indecent, or obscene words or language, or suggesting the commission of any lewd or lascivious act, shall be guilty of a gross misdemeanor, except that the person is guilty of a felony if that person has previously been convicted of any crime of harassment with the same victim or member of the victim's family or household, or any person specifically named in a no-contact or no-harassment order in this or any other state. WASH. REV. CODE. ANN. § 9.61.230 (enacted 1967).

WEST VIRGINIA: It shall be unlawful for any person, with intent to harass or abuse another by means of a telephone, to make any comment, request, suggestion, or proposal which is obscene. It shall be unlawful for any person to knowingly permit any telephone under his control to be used for such purpose. Any offense committed under this section shall be deemed to have occured at the place at which the telephone call was made, or the place at which the telephone call was received. Any person who violates any provision of this section shall be guilty of a misdemeanor. W. VA. CODE ANN. § 61-8-16 (enacted 1931).

WISCONSIN: Whoever, with intent to frighten, intimidate, threaten, or abuse, telephones another and uses any obscene, lewd, or profane language, or suggests any lewd or lascivious act, is guilty of a misdemeanor. Whoever, with intent to harass or offend, telephones another and uses any obscene, lewd, or profane language or suggests any lewd or lascivious act; or knowingly permits any telephone under his or her control to be used for such purpose, is subject to forfeiture. WIS. STAT. ANN. § 947.012 (enacted 1991).

WYOMING: A person commits a misdemeanor if he or she telephones another anonymously or under a false or fictitious name and uses obscene, lewd, or profane language, or suggests a lewd or lascivious act with intent to terrify, intimidate, threaten, harass, annoy, or offend. A crime committed under this section is committed at the place where the calls either were originated or were received. WYO. STAT. § 6-6-103 (enacted 1982).

UNITED STATES: Whoever in the District of Columbia or in interstate or foreign communication by means of telephone makes (directly or by recording device): any comment, request, suggestion, or proposal which is obscene, lewd, lascivious, filthy, or indecent; any obscene communication for commercial purposes to any person, regardless of whether the maker of such communication placed the call; any indecent communication for commercial purposes which is available to any person under eighteen years of age or to any other person without that person's consent, regardless of whether the maker of such communication placed the call; or permits any telephone facility under such person's control to be used for any such activity; shall be guilty of a felony. It is a defense to prosecution for making an indecent communication for commercial purposes that the defendant restricted access to the prohibited communication to persons eighteen years or older by requiring a previous written request to the carrier for subscription to such a service. 47 U.S.C.A. § 223 (enacted 1991).

17

Voyeurism

Voyeurism, or "Peeping Tom," statutes have been a part of the criminal law for some time, growing out of the common law action for trespass. In recent years, some states have followed the Model Penal Code in providing more comprehensive prohibitions on invasions of privacy, including invasions by eavesdropping or using eavesdropping devices. A few states have taken up the Model Penal Code focus on surveillance devices, but most still rely on the earlier concept of voyeurism by trespass with visual observation.

It is not always necessary for a person to actually see anyone inside a dwelling for a successful Peeping Tom conviction; it is only necessary that the defendant intend to attempt to see a person. That intent can be inferred from the act of peering inside a dwelling. *Chance v. State*, 268 S.E.2d 737 (Ga. App. 1980).

ALABAMA: No statute.

ALASKA: No statute.

ARIZONA: Voyeurism is a misdemeanor. A person commits voyeurism by entering a residential yard and looking into the residential structure in reckless disregard of the inhabitant's privacy rights. ARIZ. REV. STAT. § 13-1504 (enacted 1977).

ARKANSAS: Voyeurism is a misdemeanor. A person is guilty of loitering if he lingers on or about the premises of another for the purpose of spying upon or invading the privacy of another. ARK. CODE ANN. § 5-71-213 (enacted 1975).

CALIFORNIA: Voyeurism is a misdemeanor. A person is guilty of disorderly conduct if that person, while loitering or wandering upon the private property of another, peeks into the door or window of any inhabited building. A person is also guilty if he or she looks through a hole into a bathroom with the intent to invade the privacy of the persons therein. CAL. PENAL CODE § 647 (enacted 1961).

COLORADO: No statute.

CONNECTICUT: No statute.

DELAWARE: Voyeurism is a misdemeanor. A person commits trespass by knowingly entering upon another's occupied property used as a dwelling, and if he or she intentionally peeps into another's door or window. DEL. CODE ANN. tit. 11, § 820 (enacted 1953). A person is guilty of violation of privacy if he or she trespasses on property intending to subject another to surveillance in a private place, or if he or she installs any device for recording events in an unauthorized place. DEL. CODE ANN. tit. 11, § 1335 (enacted 1953).

DISTRICT OF COLUMBIA: No statute.

FLORIDA: No statute.

GEORGIA: It is unlawful to be a "peeping Tom." A person is guilty of being a "peeping Tom" if that person peeps through windows or doors on or about the premises of another for the purpose of spying upon or invading the privacy of the persons spied upon. GA. CODE ANN. § 16-11-61 (enacted 1919).

HAWAII: Voyeurism is a misdemeanor. A person commits sexual assault in the fourth degree by knowingly trespassing onto property for the purpose of surreptitiously surveying another for sexual gratification. HAW. REV. STAT. § 707-33 (enacted 1986). A person is guilty of the misdemeanor of violation of privacy if he or she trespasses in order to subject someone to surveillance, or if he or she installs any device for observing events in an unauthorized location. HAW. REV. STAT. § 707-1111 (enacted 1972).

IDAHO: No statute.

ILLINOIS: No statute.

INDIANA: Voyeurism is a misdemeanor. A person commits voyeurism by peeping (enacted as looking clandestinely, surreptitiously, or with a secretive nature), or by going upon another's land or dwelling with the intent to peep. IND. CODE ANN. § 35-45-4-5 (enacted 1977).

IOWA: No statute.

KANSAS: No statute.

Kentucky: No statute.

Louisiana: Voyeurism is a misdemeanor. A person acts as a Peeping Tom by peeping through windows or doors while on or about the property of another for the purpose of spying upon or invading privacy. La. Rev. Stat. Ann. § 14:284 (enacted 1950).

Maine: Voyeurism is a misdemeanor. A person commits violation of privacy by trespassing with intent to observe any person in a private place, or by installing a device without consent to observe events in that place. Me. Rev. Stat. Ann. tit. 17-A, § 511 (enacted 1975).

Maryland: Voyeurism is a misdemeanor. A person commits trespass by entering another's premises for the purpose of invading the occupant's privacy by looking into any window or door. Md. Ann. Code, art. 27, § 580 (enacted 1953).

Massachusetts: No statute.

Michigan: It is unlawful to be a window peeper. A person is guilty of being a disorderly person by being a window peeper. Mich. Comp. Laws Ann. § 750.167c (enacted 1931).

Minnesota: Voyeurism is a misdemeanor. A person is guilty of interfering with privacy by entering another's property, surreptitiously gazing into an aperture of another's dwelling, or installing a device for observing, and intending to interfere with another's privacy. Minn. Stat. Ann. § 609.746 (enacted 1979).

Mississippi: Voyeurism is a felony. A person is guilty of felonious trespass by entering real property, peeping through a window or other opening of a building for a lewd, licentious, or indecent purpose. Miss. Code Ann. § 97-29-61 (enacted 1942).

Missouri: No statute.

Montana: No statute.

Nebraska: It is unlawful to invade another's privacy. A person commits invasion of privacy by intruding upon another's place of solitude or seclusion, if the intrusion would be highly offensive to a reasonable person. Neb. Rev. Stat. § 20-203 (enacted 1943).

Nevada: No statute.

New Hampshire: No statute.

NEW JERSEY: No statute.

NEW MEXICO: No statute.

NEW YORK: It is unlawful to install or maintain a two-way mirror or other viewing device, where the device has the purpose of allowing surreptitious observation of another in a fitting room, restroom, shower, or motel room. A violation results in a civil penalty of not more than three thousand dollars. N.Y. GEN. BUS. § 395-b (enacted 1982).

NORTH CAROLINA: Voyeurism is a misdemeanor. A person commits voyeurism by peeping secretly into any room occupied by a female person. N.C. GEN. STAT. § 14-202 (enacted 1923).

NORTH DAKOTA: Voyeurism is a misdemeanor. A person is guilty of disorderly conduct if, with intent to harass, annoy, or alarm, or in reckless disregard of the fact that another is harassed, annoyed, or alarmed by the person's behavior, he or she engages in harassing conduct by means of intrusive or unwanted acts intended to adversely affect the privacy of another. N.D. CENT. CODE § 12.1-31-01 (enacted 1973).

OHIO: Voyeurism is a misdemeanor. A person commits voyeurism by trespassing or otherwise surreptitiously invading another's privacy for the purpose of sexual arousal or gratification. OHIO REV. CODE ANN. § 2907.08 (enacted 1972).

OKLAHOMA: Voyeurism is a misdemeanor. A person commits voyeurism by hiding or loitering in the vicinity of any private dwelling with the willful intent to watch the occupants in a clandestine manner. OKLA. STAT. tit. 21, § 1171 (enacted 1959).

OREGON: No statute.

PENNSYLVANIA: No statute.

RHODE ISLAND: A person commits a misdemeanor if he or she intentionally, knowingly, or recklessly enters onto another person's property and for a lascivious purpose looks into an occupied dwelling through an opening or window. R.I. GEN. LAWS § 11-45-1 (enacted 1979). It is unlawful for a mental health professional to engage in voyeurism. A mental health professional commits voyeurism by viewing the patient's or former patient's private anatomy. R.I. GEN. LAWS ANN. § 5-63.1-1 (enacted 1956).

SOUTH CAROLINA: Voyeurism is a misdemeanor. A person commits unlawful peeping by peeping through windows or doors on or about another's premises, for the purpose of spying upon or invading another's privacy. S.C. CODE ANN. § 16-17-470 (enacted 1962).

SOUTH DAKOTA: Voyeurism is a misdemeanor. A person commits trespass by intending to survey another in a private place, or by installing, without consent, into a private place any device for observing or recording events. S.D. CODIFIED LAWS ANN. § 22-21-1 (enacted 1877). A person commits window peeping by entering private property and peeking into a door or window of any inhabited building without having lawful purpose with the occupant or owner. S.D. CODIFIED LAWS ANN. § 22-21-3 (enacted 1976).

TENNESSEE: No statute.

TEXAS: A person is guilty of a misdemeanor if he or she intentionally or knowingly enters the property of another person or hotel premises and, for a lewd or unlawful purpose looks into a dwelling or guestroom through any window or opening. TEX. PENAL CODE ANN. § 42.01 (enacted 1973).

UTAH: Voyeurism is a misdemeanor. A person commits a privacy violation by trespassing with intent to subject another to surveillance in a private place, or by installing, without consent, into a private place, any device for observing or recording events. UTAH CODE ANN. § 76-9-402 (enacted 1953). A person is guilty of gross lewdness by performing tresspassory voyeurism in the presence of another who is fourteen or older. UTAH CODE ANN. § 76-9-702 (enacted 1953).

VERMONT: No statute.

VIRGINIA: No statute.

WASHINGTON: No statute.

WEST VIRGINIA: No statute.

WISCONSIN: No statute.

WYOMING: No statute.

UNITED STATES: No statute.

Glossary

In law, words sometimes bear a meaning that is different from their ordinary-language meaning. For example, "adultery" has a common meaning, but a statute may define the term in a way that modifies that meaning. Or, the statute may not define the term but judicial opinions that interpret the statute may do so. For example, "crimes against nature" is not commonly defined in statutory language, but state court opinions often define it and the definition may vary from state to state. Thus the definitions that we provide here should not be taken as authoritative; in any given state, some of these words may have a legal definition that differs from the one we've provided below. In a few cases, we've provided definitions that are in statutory language; we have noted where that is the case. For many words that constitute chapter titles in this book, such as "Incest," we have not provided a definition of the word in this glossary. The statutory text that we provide in the chapter itself is the best answer to the question of what the word means in a particular state.

adultery Sexual intercourse when at least one participant is married to someone else.

affinity, relationships by The non-blood relationships, including in-law relationships, resulting from marriage. See **consanguinity**.

affirmative defense A fact or condition offered by the defendant, that, if true, negates his or her legal liability.

AIDS Acquired Immune Deficiency Syndrome.

analingus A sexual act committed by applying the mouth of one person to the anus of another.

bestiality Sexual conduct by a person with an animal.

buggery Most commonly **sodomy**, but it can also refer to **bestiality**.

capital felony A **felony** punishable by death.

carnal knowledge Sexual conduct, usually intercourse, presumed to be heterosexual.

civil vs. criminal Succesful civil law suits are typically brought by private parties and lead to injunctions and/or damages, while succesful criminal law suits are brought by the state and lead to imprisonment and/or fines.

common law Law that derives its authority either from judicial opinions or from customary practices recognized in judicial opinions, as distinguished from law that derives its authority from legislative or executive action.

consanguinity, relationships by Blood relationships, implying a common ancestor. *Lineal consanguinity* describes relationships in which one person is descended from the other, as in the case of parent and child or grandparent and grandchild. *Collateral consanguinity* describes consanguineous relationships where neither party descends from the other, as in the case of siblings, or of aunt and nephew. Compare **affinity**.

consideration Something of value given in exchange for something else of value necessary to make a contract binding. Some goods or services may not serve as valid legal consideration for a contract; for, example, engaging in sexual activity.

crime against nature Refers to deviate sexual intercourse; most commonly used in legislation as a synonym for **sodomy**.

cunnilingus A sexual act in which one person applies his or her mouth to the vagina of another.

curtesy Commonly understood to mean the legal right a man acquires in his wife's estate by virtue of the marriage. At **common law**, it usually consisted of the use both during the marriage and after the wife's death of all real estate that the wife owned.

deviate sexual intercourse Anal intercourse, **cunnilingus**, or **fellatio**.

dower Commonly understood to mean the legal right a woman acquires in her husband's estate by virtue of the marriage. At **common law**, it usually consisted of the use for the rest of her life, but not the ownership, of one-third of his estate, or sometimes one-third of his real estate only, after his death.

fellatio A sexual act involving the mouth of one person and the penis of another.

felony A more serious crime than a **misdemeanor**. A felony usually carries a maximum punishment of at least one year in prison or a fine of at least $1,000.

flagellation Flogging or lashing, presumably for the purpose of sexual arousal.

fornication Sexual intercourse outside of marriage.

half blood The relationship between two people sharing only one biological parent.

HIV Human Immunodeficiency Virus. The virus that causes **AIDS**.

in loco parentis Literally "in the place of the parent." The assumption of the legal rights and responsibilities of a parent.

jointure A property provision agreed to for a wife prior to a marriage, to take effect upon the husband's death, providing for the use of the husband's real estate after his death, and sometimes its ownership.

lascivious Sexually arousing, intended to excite lust. Compare **lewd**.

legitimacy The condition of having been born to parents married to each other.

lewd Sexually arousing, intended to excite lust. Lewdness carries a connotation of immorality. Compare **lascivious**.

masochism Sexual arousal or gratification by being dominated, mistreated, or hurt by another.

mentally incapacitated Temporarily incapable of appraising or controlling one's conduct as a result of the influence of a controlled or intoxicating substance administered to one without consent or as a result of any other act committed upon the person without consent. This is a common statutory definition of the term.

mentally defective Incapable, by reason of a mental disease or defect, of appraising the nature of sexual conduct. This is a common statutory definition of the term.

misdemeanor A lower grade offense than a **felony**. A misdemeanor usually carries a punishment of no more than one year in prison or a fine of no more than $1,000.

obscene Deeply offensive, by reason of sexual or scatological explicitness, to the moral standards of the community

pander To entice a female to commit prostitution, to **pimp**; to cater to the lust of others.

per anus Literally "through the anus." Usually refers to anal sex.

per os Literally "through the mouth." Usually refers to oral sex.

physically helpless Unconscious or for any other reason physically unable to communicate unwillingness to participate in an act. This is a common statutory definition of the term.

pimp A person who obtains customers for a prostitute.

pimping The practice of soliciting customers for prostitutes. See **pander.**

profanity Language that is coarse, crude, or irreverent.

prostitute A person who engages in sexual activity with another person in exchange for a fee.

pubes The genital area covered by hair.

sadism The obtaining of sexual gratification by inflicting pain or harm on another.

sadomasochism A sexual taste that combines the characteristics of **sadism** and **masochism.**

seduction The act of enticing another (ordinarily younger) person to have sexual intercourse by means of persuasion, solicitation, promises, bribes, or other means, other than the threat or use of force.

sexual contact The intentional touching of a person's sexual or intimate parts, including breasts or buttocks; or the intentional touching of a person's clothing covering the immediate area of that person's sexual or intimate parts. Contact constitutes sexual contact only if it is intended to be, and can reasonably be interpreted as being, for the purpose of sexual arousal or gratification. This is a common statutory definition of the term.

sexual penetration Sexual intercourse, cunnilingus, fellatio, anal intercourse; any insertion, however slight, of any part of the actor's body or any object manipulated by the actor into the genital or anal openings of the victim's body; or any insertion, however slight, of any part of the victim's body into genital or anal openings of the actor's body. Seminal emission is not required as an element of sexual penetration. This is a common statutory definition of the term.

sodomy Most commonly, anal intercourse; sometimes also oral-genital contact.

STD A sexually transmitted disease.

tort A wrong or injury for which the injured is entitled to seek compensation by bringing a civil lawsuit.

venereal disease A sexually transmitted disease (STD).

wanton Reckless: acting without regard to the consequences of one's actions or the rights and safety of others.

whole blood The relationship between two people sharing both biological parents.